Praise for
BEYOND BELIEF

What kind of God do we believe in? In 1945, Clinton Gardner, an American soldier in charge of the newly liberated Nazi death camp at Buchenwald, realized that "the idea of a supreme being up there, or out there. . . ." intervening in history and our lives "made no sense to me." But this did not lead Gardner to abandon faith; it led him over a lifetime to a new paradigm. *Beyond Belief* is a moving account of the journey. It is the summation of a fifty-year encounter with remarkable figures that gave him new ways to think about God. He came to see the life-changing insights of his Dartmouth professor, Eugen Rosenstock-Huessy, concerning the "cross of reality," the "religionless Christianity" of Dietrich Bonhoeffer, and the panentheism of Vladimir Solovyov. He weaves these insights into his own new paradigm. Read it.

—M. DARROL BRYANT
Distinguished Professor
Department of Religious Studies
University of Waterloo, Canada

Eugen Rosenstock-Huessy was an immensely innovative thinker, and the current conversations in religion and philosophy are just catching up to him. He was "post-modern" before the term was invented. Gardner has organized and focused Rosenstock-Huessy's brilliant but sometimes fragmented work into a readable narrative that can be enjoyed by both scholars and non-specialists.

—HARVEY COX
Hollis Professor of Divinity
Harvard University
Author of *When Jesus Came to Harvard*

Read this volume, do! It will delight and exercise your mind, and it will give you much of value to ponder.

—FRED BERTHOLD, JR.
Religion Department
Dartmouth College

This thoughtful and wide-ranging book gains much of its power from the fact that it never forgets its home base at the Congregational Church (UCC) in Norwich, Vermont.

—AVERY POST
Former President
United Church of Christ

BEYOND BELIEF

BEYOND BELIEF
Discovering
Christianity's New Paradigm

CLINTON C. GARDNER

Beyond Belief
Clinton C. Gardner

Copyright © 2008 by Clinton C. Gardner

Foreword © 2008 by Kenneth Cracknell

Cover design by Kyle Morrison.

Front cover image by José Clemente Orozco, *The Epic of American Civilization: Modern Migration of the Spirit* (Panel 21; 1932–1934).
Commissioned by the Trustees of Dartmouth College, Hanover, New Hampshire.
Image reproduced with permission.

Text design and layout by Doug Lufkin, Lufkin Graphic Designs.

White River Press
PO Box 4624
White River Junction, Vermont 05001
www.whiteriverpress.com

ISBN: 978-1-935052-02-9

Library of Congress Cataloging-in-Publication Data

Gardner, Clinton C., 1922-
  Beyond belief : discovering Christianity's new paradigm / Clinton C. Gardner ; foreword by Kenneth Cracknell.
  p. cm.
  Includes bibliographical references and index.
  ISBN 978-1-935052-02-9 (softcover : alk. paper)
1. Christianity—21st century. I. Title.
  BR121.3.G37 2008
  230–dc22
                2008019815

CONTENTS

Acknowledgments   11
Foreword by Kenneth Cracknell   13
Prologue   17

PART I   THE CROSS OF REALITY
1   Living in the Cross of Reality   27
2   Reconciling Science and Religion   39
3   The Spirit as Speech   55
4   The Dialogical Method   73
5   The Revolutions of the Christian Era   83
6   God Is Like a Whole Humanity   96
7   From Theism to Panentheism   111
8   A Brief History of Dialogical Thinking   117

PART II   THE RUSSIAN PROVING GROUND
9   Bridges for Peace   128
10 The Solovyov Society   143
11 Metanomics: A Higher Sociology   160

PART III   THE AMERICAN BATTLEGROUND
12 Transforming Christianity   173
13 The New Transcendence   192
14 On Cemetery Hill: In Conclusion   203

Appendices
A   The Complete Cross of Reality   209
B   A Letter from Volgograd   210
C   An E-mail from Siberia   212
D   Continuing on the Web   213

List of Website Pictures   215
Biographical Notes   216
Suggestions for Further Reading   220
Selected Bibliography   221
Notes   225
Index   247

God is the power which makes us speak. He puts words of life on our lips.
Everybody who speaks believes in God because he speaks. No declaration of
faith is necessary. No religion.
Speech is nothing natural; it is a miracle.
Speech is the body of the spirit.

—Eugen Rosenstock-Huessy (1888–1973)

Spirit—the Holy Spirit—is incarnated in human life, but it assumes the
form of a whole humanity rather than of authority. . . . God is like a whole
humanity rather than like nature, society, or concept.

—Nikolai Berdyaev (1874–1948)

Christianity wholly consists in the fact that God's work has become the work
of man also. This unity between God and man is the Kingdom of God,
which comes only in so far as it is realized.

—Vladimir Solovyov (1853–1900)

ACKNOWLEDGMENTS

NORWICH, VERMONT – APRIL 27, 2008 – As befits a work that presents the spirit as speech, and introduces a dialogical method, this book is the product of numerous dialogues. While many of these were one-on-one, I would like first to recognize those that occurred in various discussion groups, ones that friends of mine and I organized, either at local churches or at Dartmouth College, just across the river from this small Vermont town.

Most of the church discussions were held at the Norwich Congregational Church, beginning in the fall of 1963; and they often had an ecumenical character, with members of Catholic and Episcopal churches joining in. All of them focused on reading innovative thinkers in the field of religion, persons who contributed to the new Christian paradigm I describe in the Prologue.

In 1981 it was a discussion group at the Norwich church that led to the formation of the Bridges for Peace project, thus creating the basis for this book's Part II.

In more recent years I've shared key pages of this work with a men's breakfast group, one that's been meeting since the early 1990s at the Norwich Inn. Organized by my friend Don Poulson, who invited men from local churches, it has the same ecumenical character that we had back in the 1960s.

Several other chapters owe a lot to discussion groups that were sponsored by the Institute for Lifelong Education at Dartmouth (ILEAD). In fact, Chapter 12's engagement with Sam Harris' 2004 *The End of Faith* was prompted by an ILEAD discussion of that book in spring 2007.

The Kendal at Hanover retirement community provided another local venue for helpful discussions. In 2006 there was a series of meetings at Kendal on issues of religion and science, focusing on the rise of fundamentalism in the United States today. These were led

11

by Fred Berthold of the Dartmouth Religion Department, and they helped me with those issues in Part III.

Besides the dialogues in those varied groups, there were certainly some individuals whose one-on-one conversations with me were equally helpful. My cousin Peyton Craighill, an Episcopal priest, introduced me to the widely admired writings of New Testament scholar Marcus Borg, thus leading me to hear him live at a conference in Georgia in January 2007, on which I report in Chapter 12. With help from Peyton and the others noted below, the last three years have brought me to the present text.

My wife Libby's common sense has toned down certain excesses, while conversations with my children—John, Jim, and Cathy—have aided me in sorting out which notes were most usable. With thanks, this book is dedicated to Libby and my children.

Thanks go also to my grandson Kyle Morrison who designed the cover.

Beyond my immediate family, certain friends who were quite familiar with my subject helped me shape this work. Freya von Moltke gave me many hints, as did Harold Berman, Fred Berthold, Darrol Bryant, Norman Fiering, Ray Huessy, Giles Jackson, and Harold Stahmer. One person who knew my subject particularly well, Frances Huessy, took on the vital task of copyediting. Her work went well beyond correcting sentence structure, substantially improving the clarity and coherence of the whole book.

I've also profited from readings and critiques by Sally Bradlee, David Briggs, Chip Fleischer, Sonja Hakala, Mary Jenkins, Carl Johnson, David Keane, Anne Margolis, Peg and Avery Post, Nicola Smith, and Ken Wolf.

The text was typed by Ruth Stalker, who also was the Office Manager of Bridges for Peace.

So thanks to all, to family and friends, to scholars here and abroad. Whatever I've discovered here owes much to my dialogues with all of you.

FOREWORD

THIS IMPORTANT AND INTRIGUING book should attract a wide variety of readers. The issues it deals with are immediately relevant both to Christians feeling uneasy with their inherited thought-patterns and those (a very great number indeed) who wish that they could find intellectual justification to become once more Christian believers. In other words, Clinton Gardner addresses the contemporary malaise in mainstream Christian theology where so many of us still in the pews find ourselves less than helped by the traditional formulations of classical theism; and in which many more people look back with a profound nostalgia for the days when "church" was central to their lives. Whether as insiders (sometimes held in the Church only by a gossamer thread) or wistful outsiders, we are all too aware of the assaults on Christian belief by neo-atheists like Sam Harris (*The End of Faith*) and Christopher Hitchens (*God Is Not Great*). In this context we need wise guides, and among such guides I nominate Clinton Gardner as one of the best. Here are some of the reasons.

First, the book is by a lay theologian who has no axe to grind to maintain the institutional structures of the Church. He is moreover a lay theologian extraordinaire, having been involved in his own quest for Christian understanding since before the USA entered the Second World War. As we learn from the autobiographical narrative so engagingly entwined as a leitmotif throughout his book, as an undergraduate at Dartmouth Gardner met one of the great original thinkers of the twentieth century. He was Eugen Rosenstock-Huessy, a German émigré and social philosopher, who spoke powerfully of God without ever invoking the supernatural. Through this great teacher Gardner entered the thought-world of vastly influential figures of that period like Dietrich Bonhoeffer and Paul Tillich, Martin Buber and Franz Rosenzweig, along with their fresh and often startling insights into the being of God and the nature of religion. At that same time he made his first explorations into the Christian thinking

of such Russians as Vladimir Solovyov and Nikolai Berdyaev. With
these encounters Gardner had started on his journey of a lifetime.
He had also begun on his lifetime journal, so many pages of which
come alive in this book.

But this young man was uprooted from his native New England,
becoming just one unit in the vast D-Day army that invaded
Normandy on June 6th, 1944. Lieutenant Gardner nearly died that
day on the Omaha Beachhead, but survived to become the com-
mandant in 1945 of the newly liberated Buchenwald concentration
camp. (What questions of theodicy cluster around these events!)
Speaking German, he became seriously "European," engaging not
only with the surviving Jewish inmates but also in depth with many
of the four thousand Russian former prisoners in Buchenwald. And
Europe becomes the wider context of this book. Gardner's thinking
from that time forward was to be on no small scale as he befriended
or was befriended by major French, German, and Russian thinkers.
As we read the book, we too can begin to live beyond our North
American context.

Gardner returned to Dartmouth to complete his academic work
with Rosenstock-Huessy. Then he set off on further studies in Paris
(he became for a time a student at a Russian theological seminary),
and later found his way to Berlin. All the time he is keeping a detailed
journal of his conversations. So he is able to offer us graphic and
vivid nutshell summaries of the thinking of this time—the late for-
ties, the fifties, and the early sixties. Even scholars of intellectual
history will be surprised at some of the connections he makes. I personally love the glimpse of Eugen Rosenstock-Huessy and Martin
Buber embracing as old friends at the train station at White River
Junction, Vermont, in 1952.

The ideas of the generation represented in this warm embrace
were seminal for the next wave of Christian thought. In 1963 the
English Anglican bishop John Robinson published *Honest to God*
and a million copies were sold to a largely receptive audience. In
the United States, the Harvard theologian Harvey Cox published
The Secular City (1965), equally warmly received by the same kind of
discerning audience. Later another Episcopal bishop John Shelby
Spong, the leading New Testament scholar Marcus Borg, and Roman
Catholic writers Gregory Baum and Leslie Dewart were to take up

similar themes, seeing God in panentheistic rather than theistic terms. Parallel developments were taking place in Eastern Orthodox thought, and Gardner shared in these developments, too.

Now it may well seem that all I have done so far is to toss out before a perhaps bewildered reader a mass of names, some of which will be quite unfamiliar. And maybe terms like "classical theism" and "panentheism" make little or no sense, either. But the good news about the following pages is that their writer is a born teacher, and he offers guidance every step of the way. He too has stood where we are, wrestling with unfamiliar concepts and striving to make sense of them in his own Christian living. He assumes no previous knowledge, never patronizes us, and takes time to explain how the whole book is shaped. What's more, he invites us into further conversation—for, as his subtitle makes clear, "Christianity's new paradigm" is still a work of ongoing discovery.

KENNETH CRACKNELL
President Emeritus
Cambridge Theological Federation, UK

PROLOGUE

Our relation to God is not a "religious" relationship to the highest, most powerful, and best Being imaginable—that is not authentic transcendence—but our relation to God is a new life in "existence for others," through participation in the being of Jesus. The transcendental is not infinite and unattainable tasks, but the neighbor who is within reach in any given situation.
—Dietrich Bonhoeffer (1906–1945)

NORWICH, VERMONT – APRIL 27, 2008 – I have opened with that epigraph from Dietrich Bonhoeffer, since his *Letters and Papers from Prison* will hover over everything I want to say. The martyred German pastor wrote that today's world has "come of age." Therefore, the time has come to articulate a "religionless Christianity" and to learn to speak of God "in a secular way." God is not like the all-powerful supreme being of traditional theism, one who is separate from us, one in whom we must try to believe; instead, he is one in whose life we participate. While Bonhoeffer has been welcomed as an innovative thinker, that epigraph echoes St. Paul, who wrote that God is he in whom "we live, and move, and have our being."

Bonhoeffer clearly anticipated the battle that is going on in Christianity today. As New Testament scholar Marcus Borg puts it, "Christians in North America today are deeply divided about the heart of Christianity. We live in a time of major conflict in the church." Describing that conflict in terms of a "paradigm change," he says that the "earlier paradigm" interprets the Bible literally and conceives of God in terms of "supernatural theism." He contrasts this with an "emerging paradigm," one that "sees the Bible metaphorically,"—and imagines God in "panentheistic," rather than in theistic, terms.

As we learn from St. Paul, as well as from the Christian thinkers who have been called mystics, panentheism is as old as theism. Traditional theism has described God as a supernatural being, with an existence separate from the natural, created world. By contrast, panentheism describes God as existing *within* the world of creation. It should not be confused with pantheism, which imagines God as being the same as everything that exists.

The term "paradigm" became popular in the 1960s through the work of Thomas Kuhn, who wrote of "paradigm shifts"—a basic change of assumptions—in the natural sciences. One example of this was Einstein's theory of relativity, which had replaced earlier paradigms in physics. Since the 1960s, social scientists and writers in the humanities have frequently used the term to describe any distinct and holistic worldview. I use it in my title because it evokes the large frameworks within which we view reality. A classic example of a paradigm shift is our 16th-century move from the Ptolemaic earth-centered view to the Copernican sun-centered one.

The earlier Christian paradigm thought of faith as *belief*; that is, believing in such things as the miracle stories of the Bible, an after-life, and an all-powerful supreme being. By contrast, the emerging paradigm sees faith as the way we commit ourselves to the Christian life. In Bonhoeffer's terms, faith is our commitment to live a "new life in 'existence for others.'"

The new paradigm, Borg writes, "has been visible for well over a hundred years" and "in the last twenty to thirty years, it has become a major grassroots movement among both laity and clergy in 'mainline'. . . Protestant denominations." That's certainly true in my own denomination, the United Church of Christ (UCC). Since I was raised as a Presbyterian, and have also spent ten years as a confirmed Episcopalian, I have seen this new paradigm emerging in a variety of settings. In fact, I have been actively promoting it since the 1940s—through writing books, convening conferences and discussion groups, even delivering an occasional sermon.

In this book, I will add some additional scaffolding to the framework of the new paradigm. As indicated by my opening epigraphs, I will draw especially on the work of Eugen Rosenstock-Huessy, Nikolai Berdyaev, and Vladimir Solovyov. Rosenstock-Huessy, who was my professor at Dartmouth College, was hailed by Bonhoeffer's twin sister Sabine as a forerunner of her brother. (Since my German and Russian guides have names that can be challenging, the reader will find pronunciations in the Biographical Notes.)

As I have noted in my Acknowledgments, these pages are an outgrowth of discussions that began at the Norwich Congregational Church in 1963. I can still remember, quite vividly, the topic we discussed that year. We read the book that introduced the notion of a secular theology, *Honest to God*, by John A. T. Robinson, Anglican Bishop of Woolwich. In that ground-breaking work of 45 years ago, the good bishop said that we had reached the time when "our image of God must go." We should give up thinking of a God who is spiritually or metaphysically above or beyond us. He turned to Bonhoeffer and the theologian Paul Tillich (1886–1965) to find ways of thinking that would overcome the common tendency to imagine God as a supernatural being. It appears that Bishop Robinson's book, selling more than a million copies, was the first widely read manifesto for Christianity's new paradigm.

That new paradigm is suggested by the secular image of Christ that appears on the cover. Here the Mexican muralist José Clemente Orozco, in a fresco at Dartmouth, depicts a clenched-fist Christ, a man who has just cut down his own cross. This contemporary Christ is challenging us to throw the idols of all religion, *including even the idol of his own cross*, onto the dark and looming scrapheap of history. There they would be piled with the equally passé idols of nationalism: the guns and tanks of war.

This secular Christ calls us to a mature and fully engaged Christianity, one that's not superstitious, sentimental, or pietistic. He is as far from fundamentalism as you can get. It is significant that St. Augustine was the first to suggest a Christ who might need to cut down his own cross.

Speaking of God in a secular way and celebrating the secular Christ have nothing to do with secularism. Secularism affirms that one can dispense with all forms of religion. What Rosenstock-Huessy and similar thinkers were doing was to translate the outdated language of 18th- and 19th-century Christianity into contemporary terms—so that it could speak to people who had outgrown the childish language that was still prevalent at the turn of the century. Of course, it is that language, in the mouths of self-styled evangelists like Jerry Falwell and Pat Robertson, that has come back to haunt us in more recent years.

After World War II, many people who thought of Christianity in contemporary terms subscribed to *Christianity and Crisis*, a magazine founded by the theologian Reinhold Niebuhr in 1941. Niebuhr's message in that magazine, that Christianity should be fully committed—politically, socially, economically, and internationally—echoed the Christianity not only espoused by Bonhoeffer, but also that depicted in Orozco's fresco.

Borg and John Shelby Spong, now a retired Episcopal bishop, have become two of today's better-known spokesmen for that kind of Christianity. Borg has proposed that we call it "transformational Christianity," rather than "liberal" or "progressive," and that suggested the title of my Chapter 12. Spong has written a book, *Why Christianity Must Change or Die*, in which he describes Bishop Robinson as a key mentor and presents panentheism as today's appropriate successor to theism.

Borg and Spong appear to take up Bonhoeffer's banner—and I am reminded of how I first heard similar ideas in Rosenstock-Huessy's lectures. He was a social philosopher, a philosopher of language, and an historian, whose interpretation of Christianity was central to all his teaching. He certainly enabled me, and many of my Dartmouth classmates, to discover Christianity in a contemporary mode. He gave us the sense that we could move *beyond belief* that God exists to a knowledge of how he lives and speaks in us.

I first listened to Rosenstock-Huessy's lectures in the fall of 1940—and I have pursued his work, quite steadily, ever since. He and his circle became my real career, although I have had to supplement that with a few income-producing ventures.

Paul Tillich once said of his friend, "Rosenstock-Huessy—when he speaks, it's like lightning." I will share that lightning here, and suggest that Rosenstock-Huessy's work might be as important a weapon as Tillich's or Bonhoeffer's in launching the needed counter-attack against the childish forms of Christianity that threaten the church and secular society today.

This book introduces Rosenstock-Huessy's work, but it is not a comprehensive study of his thought. I draw not only on Eugen (as I came to know him) but also on many others to present my own contribution to Christianity's new paradigm.

Mitch Albom's 1997 bestseller, *Tuesdays with Morrie*, contains many astonishing coincidences that resonate with my own experience and knowledge of Eugen. Mitch spent weeks with a dying professor of social philosophy, one Morrie Schwartz, thus giving wider life to his mentor's thought. In my case, I have spent decades with a professor of social philosophy, Eugen, also giving wider life to his thought. Morrie's favorite poet was W. H. Auden, while Auden's favorite thinker, apparently, was Eugen. Morrie died of ALS, the debilitating ailment now known as Lou Gehrig's Disease, which killed Eugen's best friend, Franz Rosenzweig (1886–1929). Eugen and Franz were both friends of Martin Buber (1878–1965), whose *I and Thou* was on Morrie's reading list for Mitch. And that famous book on dialogue plays a surprising role in this book's plot.

Ted Koppel's *Nightline* first called attention to Morrie—and reunited Mitch with his dying professor. Koppel's show was also the first to publicize US-USSR Bridges for Peace, as described in Chapter 9. Morrie's mantra, life's greatest lesson, was his version of a line from Auden: "Love each other or die." Eugen once put it this way: "The history of the human race is written on a single theme: How does love become stronger than death?"

I have divided this book into three parts because I take three different approaches to engaging with Christianity's new paradigm.

Part I describes how Eugen and his fellow dialogical thinkers, Rosenzweig and Buber, introduced a unifying way of thinking about *all* our knowledge. Their thinking is seen as a translation of the religious into the secular. Spirit, indeed the Holy Spirit, is presented as the kind of life-giving speech that sustains all humanity, and the biblical *Logos* is seen as the living word, becoming flesh not only in Christ but in each of us.

In the closing chapters of this part, my Russian Orthodox guides take the stage: Berdyaev and Solovyov, who were key figures in moving us toward panentheism. In Chapter 7, they are joined by two contemporary Catholic theologians, Gregory Baum and Leslie Dewart, who similarly offer ways of moving beyond theism.

Finally, Part I closes with a brief history of dialogical thinking, demonstrating how my Western and Eastern guides all had certain important 18th- and early 19th-century forerunners.

Part II will show how all the ideas in Part I were tested in Russia—between 1983 and 2000. US-USSR Bridges for Peace is described as a project exemplifying one of Eugen's key propositions:

that speech serves much more important purposes than the expression of ideas; its ultimate purpose is to establish peace.

Then Part III will take up the current development of the new
Christian paradigm. This new paradigm challenges both the religious
right, with its fundamentalism and literalism, and the atheist left, cur-
rently in full voice through the efforts of today's "Unholy Trinity":
Sam Harris, with his *The End of Faith*; Richard Dawkins, with his *The
God Delusion;* and Daniel Dennett, with his *Breaking the Spell.* Since
they have now been joined by Christopher Hitchens in his *God Is Not
Great*, I am calling the four of them "a querulous quartet."

Appendix D, "Continuing on the Web," calls attention to one
of my special hopes for this book. Not only will all of it be available on the Web, and thus easily searched, but its Web version will
have much-expanded notes, more biographical notes, many pictures,
and a related discussion group. Continue with me on the Web at
www.beyondbeliefgardner.com and www.clintgardner.net.

It's clear that Christianity has now become engaged in a war
with two fronts. On one, the mainline churches face the still-growing
forces of fundamentalism, which the media often treats as "the"
voice of Christianity today. On the other front, all who treasure their
religious heritage, be they theists or panentheists, are confronted
with the atheism espoused by Sam Harris and Company—to say
nothing of the secularism that pervades large parts of American
and European life. We who sit in the pews of mainline churches, we
centrists who reject both the right and the left, need to start taking
up our positions in this two-front war. I hope this book will help us
find the appropriate weapons.

As World War II was coming to an end, I was given an unlikely
assignment. I was put in command of the just-liberated Buchenwald
concentration camp, located near Weimar, Germany. Our troops
arrived there on April 13, 1945. If we had arrived ten days earlier, I
would almost certainly have met Dietrich Bonhoeffer. Even though he
was a prisoner at the camp during February and March, he had provided pastoral care to some of the other prisoners until he was taken
on April 3 to Flossenbürg camp, where he was executed on April 9.

My two months at Buchenwald were certainly the most for-
mative experience of my life. Shortly after our arrival there, I took
my belongings to an elegant little chalet where the Nazi camp

commander, SS Obersturmbannführer Hermann Pister, had lived. The first thing I saw in his living room, sitting prominently on a side table, was his large leather-bound family Bible. Leafing through it, I came to the pages at the back where he had faithfully recorded all his family's births, marriages, and deaths. Just as faithfully as he had recorded, in the camp's records, the names of the thousands of Jews and other "sub-humans" he had dispatched by rail for extermination at Auschwitz or had shot at Buchenwald.

The Buchenwald commander's Bible brought home to me that a 1,700-year era was coming to an end. Christianity might have a future, but no longer as the state-sponsored, all-powerful Christendom, the reign begun by the emperor Constantine.

Although I had been severely wounded on D-Day, June 6, 1944, and then wounded again in the Battle of the Bulge, my physical wounds seemed nothing compared to the psychic wounds that Buchenwald visited on me.

Four thousand Russian prisoners of war made up the largest group of inmates at the camp. I learned from them that Stalin had a gulag of similar camps—and right then I decided to make Russia's problems my own.

Returning to Dartmouth after the war, I started a college Russian club and chose courses that would prepare me for a State Department career. While I was deflected from achieving that goal, I remained an ongoing student of Russia's history—and especially of her religious tradition.

That explains why I became so deeply involved with Berdyaev and Solovyov—and why Russia became this book's Part II proving ground for all the ideas offered in Part I.

After Buchenwald and Auschwitz (and after the millions lost in two world wars), it became clear, both within and beyond the church, that we can no longer speak of an all-knowing, all-powerful, and all-loving God. The idea of a supreme being up there, or out there, one who can intervene in history or in our personal lives, made no sense to me, just as it made no sense to Bonhoeffer.

Elie Wiesel's *Night*, a classic recollection of Buchenwald and Auschwitz, describes the scene that greeted us in April 1945. Wiesel was soon put in our hospital, along with some 3,000 others, who were dying at the rate of more than 50 a day. It's likely that we saw each other—when I made my daily visits to the hospital, even though I did not meet him then.

In any event, Wiesel and I finally met in November 2002, when I had occasion to give him a copy of the camp's map, one I found hanging in Pister's office (see Picture 1 at www.beyondbeliefgardner.com; other pictures there are noted at List of Website Pictures).

Buchenwald lies behind everything I say here. In fact, I see this book as one more attempt to answer that difficult question: How can we speak of God after the Holocaust, after Buchenwald and Auschwitz?

PART I

THE CROSS OF REALITY

1 LIVING IN THE CROSS OF REALITY

Man's life, social as well as individual, is lived at a crossroads between four "fronts": backward toward the past, forward into the future, inward among ourselves. . . , and outward against what we must fight or exploit. . . . Hence both mental and social health depends on preserving a delicate mobile balance between forward and backward, inward and outward trends. Integration, living a complete and full life, is accordingly not some smooth "adjustment" we can hope to achieve once for all, as popular psychology imagines; it is rather a constant achievement in the teeth of forces which tear us apart on the Cross of Reality.

—Eugen Rosenstock-Huessy

NORWICH, VERMONT – NOVEMBER 11, 2006 – I sense an uneasy mood on the Dartmouth campus today, much like the one I sensed in the fall of 1940, when I arrived there as a freshman. Exploding airplanes have taken over from dive bombers—and Iraq, Iran, and Afghanistan have taken over from Germany, France, and England; but now as then, the campus feels uneasy at the core. My home, on a hill in Norwich, looks down on the campus, only two miles away.

In the fall of 1940, we young students had to live with the possibility that we might soon be drafted to fight the Nazis. So we found it liberating to listen to a former German soldier, one who had survived the slaughter of Verdun, as he lectured to us about what he called the Cross of Reality. This professor, Eugen Rosenstock-Huessy, liked to ride the two miles from his home in Norwich to the campus—on his horse! A mobilized scholar if there ever was one, he was a philosopher on horseback. Although he taught in the philosophy department, some of his most admired written work was on history and language. He was equally recognized as an innovative Christian thinker and a pioneer in the movement for voluntary service.

What follows is a series of journal notes from the 1940s. They recall how I first met this maverick thinker—and how his ideas quite took possession of me. (I have inserted headings into my journal whenever my notes turn into exposition of particular ideas.)

DECEMBER 15, 1940 – This would be a good time to summarize these last three incredible months at Dartmouth.

Since September, I have joined just about everything at the college: Outing Club, *Jack-O-Lantern* humor magazine, *The Dartmouth* newspaper, Dartmouth Christian Union.

In the Christian Union I have met two seniors majoring in philosophy. One is studying Nikolai Berdyaev, an exiled Russian religious philosopher now living in Paris. This senior has loaned me Berdyaev's book *The Origin of Russian Communism*. It's about the antireligious 19th-century Russian intelligentsia and some religious Russian thinkers who opposed them, the Slavophiles, led by Ivan Kireevsky and Alexei Khomyakov. It's also about Russian philosophy and Russia's leading religious philosopher, Vladimir Solovyov, a friend of Dostoevsky's. I have had long conversations with this senior about Solovyov and Russian philosophy. I'm thinking about majoring in philosophy, going to graduate school, and teaching about Berdyaev and Solovyov, as he plans to.

The other senior likes these Russians too, but is more interested in Eugen Rosenstock-Huessy, a German social philosopher. Prof. Rosenstock-Huessy left Germany when Hitler took power in 1933. My senior friend suggested I try to audit Rosenstock-Huessy's introductory course, "The Cross of Reality."

So I did that. I have been going to his class for two months now. He speaks from his heart, and he is a faithful Christian. But the way he understands Christianity is quite contemporary. There is no supernatural, no "other world" beyond this one, no life after death. Life is full of miracles, but they are not ones that run contrary to the laws of nature. *Faith* does not mean reverence for past tradition, but willingness to live for the future of all humanity.

In fact, he says that Christianity introduced the idea that humankind is working toward a common future—and therefore progress is the fruit of the Christian era. He means social, political, and economic progress, not "progress" associated with advances in science and technology.

It turns out that Rosenstock-Huessy got to know Berdyaev in 1923, soon after he had been expelled from the Soviet Union. In class, Rosenstock-Huessy refers quite enthusiastically to Solovyov, suggesting that we should read his *Lectures on Divine Humanity*.

A New Model and Method

Rosenstock-Huessy says we all live in a Cross of Reality on which we have to face backward to the past, forward to the future, inward toward our selves, and outward toward the world. He brings this cross image to life, not as an abstract idea, not as his idea, but as a new model of the human reality, a model that he invites us to discover with him. When he diagrams the cross on a blackboard, he makes a horizontal line for its time axis, then a vertical line to represent the space axis. This visual depiction becomes an icon for all his students, an icon of our human predicament—and our potential.

Since each of us lives at the center of this cross, our lives are crucial, not only for ourselves but for all humankind. With regard to the time axis of our lives, we are constantly torn between the need to be true to the achievements of the past and the need to respond to the new callings of the future. Similarly, on the space axis of our lives, we try constantly to relate our personal, subjective inner space to the objective demands of the outer world, the space around us. This model applies not only to each person but to any group, even to a nation.

From the first class in which I saw Rosenstock-Huessy draw this Cross of Reality to last week's closing lecture, the richness and significance of this model increased week by week. His books reinforced his lectures, showing us how to use this model as a method for understanding and changing ourselves and society. He said that social science, which began about a hundred years ago, had started off on the wrong foot. That is, in the 1840s Auguste Comte founded his special science for the social aspects of life (coining the term *sociology*), and sought to make it respectable by basing it on the objective and quantitative methods of natural science. These were collectively the methods René Descartes had begun to disclose 200 years earlier. But

Rosenstock-Huessy pointed out that scientific objectivity works only for nature, not for history or society. It serves beautifully to analyze the outer world, the space around us, but it is useless for exploring the inner space of the person. And objectivity is equally useless for understanding the times we live in: our present, past, and future.

The Cross of Reality, showing that times are as important as spaces, corrects the scientific subject-object model of reality, which is merely spatial, and enlarges on its limited method. All these relationships seemed crystal clear when Rosenstock-Huessy diagrammed the cross on the blackboard:

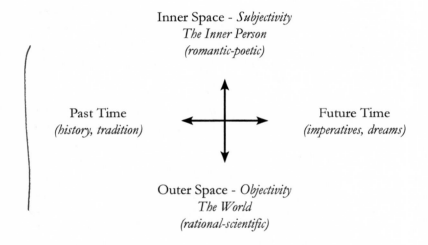

Inner Space - *Subjectivity*
The Inner Person
(romantic-poetic)

Past Time   Future Time
(history, tradition)   *(imperatives, dreams)*

Outer Space - *Objectivity*
The World
(rational-scientific)

It was not only Descartes and Comte whom Rosenstock-Huessy challenged. He said Freud draws a caricature of us by examining the psyche on the basis of our minimum powers, our animal drives, instead of our greatest powers, our gifts of the spirit. He added that upon meeting Jesus, any psychiatrist would have had him locked up.

Rosenstock-Huessy ended his *Out of Revolution: Autobiography of Western Man* with a call for a new science, a *higher* sociology, one that would have the Cross of Reality as its method. He further suggested the name *metanomics* for such a new discipline, meaning that it would go beyond (*meta*) the laws (*nomoi*) of the present social sciences.

I was completely smitten by his thought, as were many of his other students. In fact, several recent graduates are so impressed with the social philosophy of "Professor Huessy" that they are now joining with him to form a new institution to embody its principles. This new institution will be called Camp William James in Sharon, Vermont, and will be a volunteer work service program within the Civilian Conservation Corps. Approximately thirty members will come from the regular CCC; about thirty will be college boys from Dartmouth and Harvard. Page Smith, Dartmouth class of 1940, and Frank Davidson, Harvard 1939, are two of its main organizers. It is named after the American philosopher William James because, in his 1906 essay, "The Moral Equivalent of War," he proposed that all young people, as part of their education, devote a significant period to an all-out mobilization of their energies, comparable to the all-out commitment a soldier makes in wartime. As James expressed it, if we do not learn how to mobilize ourselves in peacetime, through selfless service that addresses our planet's ills, "then war must have its way."

MAY 30, 1941 – I slept very little last night. I sat up in my dorm room trying to decide whether to quit college now to join Camp William James—or to join the army. We are not yet in the war, but we all can feel it coming. France fell just a year ago. It's hard to see how England can hold out much longer. Throughout Europe men my age are fighting to stem the tide, but it looks as if Adolf Hitler's "Thousand-Year Reich" is about to begin. The contrast between this Armageddon of the human race and the peaceful atmosphere of classrooms finally became too much for me last night. I had been busy memorizing Virgil's opening lines in *The Aeneid*, "Of arms and the man I sing," while a new Sparta was destroying Athens just beyond our doors.

All spring I've been reading books on religion, history, and world affairs—at three times the speed I had ever read before. Not books required in classes, but books I felt compelled to read: such wildly different works as Solovyov's *The Spiritual Foundations of Life* and Rosenstock-Huessy's *Out of Revolution*. Last night, here in 405 Gile Hall, my fever of concentration came to a head. Just after midnight I had an experience unlike anything I've ever had before. It was a clear, distinct vision of brilliant white light—accompanied by an equally clear sense of being addressed.

During that incredible experience I felt myself being "commissioned" to attempt a contemporary restatement of Christianity, not in earlier generations' words but in my own. To see Christianity beyond the church—as a process in history. To describe the convergence of matter and spirit, the reconciling of science and religion. To show how the Cross of Reality points to that convergence and reconciliation.

So powerful was that experience last night, calling for an immediate response, that I decided to quit college this morning and spend the rest of the year at Camp William James, which has now moved to Tunbridge, Vermont. There I'd try to sort out whether I might be a pacifist, as many of my friends in the Dartmouth Christian Union are planning to be—or whether I should volunteer for the army. Also decided that one day I'll turn this journal into a book about the Cross of Reality.

At 10 a.m. I saw Dean Strong. He told me I could leave college in good standing, and mentioned that Robert Frost had done the same. Right after that I went to the Dartmouth Bookstore and bought a three-ring binder for this journal. The cover is red, the color for revolution—and for commitment! I decided I needed an epigraph on the first page, something to remember this day. I found these words near the end of *Out of Revolution*:

> The gods pass, when the individual realizes their passing, their unceasing change, he is converted to God—the living God who invites us to obey the *unum necessarium*, the one thing necessary and timely at every moment.

CAMP WILLIAM JAMES, TUNBRIDGE, VERMONT – AUGUST 15, 1941
Just a year ago I was at Goddard College in Plainfield, Vermont, with the Experiment in International Living. A Russian émigré led our morning reading group as we tackled Dostoevsky's *The Brothers Karamazov*. I decided I was Alyosha, who defends his faith against his brother Ivan's doubts. Afternoons we had a contrasting kind of experience: we dug a new septic system for the college.

Now, here at the camp, I think about Exeter, where I spent my high school years, and recall its motto, *Non Sibi*, not for oneself. I think that motto helped me decide to join this camp.

All summer I have been so on fire that I've written in my journal daily; I call my entries "morning notes," as I usually write them right after I wake up.

I've come to know Professor Huessy as "Eugen," since I have met with him almost weekly, either here or when I have visited Four Wells, his home in Norwich. Those visits are easy to make because my family moved to Norwich early this month. Fortunately, Mom and Dad like the Huessys; they've overcome their suspicions that my professor might be a sort of Svengali who manipulates his students' minds.

Yesterday was a high point here: Eleanor Roosevelt came to visit us. She has always been a big supporter of the camp, as FDR himself has been. We had good talks with her about our work. I'll write this up for the *Rutland Herald*, since I've become the camp's secretary.

I still think that parts of this journal could be used in my book about the Cross of Reality. For example, I might show how that cross explains the importance of our experience in Tunbridge.

First, we came to Camp William James because we heard a calling toward the *future*. We wanted to create a new institution, a period of all-out service as part of all young people's education. It would be the CCC plus Dartmouth and Harvard, an entirely new combination. It's a breaking-away from the ivory tower of academe into the problems and life of a real community. We heard another calling toward the future when we sent a group to Mexico to help rebuild the town of Colima—recently flattened in an earthquake. This second calling makes clearer that we're engaged in a "moral equivalent of war," not just planting trees or helping some farmers.

Second, we're creating our own *inner space* within the farm building, our headquarters. Of course, it's also the inner space of our group, the community we have formed here. The fact that most of us have memorized some verses from G. K. Chesterton's "Ballad of the White Horse" emphasizes the poetic nature of this orientation. In one stanza, Chesterton attacks academic objectivity with these wonderful words:

> *Not with the humor of hunters*
> *Or savage skill in war,*
> *But ordering all things with dead words,*
> *Strings shall they make of beasts and birds,*
> *And wheels of wind and star.*

Third, we have the experience of being connected with *past time*, with the ongoing life of a rural town whose roots go back for many generations. We go to square dances where the calling is in an Elizabethan style that's died out in England. Quite a contrast with the rootless suburbs of New York or the slums of New Haven, both places where many of us grew up.

Fourth, we are getting national publicity through stories in the *Boston Globe* and the *New York Times*. This makes our little inner group known to the outer world, objectively, with both good and bad consequences. It has helped recruiting, but it's also what led to our losing federal funding. In Congress we were attacked as just another New Deal boondoggle—and had to close our CCC "side-camp" in Sharon.

To sum up, the camp has provided each of us with a more intense experience of life, a more crucial experience, than we'd get in any ordinary college year. We have come to see that a period of such service, when integrated into one's education, would show its participants how we all live historically, drawn toward the past and the future.

I think this note about the camp makes clear that the cross is not some elaborate metaphysical concept but simply a commonsense way to interpret any experience. In fact, a person who uses common sense already interprets his or her life and history this way, from the four perspectives that the cross shows us. In other words, the cross simply codifies common sense. Unfortunately, huge numbers of people, probably the great majority—be they ideologues, fascists, or communists (all stuck on the "glorious future" front), fundamentalists (stuck on the past front), sentimentalists and pietists (stuck on the subjective front), or even rationalists (stuck on the objective front)—are not guided by common sense.

Among those who do not perceive the four dimensions of reality are people like Henry Ford who exclaimed that "history is bunk." Such people have a two-dimensional spatial view of the world; they imagine that their self, their *I*, is one pole and the world outside them is the other. They can't see that they also live in the dimensions of time.

The Multiformity of Man

The only text Eugen had us read in his course on the Cross of Reality was his *The Multiformity of Man*. In it he described how our life in industrial society makes us into interchangeable cogs in the machine, mere objects. In that world we are simply *theys*, with no more connection to time than the cog. *But we actually live in three other worlds*. Whenever we join a cause, like the labor movement, we move the human race toward a world of future time. When we marry or adopt some institutional commitment, we enter into a relationship with the world of past time, continuing the story of creation. Finally, we also have the world of our own inner space, where we become conscious of our individual souls.

To dramatize how different these worlds are, Rosenstock-Huessy offered four mathematical equations that describe the four dimensions of each singular person's life:

1. In industry, we are plural, so 3 or more = 1.
2. In a *cause*, like the labor movement, we live toward the future of *all* humanity, so infinity becomes our symbol, and so $\infty = 1$.
3. In marriage or any continuing institution, we are a dual, so 2 = 1.
4. In our inner self, we are the singular, and so 1 = 1.

His key point was that we are always balancing our roles as plural, all, dual, and singular persons. And a related point is that neither industry nor academe should treat us as one thing. We are manageable and educable only if we are treated as *multiform* beings, diverse and creative, not simply as replaceable plural cogs or simply as singular minds.

At the beginning of *The Multiformity of Man*, Rosenstock-Huessy said that Jean-Jacques Rousseau and Thomas Paine paved the road to both Stalin and Hitler. Those Enlightenment thinkers saw man as simply a part of nature, as do today's social scientists. Such a wrong understanding of man and God has social consequences, ones that can lead to social disasters.

Eugen made this same point in *Out of Revolution:* "A wrong philosophy must necessarily lead us into a wrong society."

DECEMBER 7, 1941 – With Pearl Harbor today, we realize the camp will have to fold soon. Real war is replacing its moral equivalent. Pacifism no longer attracts me. I don't think I'll wait for the draft. Probably enlist next spring. This next note is a response to our entering the war:

The Dimensions of Time

Perhaps the present war, the most engulfing historical experience of the human race, will show us the need for a post-Cartesian way of thinking, one that admits the dimensions of time. Perhaps we will learn from this experience that being primarily romantic (as we were in the 19th century) or primarily scientific (as we are in the 20th century) was dangerous. A pure romantic, focusing on his inner space, or the pure scientist, objectifying the outer world, is unable to *sense the times* in which they live and to take timely action to avert disaster.

Under the influence of natural science, we have thought of the future as if it were a mathematical forward projection of time units, of seconds, in the same sense that physical space is an outward projection of space units, of millimeters. But all our contemporary experience of war and revolution exposes that notion as a fallacy. The future is neither caused by the past, nor is it merely what happens as the clock ticks on. The future is not a fact but an act. The acts of Lenin, of Churchill, and Roosevelt, and the acts of all those who have responded to them, are what create the future.

When applied to human beings, therefore, the term *future* has quite a different meaning from when it is applied to nature. We commit ourselves to the future as an act of faith. Our life in time is just as real and full as our life in space. The experience of the two world wars might give us a deepened understanding of our relation to time, times, and timing; of how we are all children of time, caught up in the sweep of history.

So dominated are we by the slogans of science and technology, it is hard to imagine that we *do not* enter future time as we advance with our technology. Technology only improves our manipulation of matter, in the space of the natural world.

However, we *do* enter future time when we reply to the imperatives created in the past by the sacrifices, the prophecies, and the dedication of people who lived before us. We enter the future by living forward toward the unrealized dreams of our race, by taking risks, by waiting for the right time, by being willing to die for our beliefs. What distinguishes the few great revolutions of history from the many minor revolts is the way whole generations cooperated in preparing for them, carrying them out, and then preserving their accomplishments.

SOUTHAMPTON, ENGLAND – JUNE 5, 1944 – We've been locked up behind barbed wire in this camp for more than two weeks now, and our friendly American guards have orders to shoot us if we approach the gate out. That's understandable because we know the time and the place of D-Day, the greatest invasion in history. As a lieutenant, I will be a scout for B Battery of the 110th Antiaircraft Artillery Battalion, landing at 9 a.m. tomorrow. My mission is to go in with the Infantry, stake out our gun positions, then meet up with the battery when they land in the afternoon.

Almost every night we've gone to religious services. We Protestants often go to both Protestant and Catholic services, just in case. I would be graduating from Dartmouth this June had it not been for the war. By now I'd probably have written some senior paper relating to the Cross of Reality. Instead, all I've got is this journal, this record of my struggle to think my way out of theology and science into some more open way of understanding God and man, society, and history. My university in the army has been the reading of three of today's most insightful interpreters of those subjects: Rosenstock-Huessy, Solovyov, and Berdyaev.

Of course, there have been others, but those three have been my focus. If I survive this war, I'll certainly fulfill my commitment to turn this journal into a book. It will be the story of my American response to a German and two Russians who have become my spiritual fathers. I don't think it will be a formal study of their thought. Instead, I think it will be a continuation of these morning notes—as I test them against life in the postwar world.

I'll be packing this notebook in my field bag for the invasion, along with my little leather-bound New Testament. If I should die tomorrow, they'll find this journal with me—a sort of last testament. Most of my notes are secular, trying to present the Cross of Reality as a new method for the social sciences. But other notes are religious, since my long-range goal is to show how we can bridge the gap between these two modes of thought. This week's two notes are both religious, about prayer and about whether there is a life after death. Because it's quite clear to me that I may not be alive next week.

NORWICH, VERMONT – NOVEMBER 11, 2006 – Sixty-two years later, I still relive what happened to me on D-Day. At 5:00 p.m. June 6, 1944, when I lifted my head from my foxhole on Omaha Beach, a fragment from a German mortar shell sailed through my helmet, almost splitting it in two. Soaked in blood, I thought my skull was fractured—and that I would die in minutes. Then I lay on the beach for 23 hours, half-conscious, before I got any significant medical help. I still have the tiny leather-bound New Testament, full of underlinings that I carried in my backpack. And I still have my two notes on prayer and the afterlife; in fact, I plan to use them later in this book.

Finally, I still have that helmet, and have learned from the Imperial War Museum in London that the hole in it is the largest they have on record for a survivor in either world war. (See List of Website Pictures, Picture 4.)

2 RECONCILING SCIENCE AND RELIGION

The mind with its imperious urge to relate and unify everything is tempted to over-simplify life and deny the Cross of Reality by reducing the four (fronts) to one. This is the main source of viciously one-sided fallacies about man and society—sentimentalism and mysticism which engulf everything in the inner life of feeling, utopian radicalism which would bring in the Kingdom of God by violence, reactionary romanticism which dwells wholly in the feudal past, cynical rationalism which reduces man to a mere object of natural science.

—Eugen Rosenstock-Huessy

SO THOROUGHLY SMITTEN was I by Eugen in the early 1940s that I have pursued his work quite steadily ever since. Returning to finish my education at Dartmouth after the war, I took all his courses, then stayed in close touch with him throughout the 1950s and 1960s. Among our ties was that Eugen's only child, Hans, married my sister Mariot. Even in church we were close; Eugen, a deacon in the Norwich Congregational Church, usually sat in the pew just ahead of my wife Libby and me.

I turned my journal into my first book about him in the mid-1960s, and then began publishing his work in the late 1960s. My theme in all my writing about him has been to explain how he translates the religious into the secular, and vice versa. It wasn't simply that he'd shown his students how we could be good Christians without the slightest belief in the supernatural, or how we could worship God without thinking that he lived beyond the universe. Just as important was the way that Eugen showed us how everything we know is connected.

The American sociologist David Riesman, who was an admirer of Rosenstock-Huessy's work, once said: "The great religions all think in terms of *connectedness*. Everything is related to everything else." Another admirer of Eugen, Rabbi Abraham Joshua Heschel, expressed a similar thought: "All sciences and philosophies have one

39

axiom in common—the axiom of *unity* of all that is, was and will be." We students of Eugen's were smitten because he gave us a new way of perceiving that unity, the connectedness of all creation.

An Alternate Consilience

To focus on the theme of reconciling science and religion, we can turn to Edward O. Wilson's bestseller, *Consilience: The Unity of Knowledge*. His first intimation of consilience, he says, was when he experienced in college "the Ionian Enchantment," the conviction "that the world is orderly and can be explained by a small number of natural laws." Raised on Christian fundamentalism, he felt liberated by the grand picture of evolution and the empirical science of the Enlightenment.

Today Wilson sees the battle lines drawn between the two world views of "religious transcendentalism" and "scientific empiricism." The possibility that there could be a third view, *religious empiricism*, eludes him. Empiricism, of course, refers to knowledge gained through the senses, through experience or experiment, knowledge that can be tested and verified.

Wilson's grand conclusion is that "all tangible phenomena, from the birth of stars to the workings of social institutions, are based on material processes that are ultimately reducible, however long and tortuous the sequences, to the laws of physics." He envisions the unification of the natural sciences with the social sciences and humanities. As he puts it, "The human condition is the most important frontier of the natural sciences," and "the material world exposed by the natural sciences is the most important frontier of the social sciences and humanities. The consilience argument can be distilled as follows: the two frontiers are the same."

Now the Cross of Reality challenges that picture head on. The laws of physics relate only to the world of matter, the world defined by the space that lies outside us. They do not relate at all to the frontiers established by future and past times, or to the frontier of the "space" within the self. The laws of physics have nothing to say about what Rosenstock-Huessy called the obvious goal of all social science: the creation of peace among individuals, groups, and nations. We live on four frontiers, not on two that can be reduced to one. In other words, we cannot be reduced to a mere object of natural science.

Argo Books

W. H. Auden once told me that he had read everything of Rosenstock-Huessy's that he could lay his hands on. That was in 1969, when I had become Rosenstock-Huessy's American publisher, and was hoping Auden would write a foreword for one of our books. Auden came through with a fine recollection of Rosenstock-Huessy's influence on him. He cited Rosenstock-Huessy's motto *Respondeo etsi mutabor* (I respond although I will be changed) and concluded his piece with these words: "Speaking for myself, I can only say that, by listening to Rosenstock-Huessy, *I* have been changed."

Argo Books, my publishing venture, was launched with the help of Eugen's friend Freya von Moltke. Needless to say, Argo Books was a labor of love. The 37 years I've devoted to Argo and other Eugen-related activities are more than double the eighteen I spent running my own business, a mail order company called Shopping International.

Sabine Bonhoeffer's Article

In 1963, Dietrich Bonhoeffer's sister Sabine wrote an article about the similarities between her brother's thought and Eugen's. She wrote that "both men believed, hoped, anticipated, and did much in common." Their words have "come to life in many hearts, but least of all in those of German theologians."

Rosenstock-Huessy's connection with Dietrich Bonhoeffer had an important practical link. In 1929, Rosenstock-Huessy collaborated with Helmuth von Moltke, a scion of Germany's greatest military family, to found a German movement for voluntary service. Several members of that movement later formed the Kreisauer Kreis (Kreisau Circle), one of the few resistance groups against Hitler.

Rosenstock-Huessy has rightly been called the spiritual father of that group, whose common enterprise resulted in work camps that brought university students, young farmers, and miners together for community service and discussions of pressing social concerns. As Sabine Bonhoeffer reported, her brother knew all about the Kreisauer Kreis—and met with Helmuth von Moltke several times. And whereas Bonhoeffer was not a member of the group, he certainly supported its goals. Bonhoeffer was finally arrested by the Gestapo in April 1943 and executed in April 1945; von Moltke was arrested in January 1944 and executed in January 1945. It was Moltke's widow, Freya, who later became Eugen's friend and companion at the end of his life.

The historian and political advisor, George Kennan, who had served in the US embassy in Berlin just before the war, later wrote a remarkable testimonial about Helmuth von Moltke: "I consider him... to have been the greatest person, morally, and the largest and most enlightened in his concepts, that I met on either side of the battle lines in the Second World War."

Three Thinkers for the Third Millennium

That bit of history around Helmuth von Moltke, Dietrich Bonhoeffer, and Eugen Rosenstock-Huessy undoubtedly had something to do with what the American theologian Harvey Cox learned when he attended a 1961 conference in Berlin. Convened to consider the future of theological thought, the assembled church leaders took a vote at the end of their conclave; they selected Bonhoeffer, Tillich, and Rosenstock-Huessy as the three 20th-century religious thinkers who would still be important in the third millennium.

The Problem with Genius

When I wrote in December 1940 that many of his students and I were "completely smitten" by Rosenstock-Huessy, I might have added that we were more aware that we were hearing something important than we were sure about how we would describe just what that "something" was. We sensed that the Cross of Reality was, indeed, a model of how we experienced life in all its richness, and we also sensed that this model could be turned into a method to address any human problem, be it in the realm of religious or secular life, be it personal, social, or international. Since it did not exclude, but in fact *included*, the scientific method we use to deal with raw nature, we sensed that the Cross of Reality showed how everything is connected.

Yet, for most of us, there would have to be many years of further reading in Eugen's work, especially his works on language, before we could say in our own words exactly how the Cross of Reality gave us such a unifying perspective. Eugen spoke as a prophet, with the volcanic eruptions of what were clearly original thoughts. He was not one who tidied up after these eruptions.

I think that helps explain why Rosenstock-Huessy remains undiscovered to this day, as a social philosopher or as a theologian, while his friends Tillich and Karl Barth (1886–1968) became perhaps our best-known theologians. Tillich put his finger on it when he said, "Rosenstock-Huessy—when he speaks, it's like lightning." Flashes of genius need to be clarified by their author or the author's circle. This issue was addressed by the prominent Lutheran scholar Martin Marty in 1967, when he reviewed Rosenstock-Huessy's most popular book, *The Christian Future* (first published in 1946). Welcoming a new edition of that work, Marty noted that he had been a long-time admirer of Rosenstock-Huessy's work. But then he went on to say:

> It has never been possible to pigeon-hole Rosenstock-Huessy. . . . His juxtaposition of conventional genius and genial unconventionality is both disconcerting and creative. In 1946 Rosenstock-Huessy was ahead of his time—and he still is today. In this book he writes about secularization, hermeneutics, the gift of language, the meaning of personhood, and Christianity, without old-line appeal to transcendence.

Marty recently returned to the question of Rosenstock-Huessy's disconcerting originality when, in 2006, he wrote: "I always tell people that nine pages of RH are genius, and the tenth is so idiosyncratic, one knows not where to fit it. But that, too, was part of the genius."

Even more recently, in fact just as this book was being readied for the printer, Marty took a surprising initiative. He devoted his entire April 22, 2008, column in *The Christian Century* to Rosenstock-Huessy. Under the title "Grace in the center," Marty writes, "I was influenced enough by him to write a now forgotten book on his theme *Respondeo etsi mutabor*, 'I Respond Although I Will Be Changed.' The motto would be on my coat-of-arms if I had one."

Marty goes on to suggest three of Rosenstock-Huessy's books to his readers: *The Multiformity of Man; The Christian Future;* and *I Am an Impure Thinker*, "with its provocative essay 'Farewell to Descartes.'" He ends his piece by offering some of his favorite Rosenstock-Huessy sayings. One of those is: *"As soon as we place grace where it belongs, in the center of life, as its inspiration, life ceases to be arbitrary or accidental or casual or boring."*

Having Marty, a former president of the American Academy of Religion, suddenly decide to call attention to Rosenstock-Huessy once more, on the eve of this book's publication, makes me feel a touch of that grace at the center, an increasing confidence that this work may be coming at just the right time.

One Rosenstock-Huessy student has explained his relative obscurity as follows:

> I think it is just that there are too many ideas on the page, like someone telling ten stories at once. And he is too historical/sociological for philosophers, too Christian for a lot of academics, and too this-worldly for most Christians, and he is too anti-theological for theologians—Loewith says of *The Christian Future* that it is Goethean, not Christian. But I am attracted to Goethe and Blake, and think that Rosenstock-Huessy's view of the church as a living organism takes building the New Jerusalem as our allotted task.

Eugen was not unaware that there would be such problems in the acceptance of his work. He constantly said that genuinely new thought took at least three generations to introduce—and always required restatement by a second generation. We who have made up the circle gathered round him, so far largely unsuccessful in making the breakthrough, comfort ourselves with that thought. When I wrote to thank Marty for his column, he wrote back: "Bruce Boston (and others) wrote after the column appeared. May his and your and my tribe increase." (Bruce Boston wrote the first doctoral thesis on Rosenstock-Huessy's work.)

Speech Is the Body of the Spirit

Perhaps it *was* because he told so many stories at once that Rosenstock-Huessy seemed to me like an Einstein of the human sciences. He reoriented his students' post-Enlightenment minds by showing us quite fresh ways to see how everything is connected—and thus how to end the 300-year conflict between science and religion.

To introduce my justification of that bold claim, I'll quote the mathematician Blaise Pascal (1623–1662), whose thoughts on religion still seem alive today: "*Man is to himself the most amazing thing in nature; for he cannot imagine what a body is and still less what a spirit is, and least of all how a body can be united to a spirit.*"

Pascal is not simply making a statement here. He really is asking us to answer a difficult question: How *can* we imagine a body united to a spirit?

I think we can find the answer to Pascal's question by turning to the Cross of Reality. *That cross shows us that the actions of the spirit in us are parallel to, indeed the same as, the actions of language in us.* Once we grasp that, we are well on our way to understanding how everything is connected, from the most material to the most spiritual.

The quotations at the front of this book bear repeating now, because they clarify what it means to equate the spirit with speech:

God is the power which makes us speak. He puts words of
life on our lips.
Everybody who speaks believes in God because he speaks.
No declaration of faith is necessary. No religion.
Speech is nothing natural; it is a miracle.
Speech is the body of the spirit.

When we reflect on the full import of those propositions, we realize that God as spirit, indeed as the Holy Spirit, *is already within us*, the very source of our humanity. Thus, we do not need to struggle to believe in God; we have only to recognize his constant creative presence in us. Of course, there is a further step: We need to respond to the fact of that presence by living inspired, responsible, and creative lives.

Just how does the spirit, as speech, work its miracles within us and within history? It is speech that creates future time and ties us to the past; it is speech that enables us to have an inner space and deal with the world outside us. And it is *grammar* itself, that apparently mechanical thing, that creates and organizes these realities for us. In fact, we live in a four-fold reality, created by four basic kinds of speech:

1. Imperative (or vocative) speech, calling us to the future.
2. Subjective speech, addressing the inner self.
3. Narrative speech, telling our history.
4. Objective speech, analyzing the world outside us.

First, as we listen to the imperatives or vocatives we hear from others, initially from our parents, then from others who love us, later perhaps from clergy or other people we admire, we hear ourselves being addressed as *thou*. (This intimate form for "you" sounds archaic in English but is perfectly normal, indeed required, in most European languages; for example, in German, it is the familiar *Du*, as contrasted with the formal *Sie*. Whenever I use "thou" in this book, think of it as "you" spoken from the heart.)

When we hear ourselves being addressed personally as thou, such speech comes to us with force; imperatives and vocatives establish our *calling* to make the future, not only for ourselves and our loved ones, but for all humanity. In *The Multiformity of Man*, this was our infinity equation: $\infty = 1$.

In response to having been so called, we discover our I, our subjective and inward self (our inner space), the singular: $1 = 1$.

We then seek to return the gift of having been called by being creative ourselves, by contributing to the narrative of history. As we do so, we must form a *we*, as in marriage or any other history-making attachment, the dual: $2 = 1$.

Finally, in the outside world, we become known objectively in the third person, as *he* or *she*. In effect, we become part of *they*, the plural: $3 = 1$.

These four orientations to reality—to future and past in time, to inward and outward in space—form the Cross of Reality in which we live. Those orientations are not simply out there, waiting for us to discover them. Instead, the four basic forms of language create those four different orientations and mold us into those four different grammatical persons. It is speech that creates inward and outward space as well as backward and forward time. (In nature, time has no forward movement.)

Rosenstock-Huessy provided a beautifully concise description of this progress of speech through us when he wrote:

The soul must be called "thou" before she can ever reply "I," before she can ever speak of "us," and finally analyze "it." Through the four figures, *thou, I, we, it*, the word walks through us. The word must call our name first. We must have listened and obeyed before we can think or command.

Those words bring us back to Pascal's question: How can we imagine a body united to a spirit? We can answer his question when we recognize that the spirit is not something ethereal; it comes out of our mouths and into our ears. The spirit is speech; it is the word that calls our name.

Of course, Rosenstock-Huessy had the Cross of Reality in mind when he wrote that description of how the word walks through us—in the four figures *thou, I, we,* and *it*. Following him, throughout this book I'll continue to show how the Cross of Reality connects all our experience and knowledge, both religious and secular, both personal and historical. Let me now offer some brief previews of those connections.

Universal History

My favorite course with Eugen was his "Universal History," in which he described how humankind had been created by four kinds of speech.

During some 40,000 years before Christ, tribal speech, with its totems and taboos, had oriented us to our ancestors, to the narrative of our past.

Then, in the great empires, such as China and Egypt, already flourishing by 3000 BC, the speech of the temple oriented us to the stars, the rivers, and the fields, the universe of nature, the world outside us.

By 600 BC Greek speech had begun to orient us to our inner selves, through poetry and philosophy.

During that same millennium before Christ, the speech of Israel emerged, orienting us to our future by way of prophecy.

With the coming of the Christian era, those four ancient modes of speech were fused, and after Christ, we no longer felt bound by a single orientation. We were no longer simply Greek or Jew, Egyptian or tribesman. For 2,000 years now, we have been moving steadily toward spiritual unity, as we have become increasingly able to articulate all four forms of speech.

Four great types of civilization had reached dead ends at Year Zero of our common era. Christ and his apostles came at the right time. They translated those dead ends into new beginnings, becoming in effect the narrow middle in the hourglass of history. Since that center-time, human history has become one story.

Eugen's friend, the German philosopher Karl Jaspers (1883–1969), described the period 800 BC–200 BC as "the Axial Age," the time when most of the great religions and philosophies were born. Among the founders he cited were Heraclitus, Socrates, Plato, Aristotle, Confucius, Lao Tzu, the Buddha, Zoroaster, and Isaiah. Eugen agreed with Jaspers, seeing these pre-Christians as necessary preparers for the narrow middle when Christ was born.

Western History

Just as he told pre-Christian history in terms of four kinds of speech, so Rosenstock-Huessy saw these four kinds of speech given different emphases in each of the great Western revolutions. The imperatives established in the first millennium of the Christian era made all those revolutions necessary, from what he called the "Papal Revolution" of the High Middle Ages to the Russian Communist revolution of our own time. Each of the six great revolutions had different impulses:

1. The Papal Revolution had a messianic orientation toward the future.
2. The German Reformation emphasized our inner conscience.
3. The British Parliamentary or Puritan Revolution celebrated the laws and traditions of the past.
4. The French Revolution focused on the outer front, where reason and objectivity hold sway.
5. The American Revolution was a happy combination of impulses from both the French and the British.
6. Finally, the Russian Revolution turned into a rather unhappy combination of future messianism with the new language of objectivity. People became statistics.

Jung and Psychology

From 1962 until his death in 1973, Eugen and I visited frequently at Four Wells. We would talk for an hour or so in his sunny study on the second floor. Sometimes I would bring a book like Carl Jung's *Memories, Dreams, Reflections.* Eugen did not dismiss Jung the way he did Freud and Comte. After all, Jung retained great respect for religion.

Still Eugen was not happy with Jung's three main contributions to psychology: the significance of dreams, the exploration of the unconscious, and the role of archetypes. In Eugen's view, dreams were the "garbage heap" of the human mind, not revealing anything important about ourselves. Nor is there any hereditary unconscious that influences our actions. We enter the world pretty much as a tabula rasa, a blank slate, and become what has been spoken into us.

Jung's conviction that there are always four aspects of psychological orientation has more than a hint of the Cross of Reality in it. Jung also had a compelling idea that something resembling religion was needed and present in everyone, whether they liked to call it religion or not. Eugen, however, seemed to be quite on target in his thought that there was only *one* great archetype: Our brain was shaped, from the beginning, to recognize speech in its four distinctive modes. We did indeed inherit this crucial archetype, engraved in our hearts and minds.

Teilhard and Evolution

Besides Jung, another important thinker I discussed with Eugen was Pierre Teilhard de Chardin. In *The Phenomenon of Man*, this great Jesuit paleontologist had described evolution as the progressive "inspiriting" of matter. In fact, I had compared Eugen's thought with Teilhard's in one of our church discussion groups. Not surprisingly, I had detected what I thought was a version of the Cross of Reality in Teilhard's book. His "Omega Point," toward which evolution is moving, of course relates to the *future*. His category of *the within*, which he equates with spirit's existence in raw matter, he called *radial energy*. In humans he called it *consciousness*. The story of evolution, our narrative history, he described as the continual growth of that spiritual energy. It takes form in the outer world, which he called *the without*. I concluded that Teilhard, like Tillich, helped us move away from thinking of God as a supreme being.

Teilhard's view that man was evolution's leading edge seemed to enhance Darwin's drabber picture, without denying what the great naturalist had discovered.

Similarly, Eugen's view of evolution did not deny Darwin's discoveries. But "survival of the fittest" did not mean something like being the fastest at scurrying away from danger—or the strongest at bashing in the heads of one's opponents. Rather, the "fittest" among us are those who are the most inspired and successful in speaking toward the past and the future, toward the inner self and the world around us.

Teilhard had described today's earth as a "noosphere" (from the Greek *noos*, "mind"). I thought it would be better to call it an "orasphere" (from the Latin *orare*, "to speak."), a shift Eugen liked. Nor did I share Teilhard's optimism about the inevitability of progress. One of Teilhard's propositions was that it would be irrational to imagine "the universe committing abortion upon itself." However, he wrote that in the 1930s, before we knew of the hydrogen bomb.

Beyond Theology

Rosenstock-Huessy felt that, after our overwhelming experience of the First World War, we should seek quite new directions in our religious and social thinking—and not simply attempt to revive theology, as his friends Tillich and Barth had proceeded to do. Instead, he thought that the old concerns of theology should be taken up by new disciplines, such as the higher sociology he envisioned as metanomics. He once described the purpose of that future discipline as "the search for the omnipresence of God in the most contradictory patterns of human society."

Rosenstock-Huessy's most accessible thought on Christianity is in *The Christian Future*. One line in that book has been running as an undercurrent in my mind as I have been writing this one: "The supernatural should not be thought of as a magical force somehow competing with electricity or gravitation in the world of space, but as the power to transcend the past by stepping into an open future."

Those words sum up what Rosenstock-Huessy told his students about the supernatural. He said that the laws of nature cannot be interrupted by miracles, faith, or prayer. While there is no supernatural in that sense, he said that *all creative human speech is supernatural.*

As he put it, "speech is the only supernatural." Since we are the animal that speaks, we are "the uphill animal," the only one able to rise above its natural environment.

Rosenstock-Huessy's thinking about God resembled Berdyaev's, since both of them sought to get beyond our heritage of theism. In fact, Solovyov, Berdyaev's spiritual father, joins with them, making up a triumvirate. All three contributed to a panentheistic understanding of God, one that is expressed in Berdyaev's proposal that we think of God as being "like a whole humanity."

Rosenstock-Huessy's thinking about God also resembled Berdyaev's in that both of them could be called "trinitarian thinkers." As I listened to Rosenstock-Huessy, I realized that imperative speech, calling us to the future, relates to revelation and the Holy Spirit; subjective speech of the inner person relates to redemption and the Son; and narrative speech, carrying the past forward, relates to creation and the Father.

Answering Pascal's Question

The preceding reflections on the subjects of history, psychology, evolution, and theology—all aimed at showing the *connectedness* of Rosenstock-Huessy's thinking—were triggered by Pascal's question of how we can think of a body as being united to a spirit. I have answered that the Cross of Reality shows us just how that can be. The cross is an image of how *everything is connected*. Descartes, natural science, and reason have not been dismissed in this post-Cartesian perspective. They have simply been relegated to the objective front of our four-front experience.

Respondeo etsi Mutabor

In sum, the Cross of Reality offers us a third framework for our thinking, beyond those of natural science and theology. Rosenstock-Huessy sought to capture the character of this third framework in that motto that Auden and Marty cited, *Respondeo etsi mutabor*. My early notes on this motto, written just after the war, tried to explicate it, as follows.

For several generations now, we have been thoroughly "scientific." We have pretended to be sitting on a bridge above the stream of reality, watching the waters roll past. Occasionally we moistened a toe in the stream, but still imagined ourselves above it, observing it from outside. Our belief that there was such a position stemmed from Descartes' 17th-century *Cogito ergo sum* (I think, therefore I am). And *doubt* everything else.

Only a few generations ago we had a different viewpoint. From the theological perspective we certainly did not think of ourselves as doubting or being above it all. Instead, we saw ourselves as believing and subservient. The ultimate reality was like clouds in the heavens, shining above. That theological perspective was summed up in Saint Anselm's 11th-century *Credo ut intelligam* (I believe, in order that I may understand).

But for many of us today, neither the strictly scientific nor the strictly theological viewpoints make sense. We are struggling to find a third perspective on where we stand in the order of reality, a new way of expressing how we are beginning to see things. To help us discover and articulate a new standpoint, Eugen proposes an updated Latin formula to replace the *Cogito* and the *Credo*. Like them, it is a motto expressed in just three words: *Respondeo etsi mutabor* (I respond although I will be changed).

In this new perspective we are neither above nor below reality. We stand at its center. We are addressed by it and we must reply. In the process of replying, by speech and act, we find that we have been changed. We make progress insofar as we make truthful (and that means *timely*) replies.

In this new perspective, God is not a being dwelling above us, but rather "the power which makes us speak." *And* the power that forces us to answer. The Cross of Reality shows us that any significant experience in life starts with an imperative or vocative, calling us toward the future. The motto *Respondeo etsi mutabor* describes what happens when we hear such a call. At first we are not sure whether we should respond. We are comfortable with the past, with what we already know. To do something new may be painful; in fact, it *usually* is. That's why Eugen used the word *etsi, although*. But there's never any progress, personal or social, without people taking the risk and responding to some new calling in their lives.

Can These Ideas Be Tested?

The professional attackers of religion like to make much of the "fact" that no religious propositions can be tested. In Sam Harris's 2004 blockbuster book, *The End of Faith*, he says you cannot prove that any religious propositions are true; there's no evidence for them. If you frame such propositions in traditional language, perhaps Harris has a point. However, everything I have been saying here, framed as it is by the Cross of Reality, is *eminently testable!* No matter how spiritual, it can still be *proved to be true*—by combinations of logic and experiment. This theme is taken up by Rosenstock-Huessy in one of his finest essays, "The Uni-versity of Logic, Language, and Literature." Like him, in this book, I try to speak no words that abandon the tests of logic, evidence, and verification. Rosenstock-Huessy addressed this point when he wrote:

> Language is a process that can be weighed and measured and listened to and can be physically experienced. It goes on before our eyes and ears. Is it not strange that the science of this lifeblood of society should not be exalted to the rank of social research?

If you can weigh and measure, you can test. I have been testing these ideas for some 67 years.

The Complete Cross of Reality

Appendix A displays a more complete version of the Cross of Reality than I showed in Chapter 1. While the reader might want to glance at that version now, the many subjects covered in it will make more sense after reading the first seven chapters. I have called this the "complete Cross of Reality" because I liked the alliteration of two c's, and it *is* complete as far as *this* book's topics are concerned. But there are countless further categories of human experience that could be added to it; the ones shown here are simply those I have found to be the most important.

Now I should enter a sort of quit-claim on this cross. Certainly life, and especially the life of the spirit, cannot be reduced to a diagram. The Cross of Reality is no automatic "Open, Sesame" to perceiving all the truth or solving all our problems, be they secular or religious, personal or social.

In other words, its usefulness as a model or method depends entirely on the imagination, resources, and energy with which we apply it to understanding and dealing with those problems.

3 The Spirit as Speech

All speech is the precipitation of the intensified respiration which we experience as members of a community, and which is called the Spirit.

—Eugen Rosenstock-Huessy

The spirit of man is the Holy Spirit.

—Eugen Rosenstock-Huessy

One knew that the distinction between immanence and transcendence disappears in language.

—Franz Rosenzweig

It was during the First World War that the ideas presented in those epigraphs, about the spirit as speech, first saw the light of day. Eugen Rosenstock was fighting on the western front at Verdun, while his close friend, Franz Rosenzweig, was stationed on the eastern front in Macedonia. (Eugen Rosenstock added "Huessy" to his name in 1925, having married the Swiss Margrit Huessy in 1914.) Throughout the summer of 1916 these two young men engaged in an intense trench-to-trench correspondence on Judaism and Christianity. Their letters were later published, and have been widely discussed. The Jewish scholar Hans Schoeps described them as "the purest form of Judaeo-Christian dialogue ever attained, perhaps even for ages to come."

In his final letter of this correspondence, dated December 1916, Rosenzweig asked Rosenstock to tell him more about his new understanding of language. Rosenstock replied in early 1917 with such a long letter that it eventually became the text for a book, published in 1924 as *Angewandte Seelenkunde* (Practical Knowledge of the Soul).

After the war, Rosenzweig became famous for the book he completed in 1921, *The Star of Redemption*, a contemporary interpretation of Judaism and Christianity based largely on understanding speech as God's action in us. Revelation, redemption, and creation, he said, are continuing processes in human life, not one-time biblical events.

"Man became man when he first spoke," Rosenzweig wrote. True speech is revelation itself. As he put it, "one knew that the distinction between immanence and transcendence disappears in language." Rosenzweig actually began writing *The Star* in 1918, over a year after his correspondence with Rosenstock on Judaism and Christianity had ended. And he gratefully acknowledged that "the main influence" for his book had been that letter on language, which Eugen had sent to him early in 1917.

Shattered by their experience of the war, both Rosenstock and Rosenzweig felt that timeless abstract philosophizing and theologizing no longer addressed what really happened in our lives. Rosenstock-Huessy addressed this theme in many works. For example, in his *Speech and Reality,* he points to how Rosenzweig had opened *The Star* with these words: "From death, and from the fear of death alone, springs all knowledge. Philosophy tries to throw off the fear of things earthly, to rob death of its poisonous sting."

The dialogue between Rosenstock and Rosenzweig was remarkably deep and creative. Rosenstock's parents were Jewish, but they were not religious observants. He had first met Rosenzweig, two years his senior, in 1910, when they had both gone to a scholarly conference in the German spa town, Baden-Baden. On the evening of July 7, 1913, in Leipzig, they had a long conversation on religion, as a result of which Rosenzweig decided that he should abandon his Jewish heritage, to which he felt little attachment, and adopt Christianity. However, he wanted to attend one final synagogue service, the Day of Atonement, October 11. Hearing the sound of the ram's horn at that service so moved him that he reversed his decision. He proceeded to become a profoundly believing Jew. As *The Star* reveals, however, his profound belief was matched by a profoundly contemporary conception of what belief really means.

In a 1924 essay entitled "Das neue Denken" ("The New Thinking"), Rosenzweig clarified the ideas he had presented in *The Star*. One bold claim he made in "The New Thinking" was that the "method of speech" he and Rosenstock were developing "replaces the method of thinking maintained in all earlier philosophies." Whether Rosenzweig's extravagant claim can be justified is an underlying theme of this book.

The last decade has seen an explosion of interest in Rosenzweig. Mark Lilla, an essayist and historian of ideas and currently teaching at Columbia University, reviewed eleven recent books by or about Rosenzweig in the December 2002 *New York Review of Books*. Unfortunately, Lilla showed not the slightest interest in Rosenstock-Huessy. Instead, he calls him Rosenzweig's "confused young friend." Dismissing the "new thinking" on language as of little significance, Lilla sees Rosenzweig primarily as an innovative thinker on religion. Lilla's flippant remark about Rosenstock-Huessy is a classic example of academe's response to him.

The Law of Motion of the Spirit

Academics generally do not want language to be tainted by "spirit," which evaporated for most of them with the Enlightenment. For a Lilla, "new thinking" about speech and the spirit, giving rise to "the method of speech," is simply confusing.

Of course, it is the method of speech that is made visible on the Cross of Reality. Indeed, that cross is best understood as a dynamic model of just how speech works in us. It shows us that we live in an infinitely richer realm than that described to us by natural science or by most traditional theology. We are neither the cold observers of the world outside us nor the faithful children of a God above. Instead, we live at the heart of reality. We are the agents for the evolution as well as the revolution of matter and spirit. There is no outside prime mover like the God described by Descartes, Spinoza, or the deists. Nor is there a supreme being, above and beyond, like the God of theists. The only motion of the spirit is within human souls and between human souls. God speaks, or fails to speak, in each of us. He is infinitely close, not infinitely distant.

Now, if the only motion of the spirit is in and between us, is it possible to describe that motion? Rosenstock-Huessy suggests a specific law of motion of the spirit. This law, showing us how the spirit moves within us and how the soul is formed, becomes clear only when we realize that *spirit* is not something nebulous in the air. Rather, spirit is audible; it is the higher kind of all human speech. And such speech does not have an infinite variety of forms. Again, there are only four basic kinds of speech, and they move us through the four stages of any significant experience:

1. Imperative (vocative) speech is what calls us to the future. We hear ourselves addressed as *thou (you)*. Such speech wakes us up and inclines us to respond. *Go thou!* Fulfill what you are called to do.

2. Subjective (poetic, prayerful, and philosophical) speech is what we use to address our inner self, our *I*. Now the grammatical mood becomes subjunctive. *What if I were to go?* Inner questioning arises in response to the pressure of imperatives.

3. Narrative (historical) speech enables us to recall past time or tell the current history of our lives. *We* becomes our grammatical person because creative action requires more than one person. *We went, or we are going.* Learning from what has happened in the past, we start interacting with others.

4. Objective (scientific) speech makes it possible for us to analyze the world outside us. Now we and others can see ourselves as *he, she* or *they*. *She went; they went.* No longer "moved" by speech, we step back and assess what is going on.

Those four stages of any memorable experience are universal and inevitable for all of us. As we move through them, we are conjugated into those four different grammatical persons: *thou (you), I, we, he* or *she.*

This law of motion of the spirit is central to a dialogical method. Rosenzweig called it "the speech method," and Rosenstock-Huessy called it "the grammatical method." All three names refer to the same thing. Sometimes this focus on language has been called "dialogical thinking" or "speech thinking." Whatever it is called, it appears that its first 20th-century expression was in that 1917 letter of Rosenstock's to Rosenzweig, which was subsequently published as *Practical Knowledge of the Soul.*

> Does the soul have a grammar? Now, as the Word comes out of the soul, and the truest Word comes straight from the very depths of the soul, . . . then, just as the mind has logic, the soul will have a sense of the way words fit together—that is, "grammar"—as its inner structure. . . . He who would explore the soul must fathom the secrets of language.

This passage reveals those secrets, in their simplest form. A key secret is that language turns us into the four grammatical persons: *thou, I, we, he or she*—and in that order. A related secret is that language, more surely than reason, creates our sense of the future and the past, our inner selves, and the outer world.

Revelation Is Orientation

Of the many seminal ideas that Rosenstock gave to Rosenzweig, there is one that seems immensely fruitful, and incredibly concise: "Revelation is orientation." Rosenzweig considered this a breakthrough insight, one that integrated religious revelation, creation, and redemption with what goes on in our daily lives.

Reflecting on what Rosenstock meant by "revelation is orientation," I have come to see it as telling us what happens to us in the interior language of prayer. Not prayer as sponsored by organized religion, but prayer as engaged in by all human beings, whether they are religious or not. Prayer in this larger sense is not like reaching up to be in touch with an all-powerful divine Father who can advise, guide, intervene, and save. Instead, it is like centering oneself at a place where one's interior life meets one's tasks in the exterior world. And like drawing strength from one's own past, and the past of the whole race, as one seeks to find the way into a meaningful future. At this center of the cross in which we live, God reveals himself to us. Revelation becomes a new orientation to the times of our personal history and all history, just as it becomes a new orientation of our inner self to the world outside us.

High Speech

We can now see that Rosenstock and Rosenzweig have raised our understanding of language from being simply a mode of communication to something at a distinctly higher level. They have enabled us to perceive speech as the body of the spirit, indeed as the body of the Holy Spirit.

But their concerns were not simply in the realm of spirituality or religion. Both Rosenstock and Rosenzweig were clear that they were working toward disclosing a method for the human sciences, including philosophy and theology, just as surely as Descartes perceived that his goal was a new method for natural science (one he thought would apply to all realms of knowledge).

At the time of the First World War, when Rosenstock and Rosenzweig began their conspiracy against the accepted wisdom of that era, anthropology and psychology were quite new disciplines. The leading lights in each were inclined to treat language simply as a wonderful tool, the means by which we communicate with each other, a way of transferring ideas out of one mind and into another. Rosenstock and Rosenzweig, by contrast, saw language as something much more fundamental and more marvelous: Language had turned us into human beings—and eventually into religious human beings.

Rosenstock-Huessy's essay, "The Origin of Speech," distinguishes between two kinds of speech. On the one hand, we have the formal or high speech that we use "to sing a chorale, to stage tragedy, to enact laws, to compose verse, to say grace, to take an oath, to confess one's sins, to file a complaint, to write a biography, to make a report, to solve an algebraic problem, to baptize a child, to sign a marriage contract, to bury one's father." On the other hand, we have the informal or low speech that we might use to show "a man the direction to the next farm on the road" or to stop "a child from crying." Such low speech, which makes up "our daily chatter and prattle," often serves "the same purposes as animal sounds."

It was only after reading that "Origin" essay that I came to understand what Rosenstock-Huessy meant by "high speech." He meant the intentional, relational, and dialogical speech, the fully articulated speech we use when we seek to tell the truth or establish relations with others. It is the language we use to advance any cause, large or small, social or personal. It is not the language we use when we say, "Please pass the salt" or "Goodbye." But it is rare to go through a day without using this higher form of speech. As a matter of fact, there is a vestige of high speech in "Please pass the salt," since "Please" establishes a cordial relationship. Similarly, "Goodbye" is a vestigial remnant of its origin in the heartfelt blessing, "God be with you."

The higher kind of speech is "bound to time and nourished by time," as Rosenzweig expressed it. Whenever we use such speech, we create a tension between past and future; we speak to change the listener and our times.

It also helps to grasp the idea of high speech when we make a distinction between what we mean by *language* and what we mean by *speech.* Language can be simply any use of words, while true speech involves not only speaking but *listening.* The word that we have heard from another stays with us and frames what we do, from our smallest to our largest actions.

In other words, high speech always implies its own enactment. The words that initiate such speech stay alive and guide us through their realization. We never leave the fields of force created by high speech, from a well-timed word of encouragement from a parent or teacher to an order given in combat.

While it is certainly not always the higher form, even what goes on inside our minds is speech. As Rosenstock-Huessy puts it, "thinking is nothing but a storage room for speech."

The Many Kinds of High Speech

Although Rosenstock-Huessy emphasizes the spoken word in his writings, he certainly suggests that all intentional and truth-telling human expression is high speech. From the first drawings of a bison in caves, to tribal dancing and chanting, to a symphony by Beethoven, to a painting by Paul Klee, to a house by Frank Lloyd Wright, to a book by Dostoevsky, to a poem by Robert Frost, we speak about who we are, we keep the past alive, and we feel called to our future.

So speech is not simply words. It is not simply our informal chatter or the tool we use to survive, though those are "low" speech. It is not simply earnest dialogue, debate, drama or sermon, although those are "high" forms of speech. It is not only what we say with our mouths; it is also what we write on paper as poetry, literature, or drama. Beyond all those word forms, speech is any fully serious human expression, from a hug or caress to a dance or a symphony.

High speech is even serious humor. Garry Trudeau's "Doonesbury" is a good example. In humor we show that we can juggle the different kinds of speech; we play with them. Indeed, humor is a vital kind of speech, lubricating, as it were, the transmission of all the others. As serious a philosopher as Solovyov wrote a humorous satire about himself—and once defined man as the *laughing animal.* Rosenstock-Huessy's culminating chapter in *Out of Revolution* is titled "The Survival Value of Humour." There he says, "Common sense. . . acts on the principle that a man who fails to apply laughing and weeping in the discovery of vital truth simply is immature."

High speech becomes frozen in the architecture of our buildings and the environments we create in our towns and cities; it is expressed by our monuments and gravestones. In fact, everything we create, every form of human expression, is a form of speech. Even thinking and prayer, or reading, are acts of speech inside us. They resonate and reflect on the open speech that carries us through life.

This understanding of speech accounts for the deaf and blind, people like Helen Keller. The miracle of Helen Keller's life was brought about by the loving care of her family and her teacher-friend Anne Sullivan. If they had never "talked" to her, she would never have uttered a word, and the name *Helen Keller* would mean nothing to us.

So high speech includes all language, verbal and non-verbal, that serves a constructive social purpose, all language that is intentional, relational, or seeks to tell the truth. Examples of what it does not include are chatter, gossip, ranting, lying, propaganda, and advertising.

The most important thing to say about high speech is that it frames and determines all our actions in life. Any social act is the carrying out of an intention that had been created in us through listening first, then responding inside ourselves, and finally deciding to do something. The action is simply the outer completion of the speech that began as an inner listening. All our experiences from birth to death are framed by what is spoken to us and what we reply. We are the most plastic of all creatures; we are the receptacles and organs of speech.

If our personal lives are framed by speech, so our history has been created through speech. Our entire organization and interpretation of the world are accomplished through what we have heard from preceding generations and what we say to the next. Through speech we learn what it is to have a future and a past. Without speech we would not be conscious of historical time. With our consciousness of time, of timing, of seizing the right moment, and saying the right word, we place ourselves at the center of the creative process. The story of human progress is the story of when we have said the right words at the right time.

Politics is not so much the art of the possible as it is the art of the spoken word. We attain political office, or any significant position in life, through what we are able to say, and especially through what we are able to say without advance preparation. It is what we say without a written speech, when we are on our feet before an audience, that enables our listeners to decide whether we can be trusted as leaders in our times. If we cannot think and talk on our feet, then the public quite rightly knows that we will not be able to act on our feet when the time comes for us to take immediate action. The complete person, the whole person, the person who can be trusted with great responsibility, is the person whose speech comes so naturally that one senses his or her integrity. Indeed, a person's integrity is the coincidence of thinking, speaking, and acting.

The Four Forms of High Speech

Rosenstock-Huessy has shown us that all high speech takes just four forms—imperative, subjective, narrative, and objective. Those forms, taken together, create the Cross of Reality in which we live. Now we might focus, even more closely, on how these quite different ways of speaking orient us throughout our lives.

1. Imperative Speech: Toward Future Time

Imperative speech is what calls us to any important undertaking in life. It establishes our commitments, loves, avocations, and (if we are fortunate) our vocations. Thus, "vocative," which emphasizes "calling," is another name for the imperative. We hear such speech from parents, teachers, or any other person whose guidance we seek. We hear it as the Ten Commandments or Isaiah; as Luther's 95 Theses or the Declaration of Independence.

To give us a fresh sense of this future-creating speech, and to contrast it with subjective and objective speech, Rosenstock-Huessy has proposed that we also call it "prejective" speech.

We hear such speech in the words of anybody who cares for us, addressing us as *thou.* Any speech that casts a net of faith into the future is a vocative, like "Will you marry me?" That is not a request for information.

A person who is starved for such speech cannot discover who he or she is and therefore cannot speak his or her own imperatives. A society that cannot speak its own imperatives gives way to decadence. Decadence is the inability of one generation to communicate imperatives to the next. All education, therefore, that is not simply technical, aims to create and maintain imperatives. *This future-creating speech precedes and determines all the others.* Until we sense this orientation and feel overwhelmed by it, we never really begin anything new in our lives.

In religious terms, it is hard to imagine a resurrection for the person who has not been moved by the imperative, and lives simply for his or her own time. We are only a little lower than the angels, and we *are* supernatural, because we are the creature that can hear the call to enter the future.

2. Subjective Speech: Toward Our Inner Space

Subjective speech arises in response to imperatives and vocatives. It creates the inner space where we begin to feel personally responsible for the appropriate answers to life's questions.

Now just why is it that subjective speech *follows* the imperative in a necessary sequence? What is the connection between listening to the imperatives of a leader or a teacher who inspired you, and going to the theater, listening to music, or simply going for a walk? Well, after you hear somebody tell you to change your ways, you want to stop and sort things out. That is why the speech that takes us from the call of the future to our inner orientation is in the subjunctive, conditional, or optative mood. We turn inward, start questioning, and consider different responses.

Art, music, literature, poetry—in fact, all the voices of culture—are subjective speech. The arts remind us of all the possible ways to reply to imperatives. We can be the doubting Ivan Karamazov or we can be the faithful Alyosha.

A critical kind of interior speech is prayer. Prayer is a concentrated pondering of one's reply to the callings of the future. For the religious, prayer means a listening to God's imperatives, a recognizing that we are being addressed. How should I respond—although I know I will be changed?

However, we *all* participate in prayer, even if we profess no religion. Constructive prayer does not aim to carry us deeper and deeper into an interior life. It aims to take us momentarily into this interior, and then to become more purposefully engaged in solving the crises of our own lives—and the larger crises of society.

We develop our unique personality by selecting, from the many imperatives that address us, the particular callings and the particular causes that move us to respond. We are not just bundles of nerves, but we are just bundles of responses.

"Go thou," the prophets of preceding generations say to us. "I'm not sure whether I'll go," we reply. As we question and decide just what we will do, we discover our identity, our *I*. We then feel different from "the establishment" of any preceding generation. From an orientation toward the future of the whole race, created by the imperative *thou*, we proceed to the singular, inward space of the individual who replies, the *I*.

3. Narrative Speech: Carrying the Past Forward

We enter historical time when we leave the subjective orientation of *I* and decide to express ourselves openly in the world. That means taking responsible action with some other person or group. This is our answer to the questioning that went on in our second, interior orientation. It may mean marriage or becoming wedded to one's career, but in every case it forms a *dual* relationship: You cannot act historically by yourself. You incorporate, you embody. Therefore, our speech and actions are now in the narrative mood and the grammatical person of *we*.

Marriage is the most obvious dual required to continue creation, but unmarried persons form generative attachments whenever they relate themselves to some significant cause or institution.

Through narrative speech we participate in past time, not only as a part of the world's history but also as a part of the "current history" of our own lives. Let us consider why narrative speech does not face backward but *carries forward*. Rosenstock-Huessy suggested that we name our orientation to past time as "trajective." There is no better statement of what trajective speech means than the one made by Vladimir Solovyov in his story, "The Secret of Progress," about a hunter lost in a forest. Despairing of getting out, he is offered help by a repulsive old woman. She assures him that she can show him the way if he will only carry her across a stream. As he does so, the heavy old lady becomes lighter and lighter; at the other side she is turned into an enchanting maiden.

Here are Solovyov's moving words as he comments on this story:

The modern man, hunting after fleeting, momentary goods and elusive fancies, has lost his right path in life. The dark and turbulent stream of life is before him. Time like a woodpecker mercilessly registers the moments that have been lost. Misery and solitude, and afterwards—darkness and perdition. But behind him stands the sacred antiquity of tradition—oh, in what an unattractive form! Well, what of it? Let him only think of what he owes to her; let him with an inner heartfelt impulse revere her grayness, pity her infirmities, feel ashamed of rejecting her because of her appearance. Instead of idly looking out for phantom-like fairies beyond the clouds, let him undertake the labor of carrying this sacred burden across the real stream of history. This is the only way out of his wanderings—the only, because any other would be insufficient, unkind, impious: He could not let the ancient creature perish!

The modern man does not believe in the fairy tale, he does not believe that the decrepit old woman will be transformed into a queen of beauty. But if he does not believe it, so much the better! Why believe in the future reward when what is required is to deserve it by the present effort and self-denying heroism? Those who do not believe in the future of the old and the sacred must, at any rate, remember its past. Why should he not carry her across, out of reverence for her antiquity, out of pity for her decay, out of shame for being ungrateful? Blessed are the believers: While still standing on this shore they already see through the wrinkles of old age the brilliance of incorruptible beauty. But unbelievers in the future transformation have the advantage of unexpected joy. Both the believers and the unbelievers have the same task: to go forward, taking upon their shoulders the whole weight of antiquity.

4. Objective Speech: Toward the Outside World

Our life in the first three speech orientations—imperative, subjective, and narrative—comprises all of our "high" experience. But we cannot live through these experiences, we cannot complete them, understand them, or be open to new experience without our fourth orientation via objective speech. Thus, this strictly rational orientation plays as vital a role in our lives as the first three. The only mistake made by today's academic, scientific, and technology-obsessed minds has been to identify such speech as the primary and supremely "real" one.

Objective speech states as an outward fact what was first a powerful calling *(thou)*, then an inner secret *(I)*, next a shared experience *(we)*, and now is simply a commonplace for everyone *(they, he, she,* or *it)*.

In our daily lives we hear objective speech whenever we analyze our own or somebody else's experience. Most journalism is objective speech. So are all the facts and figures, all the data that we use to organize our lives and our economies. Mathematics and statistics are necessarily objective.

The natural sciences are, of course, quite properly objective; but today's social sciences suffer from being *improperly* objective. They imitate natural science by adopting its numerical, statistical, and analytical method.

While he devoted all his energies to attacking the dominance of objective speech in today's world, Rosenstock-Huessy never suggested we retreat to our inner orientation or reject our outer one. In fact, he positively celebrated the role of rational, analytical speech:

> The fourth phase, analytics, is indispensable, too. . . . In this phase the movement dies and is discarded as merely natural. "Nature" we call everything which exists without "you," without "me" and without "us.". . . In the "natural" the act is dismissed. . . . The fourth phase of speech is the spirit's death. If we call the impetus by which a total experience subjects one man to the four phases through which the experience is realized "spirit," i.e., a breath of life, then phase four is the phase in which the spirit dies but the specimen recovers. If phase four did not abstract us from our spells, freedom could not exist to start a new phase.

The Four Moods of Literature and Theater

Rosenstock-Huessy made clear that high speech is more than aural when he described how all literature and theater express themselves in just four moods, four primary kinds of speech.

First, there is the *dramatic*, heavy and imperative in style, challenging us to move toward the future.

Second, we have the *lyric*, which is light, personal, and includes comedy. Its inner orientation is subjective.

Third comes the *epic*, the historical narrative, such as the *Iliad* or the *Odyssey*.

Fourth, and finally, we have the *prosaic*, the outward and objective presentation of life, the "realistic."

It is not simply that literature and theater divide into those four ways of speaking. Almost every human language has at least four moods that change the verbs of any sentence. In English we have the *imperative* "Go!"; the *subjunctive* "Were I to go?"; the *narrative* "I am going"; and the *indicative* "He went."

Language Does Not Describe

To sum up, we can now perceive why Rosenstock-Huessy called speech the "only miracle." As we speak in future, past, inner, and outer directions, we actually *create* those directions. They were not there before we said so! History exists because we tell it. Without prayer, music, and poetry, there would be no inner self. Without vocatives and prophecy, no future. Without measurement and analysis, no science. In Rosenstock-Huessy's concise formulation: "By speaking we create times and spaces. Language does not describe. It creates a before and after as well as a here and there."

I Have Been Spoken to, Therefore I Am

We can now also perceive why speech is a more fundamental category in the human phenomenon than reason or thinking. All significant human experience—personal, social, and historical—takes place in the context of speech and can be interpreted by a full understanding of speech. Our lives are framed by the speech of others; our own contribution to history is what we "say" by word and deed. As persons we are simply the embodiment of speech. Descartes said, "I think, therefore I am." We reply, "No, René, you have it wrong. What you really mean is, 'I have been spoken to, therefore I am.'"

Our presentation of the four forms of speech tells us that, in the human community, *speech does much more than express ideas; it establishes relationships*. When used for its purpose, such "high speech" establishes peaceful or healthy relationships—for us as individuals, as groups, or as nations—with all our speech partners.

When we perceive speech in it fullness, we overcome our inheritance from Aristotle and Descartes: imagining that being rational is the main goal of the human mind. What the Cross of Reality shows us, as it arrays the four forms of speech—in their relationship to changing the times and renewing the self and the world—is that our goal is to be "supra-rational." That is, reason (with its objectivity) should always be present in any complete experience of thinking, speaking, and acting. *It is simply that reason does not trump the other three ways we apprehend reality or tell the full truth.*

William James on the Soul

The philosopher and psychologist William James (1842–1910) said he would rather not say anything about the soul until he could grasp the pragmatic significance of that term. What we have described above as our four speech orientations, seen as one sequence informing any important human experience, may also be seen, quite pragmatically, as describing the formation of the soul.

Our soul—or in secular terms, our psyche—is what we form when we move responsively through all four speech orientations. It is our power, expressed by speech and act, to live so that we represent past and future times and inner and outer spaces. Our soul grows larger the more we feel compelled to listen and speak imperatively, subjectively, narratively, and objectively. Our soul does not belong to some other world, or go to some other world, as religious thought often suggests. No; the soul is the way we incarnate the word down here.

Logos: In Heraclitus and St. John

While it is quite correct to see Rosenstock-Huessy's and Rosenzweig's understanding of language as something genuinely new, it is also, paradoxically, quite correct to see it as something very old. Indeed, it dates from one Greek man who is often called the first philosopher, Heraclitus (530-470 BC), and another man whom we might call the first Christian theologian, St. John of the Fourth Gospel.

Heraclitus had used the word *Logos* when he said: "We should let ourselves be guided by what is common to all. Yet, although the

Logos is common to all, most men live as if each of them had a private intelligence of his own." We will never know for sure whether Heraclitus meant "speech" or "reason" when he wrote those words about *Logos*, but they seem to make more sense if he meant "speech," something that links us with one another, overcoming our tendency to live privately.

The Gospel of St. John opens with the imperishable words: "In the beginning was the Word, and the Word was with God, and the Word was God. . . . And the Word was made flesh, and dwelt among us." In the original text, St. John used *Logos* for *Word*. Here it is more certain that he meant "speech," since it is hard to imagine "reason" becoming flesh in Christ. It was "the living word" that came to dwell in the flesh. (I am capitalizing *Logos* throughout this book since I am presenting it both as the religious Word of God *and* as the living word spoken by all humankind.)

In view of what St. John and Heraclitus said of speech, what Rosenstock and Rosenzweig were "discovering" in 1916 could hardly be older. They were rediscovering something that had become obscured by more than two millennia of timeless Platonic philosophizing and Aristotelian metaphysics.

That is why Rosenzweig was justified in his extravagant claim about replacing the methods of all earlier philosophies. The two millennia of obscuring also explain the slowness in the recognition of what these two men were discovering. Our minds have been supersaturated with the abstract, objectifying thought of Plato, Aristotle, and Descartes.

Sin as the Abuse of Speech

It is easy to suggest fault in Rosenstock-Huessy's "Everybody who speaks believes in God because he speaks." For example, how does one reconcile that with Adolf Hitler, a man whose powers of speech intoxicated most of Germany?

The answer is that Hitler was not really speaking in his tirades to the German public. Instead, he was ranting; he was abusing speech. Rosenstock-Huessy said that speech exists primarily to establish relations with others, to make peace, and to tell the truth. But speech can also be abused if it is used to destroy relations, to make war, and to lie. Everybody who abuses speech, like Hitler, shows our capacity for sin and evil, the power of the devil in us, if you don't mind an old-fashioned reference.

The Cross of Reality and the Cross of Christ

Is it appropriate or effective to describe the Cross of Reality as a secular image? I have been describing it as an image of how the spirit, even the Holy Spirit, is at work in us. But should we go further and think of it as an image of the Cross of Christ?

Since Rosenstock-Huessy's work has been bedeviled by confusion on this question, it bears looking at. It is certainly true that, in *The Christian Future*, he described the Cross of Reality as a secular translation of the Cross of Christ. That is, we are all crucified, we all have to bear a cross, no matter what our religion—or even if we profess no religion.

But the Cross of Reality is not something to which one makes a commitment, as one does to the Cross of Christ. Before one starts to talk about any topic, be it religion, the person, or history, one can turn to the Cross of Reality as a basic model of the human condition. It shows us what faces the animal that speaks. It shows us that this animal acquired language and grammar, that it now understands how to sing and pray and draw pictures. It tells us that we became the human animal when we learned to speak, to hear imperatives, to think subjectively, to tell history narratively, and to build homes in the outer world.

Thus, one can use the Cross of Reality to investigate and clarify any matter of human concern, as Rosenstock-Huessy did when he compared Christianity with the other great religions. He said that Christianity was primarily concerned with the future front, while Judaism was more related to our roots in the past. By contrast, we have two spatial religions in Buddhism and Taoism. Buddha wanted to save us from strife on the outer front, while Lao Tzu told us how to be content with self-effacement on the inner.

In sum, the Cross of Reality is not a uniquely Christian image, nor is it the Cross of Christ. It is simply an image of the human condition, one that is crucial at its core. As we study the orientations on it, and especially the tensions among those orientations, we perceive that this model can be turned into a method able to address any subject of human concern.

A Complex Grammar

We have said that poetry can be high speech. After Rosenstock-Huessy died in 1973, Auden wrote the poem, "Aubade," as a tribute to him. Published in *The Atlantic*, its last stanza reads:

> But Time, the Domain of Deeds,
> calls for a complex Grammar
> with many Moods and Tenses,
> and prime the Imperative.
> We are free to choose our paths,
> but choose We must, no matter
> where they lead, and the tales
> we tell of the Past must be true.
> Human Time is a City
> where each inhabitant has
> a political duty
> nobody else can perform,
> made cogent by her Motto:
> LISTEN, MORTALS, LEST YE DIE!

4 THE DIALOGICAL METHOD

Our defense of grammar is provoked by the obvious fact that this organon, this matrix form of thinking, is not used as a universal method, hitherto. . . . The originality of social research hinges on the existence of a method that is neither stolen from theology nor from natural science.

—Eugen Rosenstock-Huessy

AS I MENTIONED IN THE ACKNOWLEDGMENTS, in 1963 I began an ecumenical church discussion group, one intended to provide a forum for discussing thinkers like Rosenstock-Huessy and Rosenzweig, Martin Buber, Paul Tillich, and Dietrich Bonhoeffer, all of whom have made important contributions to Christianity's new paradigm. Early in 1965, we turned to Buber's *I and Thou*.

Buber's leading US interpreter, Professor Maurice Friedman, addressed one of our sessions. Ten years earlier, he had published *Martin Buber: The Life of Dialogue*, and had accomplished for Buber something none of us students had so far accomplished for Rosenstock-Huessy. That is, Buber was being widely read and discussed on campuses and in study groups like ours.

"A third Copernican revolution" was how Friedman described Buber's thought, a revolution as momentous as Immanuel Kant's had been. Kant, he reminded us, had reoriented Western thought with his assertion that the individual mind itself has an inner order (presumably in the way our brain is made) that determines the order it perceives in the world outside it. Buber had gone beyond Kant with his "social conception of knowledge." The isolated individual mind cannot even begin to perceive external order until it has entered into social, dialogical relationships. The feral child, brought up by wolves, unspoken to, is speechless and hardly human.

Friedman had generously acknowledged that Rosenstock-Huessy, Rosenzweig, and others had been cofounders of "dialogical thinking." However, it could be argued that this "third Copernican revolution" had really been begun by Rosenstock-Huessy, who had more profound insights than Buber into the ways we are shaped by speech, not only personally but also *historically*.

There is a great difference between Buber and Rosenstock-Huessy. Buber said that any person, an independent *I*, can choose to have either warm dialogical *I-thou* relationships or cold objectifying *I-it* relationships, with others or with God. One does not become a fully realized person until one chooses the *I-thou* relationship. As Buber expressed his key insight, "as I become *I*, I say *thou*."

Rosenstock-Huessy, by contrast, said that there is no such thing as an independent *I*. One becomes an *I* only as one is addressed by others, and by God, as *thou*. The proper grammatical order is *thou-I*, not *I-thou*. It is when we hear imperatives, when we hear ourselves addressed *personally* as *thou*, that we enter into the human story. As Eugen describes it, "The first form and the permanent form under which a man can recognize himself and the unity of his existence is the Imperative. We are called a Man and we are summoned by our name long before we are aware of ourselves as an Ego."

In further contrast with Buber, Rosenstock-Huessy said that, after hearing oneself addressed imperatively (or vocatively) as *thou*, and then realizing oneself as *I*, one then goes on to become two further grammatical persons: *we* and *he* (or *she*). In other words, Eugen describes us as living in a four-fold reality, a Cross of Reality, while Buber describes only a two-fold reality.

A great deal depends on whether we see our speech universe as two-fold or four-fold. Rosenstock-Huessy addressed this issue by contrasting what he called Buber's "concept" with his "method." And a great deal depends on whether we see the beginning of speech as *I-thou* or *thou-I*. Their order relates not only to our understanding of language but also to our understanding of God. As Rosenstock-Huessy put it, "God can never communicate something to me as long as I think of myself as an *I*. God recognizes me only as a *thou*."

While Rosenstock-Huessy and Buber had their differences, Buber was quite generous in acknowledging Rosenstock-Huessy's work. In fact, the back jackets of numerous Argo Books publications contain his endorsement:

> The historical nature of man is the aspect of reality about which we have been basically and emphatically instructed in

the epoch of thought beginning with Hegel. . . . Rosenstock-Huessy has concretized this teaching in so living a way as no other thinker before him has done.

One of Rosenstock-Huessy's students, Marshall Meyer, lived at Four Wells during 1952, when he was a Dartmouth undergraduate. He went on to become a prominent rabbi in Buenos Aires and then in New York. Part of his life at Four Wells involved driving Rosenstock-Huessy to events and meetings. Meyer recounted a story about driving Eugen to the train station in White River Junction, Vermont, to pick up Buber for a visit. Meyer described his feelings when he watched their warm embrace on the platform. He said their arms seemed to reach back to the early 1920s—to include Franz Rosenzweig, who had collaborated with both of them during those postwar years.

Speech and Reality

Rosenstock-Huessy's lead essay in *Speech and Reality* (Argo, 1970) was called, "In Defense of the Grammatical Method." In it, he made a strong case for his envisioned unifying science—his metanomics—contrasting its basic assumptions with those of theology and natural science. My introduction to that book included large claims for the author, saying that the book's purpose was to "dethrone the Cartesian method as the basis of all science." The theologian John Macquarrie reviewed the book in *Commonweal* magazine, and took me to task for claiming that Rosenstock-Huessy had "made an epoch-making discovery for the future of man's knowledge about himself." Nevertheless, Macquarrie summed up the book's main point with a telling clarity:

> The author believes. . . that the social sciences suffer from being forced into the methodological mold of the natural sciences. Anyone acquainted with the kind of psychology and sociology commonly taught in the United States today could hardly fail to agree. . . . But where do we look for a better method? Rosenstock-Huessy suggests that we look to language. Speech is the basic social reality. Grammar, in turn, is the science which describes and analyzes the structures of

language. Hence, grammar is the foundation for developing a methodology for the social sciences.

Applying the Dialogical Method

Just what would that methodology look like? Rosenstock-Huessy made such diverse approaches to presenting his "grammatical method" that it takes a close reading to understand the scope and breadth of what he was saying.

The dialogical method, based as it is on the Cross of Reality, assumes that all four forms of speech—imperative, subjective, narrative, and objective—are *equally important* and are *interdependent*. It follows that, in applying this method, we should attempt to understand and answer any human question in terms of its four speech-created orientations.

First, the most general way of applying the method is to examine any human question in terms of its relation:

1. To the past, to history and tradition, to its *narrative*.
2. To the future, to the *imperatives* involved.
3. To the *subjective* inner feelings and convictions of the participants.
4. To the *objective* facts—and the action now needed in the world.

Second, we can examine any question in terms of the four stages in any significant human experience. Specifically, any problem, from the collapse of a nation's economy to an individual's nervous breakdown, can be examined:

1. Initially, in relation to the future-oriented imperative(s) that set it in motion.
2. Then, how it entered a subjective phase, within the society or person.
3. Subsequently, how it became institutionalized in historical time.
4. Finally, how it played out, objectively, in the outer world.

Third, we might ask which of these four orientations has become dominant in an individual or group. Which consciousness is most evident? Is the person or group experiencing themselves as a *thou*, an *I*, a *we*, or a *they*?

One is likely to find that all three of these ways of applying the dialogical method are relevant in a given situation. In any case, it is attention to *all four* of our speech-created orientations, and especially to their interrelation, that makes the method different from what is generally understood as the scientific method today. That method, the approach enthroned by natural science and still dominant in the academic mind, is simply one step in the more all-embracing dialogical method. Its prized objectivity overlooks, ignores, or denigrates the significance of the imperative, the subjective, and the narrative.

A New Method for Psychology

Rosenstock-Huessy's son, Hans Huessy, described an application of the dialogical method in a paper he wrote in 1965 for the first public seminar on his father's work. The event was convened by the theologian Harvey Cox. Huessy showed how the Cross of Reality would provide the key to a new method for both psychiatry and psychology.

Huessy pointed out that modern psychology began by imitating the natural sciences. It constructed its pyramid of knowledge by starting with the most elementary building stones, the most trivial, objective raw data. This approach put all the emphasis on the physiological level of human functioning: seeing, hearing, eating, sleeping, and sex. While much can be learned by studying our behavior on this objective or outer front, the dialogical method posits that there are three other fronts of *equal* importance. For example, in our prejective orientation, as we attempt to create the future, we live at the level of love and self-sacrifice. Hans Huessy said that most psychological and psychiatric theory ignores these higher levels of human performance or "explains them away as pathology." Thus, psychoanalysis is likely to think of our personal and subjective "artistic creations as a compensation for neurotic complexes." Similarly, "heroic deeds are explained as defenses against psychopathology."

He then showed how the Cross of Reality revealed the normal and desirable sequence of any human experience. Emotional disturbance may be described as getting stuck in one particular phase, or it might be the result of an attempt to skip one. The dialogical method reveals four basic phases in any significant experience: (1) inspiration, (2) communication, (3) institutionalization, and finally, (4) history.

We see this sequence when we fall in love and get married. Our falling in love cannot be an objective or logical experience. We must be swept off our feet, inspired. Then we enter a subjective phase in which we must communicate our new relationship through love letters, singing, and talking. In the third phase, institutionalization, when we marry before witnesses, our experience has begun to enter recorded history. Finally, usually after our first child is born, we experience ourselves as an objective family unit. In each phase we have had new and different emotions.

Huessy said, "I would view these meaningful experiences as tying up considerable emotional energy, to borrow from psychoanalytic theory, and I think it is essential for us to see these experiences through all four stages so that this emotional energy becomes freed and available for new experiences." As we go through any important experience, the movement from one phase to the next always involves some change, and change is usually accompanied by pain or "psychiatric symptoms." But such symptoms are not necessarily indicators of pathology. Psychiatrists may do positive harm by mistaking the symptoms of healthy change for psychiatric illness.

Finally, he challenged Freudian psychology's assumption that one begins with the ego or *I* and then works out to include additional members of the social group. The *I*, he said, is *not* the first form in which we come to consciousness of ourselves. As a child, and even later in life, we become a subjective *I* only after having first been addressed vocatively as *thou*. "One might say that children are spoken into membership in the human race. They are not born into such membership." In other words, our ego does not produce itself. It is produced by the vocative or imperative address of our parents, our society, and our tradition. Since his specialty was child psychiatry, he was able to document these points. Children, he says, learn the pronoun *I* last. Autistic children do not learn to use *I* until very late in their development.

The Four Breakdowns of Society

Turning now from the individual to society as a whole, the Cross of Reality becomes increasingly understandable as a method when we realize that peace in society is constantly threatened by a breakdown on one of the four fronts created by our speech orientations.

An examination of society reveals that it always faces four speech-related threats:

1. *Revolution*—A breakdown on the *future* front; loss of respect for the past; expressed as an excess of *imperative* or future speech. The antidote for revolution is to create respect, a loyalty to the past that enables a future to be created.
2. *Anarchy*—A breakdown on the *inner* front; loss of respect for objective, exterior order; an excess of inward or *subjective* speech. The good that cures this ill is unanimity, unity, or harmony.
3. *Decadence*—A breakdown on the *past* front; loss of faith in the future; an excess of *backward-looking* speech related to the past. Again, decadence is the inability of one generation to communicate future imperatives to the next. The corrective for decadence is faith, which is not a belief in the past but a belief in the future.
4. *War*—A breakdown on the *outer* front; loss of any interior agreement; an excess of speech that *objectifies* the other. The good that counteracts it is government, the efficient organization of territory.

It follows that a new discipline employing the dialogical method would see the creation of peace on these four fronts of life as its necessary purpose. Thus, this higher sociology would *not* be objective. It would break free of Cartesian rationalism, the isolated and doubting *I* coldly observing the *it*. It would correlate and interpret our poignant relationships with future and past times as well as with our inward and outward spaces.

The Lamina Quadrigemina

Thus far, we have seen that the dialogical method derives from the patterns of speech. We can probably take this argument a step further: It seems likely that these patterns of speech are caused by different functions within the human brain. Rosenstock-Huessy had no problem imagining that the lamina quadrigemina, a small structure in the middle part of the brain, might be the part of our anatomy that sorted out the four basic kinds of speech, thus making us conscious of the Cross of Reality.

Eugen talked about the lamina quadrigemina in a lecture I attended in 1947, saying he had recently received a letter from an old friend, Richard Koch, who had been Franz Rosenzweig's doctor. In his letter, Koch said that his wartime operations on soldiers with damage to their brains had suggested to him that the lamina quadrigemina might act as a brake and sorting center for our reception of speech.

This primitive organ is found in all vertebrates, and its function has never been clear. Koch suggested that the quadrigemina might provide the anatomical proof for the Cross of Reality.

As Eugen reported all this, in great detail and with great enthusiasm, it truly sank in on me, how *grounded* in matter he perceived both speech and spirit to be. He was willing to answer Pascal's question about how a body can be united to a spirit by imagining a particular *physical organ* where this occurred. To borrow a term from the best-selling author Gary Zukav, that organ would be "the seat of the soul."

Whether or not the lamina quadrigemina is proven to be the place where the four forms of speech are sorted, it is almost certain that further studies will eventually determine that particular parts of the brain enable us to perform that critical function.

The Language Instinct

The American linguist and author, Noam Chomsky, and his colleague, the psychologist Steven Pinker, have each written popular books that suggest that our brains do indeed contain something like sorting organs, with the corollary that the patterns of grammar are built into us. Chomsky's widely accepted thesis that the patterns of grammar were hard-wired into us had obvious similarities to Rosenstock-Huessy's ideas. I brought *Speech and Reality* to Chomsky's attention in 1972, and although he had initially seemed quite interested, I was not too surprised when I heard nothing further from him. I am afraid Rosenstock-Huessy loses most academics the moment he mentions God.

Pinker's *The Language Instinct: How the Mind Creates Language*, published in 1994, reconfirms Chomsky's thesis and supports some of the points here about the universality of grammar and how it shapes the patterns of our thought. He is more interesting than the anthropologists who think of language simply as a tool. But there is no hint that he sees beyond the technical aspects of his subject. That speech has anything to do with spirit—or, God forbid, the Holy Spirit—is not the kind of thinking that could fly at MIT, where he was at the time of that book's publication.

Ten Theses on Language

The dialogical thinking embodied in the Cross of Reality can now be synthesized into ten theses on language:

1. There are four basic kinds of speech: (a) imperative, (b) subjective, (c) narrative, and (d) objective.
2. In any significant human experience we experience all four of those kinds of speech in that order.
3. Each kind of speech relates to a different personal or group orientation toward times and spaces: (a) imperative toward the future, (b) subjective toward our "inner space," (c) narrative toward the past, and (d) objective to the outside world.
4. Each kind of speech also relates to a particular person of grammar: (a) the imperative to *thou (you)*; (b) the subjective to *I*; (c) the narrative to *we*; and (d) the objective to *he, she,* or *they.*
5. When we examine the pattern of those speech orientations and grammatical persons, we see that they form a Cross of Reality, at the center of which any person or group finds itself.
6. A corollary to the axiom of the cross is that its future orientation is the most important; as we hear vocatives or imperatives, we are moved to respond.
7. What we call the human psyche, or soul, is formed as it lives through the "crucial" speech experience posited by the Cross of Reality.
8. When we realize that the Cross of Reality shows the essential patterns of language in the human mind, we can also perceive that it makes visible a dialogical method for the human sciences. It tells us that any question should be examined in the light of all four orientations, and especially we should take into account the *tensions* between or *among* them.
9. The Cross of Reality depicts the action of high speech, fully-articulated speech, in any person or group; such speech

establishes relations with others, creates peace, and tells the truth. And such speech can be recognized as the way spirit is present and active in human beings. Thus, we can call speech the body of the spirit.

10. In religious terms, we can come to see that high speech is the embodiment of what Christians call the Holy Spirit. It follows that the Trinitarian God is not something in which we need to believe; that God is already within us, as the very source of our humanity, as the grace we find at the center of our lives. The theological categories of Father (Creation), Son (Redemption), and Spirit (Revelation) relate, respectively, to three kinds of speech and their related grammatical persons. Thus, Father relates to *narrative* speech of the past and *we*; Son relates to *subjective* speech of the inner person and *I*; Spirit relates to *imperative* speech toward the future and *thou (you)*.

All ten of those theses, when taken together, establish the dialogical method as a fundamentally new way of thinking about human reality. From elementary observations about language and grammar, and about the inner person and the outer world, they proceed to the realization that high speech is the embodiment of the Holy Spirit. If we embody that Spirit, it follows that we also embody the Trinitarian God.

Those theses present the Cross of Reality as an image of how the Spirit works in us and how God speaks in us. Thus, it is a thoroughly panentheistic image, one that reinforces the emerging Christian paradigm, as described early on by Bonhoeffer and Tillich—and more recently by Borg and Spong.

In the next chapter we'll see how these theses lie behind the story told in Rosenstock-Huessy's *Out of Revolution*. There he describes how new kinds of inspired and impassioned speech have formed and reformed us over a millennium. This story enables us to see just how the Holy Spirit is at work in our history.

5 THE REVOLUTIONS
OF THE CHRISTIAN ERA

The French and Russian revolutions are results of the Christian era. They depend upon it, they complete it.

—Eugen Rosenstock-Huessy

Revolutions do nothing but readjust the equation between heart-power and social order. They come from the open and happen under the open sky. They bring about the Kingdom of God by force, and reach into the infinite in order to reform the finite.

—Eugen Rosenstock-Huessy

OUT OF REVOLUTION WAS CERTAINLY Rosenstock-Huessy's most important book, but its 800 pages can seem daunting. In this chapter I will suggest why it is worth the effort.

Harvey Cox was one of the several prominent theologians to understand and use *Out of Revolution*. I first met Cox in 1964, the year before he woke up the American religious establishment with his book *The Secular City*. He was the speaker at the annual meeting of the United Church of Christ in Vermont, and his theme was that the great Western revolutions and today's secular society were the fruit of the Christian era. When I approached him after his talk and said it reminded me of Rosenstock-Huessy's *Out of Revolution*, he immediately acknowledged Rosenstock-Huessy as his main source. He also mentioned how he had first heard of Rosenstock-Huessy at a meeting in Berlin in 1961. Since that meeting, Cox said, he had been reading Rosenstock-Huessy's work quite avidly.

A few years after that meeting with Cox, I called on Reinhold Niebuhr at Union Theological Seminary, to ask for a jacket blurb for a new Argo Books edition of *Out of Revolution*. We had a good, long talk, especially about the difficulties of introducing Rosenstock-Huessy to a wider public, difficulties that arose partly because of his

wide-ranging thought and partly because he was often assumed to be
an idealist, a latter-day Hegelian.

The statement that Niebuhr later sent was put right on the
book's front cover; it certainly suggested that Rosenstock-Huessy
was more realist than idealist:

> Really a remarkable book, full of profound insights into the
> meaning of modern European history. I have not read a
> book in a long time which is so imaginative in relating the
> various economic, religious and political forces at play in
> modern history, to each other. Ordinary historical interpre-
> tations are pale and insipid in comparison with it.

During Argo's early years, there was a sort of reassembly of the
troops from Camp William James. Page Smith, one of America's
leading historians, was Provost of Cowell College at the University
of California at Santa Cruz. He described *Out of Revolution* as "the
most remarkable book of our time." His enthusiasm enabled Argo
to find many readers for the book on the West Coast. The Whole
Earth Bookstore became our biggest customer, partly because
of Page, and partly because their guru, Stewart Brand, wrote that
Rosenstock-Huessy's book was "personal, passionate, deeply uncon-
ventional, and I'm convinced, deeply right."

Two other prominent admirers of *Out of Revolution* were the
social critic Lewis Mumford and the political scientist Karl Deutsch.
I recall how Deutsch described Eugen as a genius in seeing patterns
in history. Mumford wrote: "What is most important in his work is
the understanding of the relevance of traditional values to a civilization still undergoing revolutionary transformations."

Autobiography of Western Man

Whereas Rosenstock-Huessy makes only passing reference to
the Cross of Reality in *Out of Revolution*, and only hints that he is
using its dialogical method, it is evident that the new method enabled
him to see certain patterns in the way that each revolution unfolded.
Each of the great Western revolutions went through four phases:

First, there was an imperative calling to remake the future, not only of the revolution's birthplace but eventually of the whole race. Each revolution's leaders felt called as thou.

Second, there was a subjective reply to this calling, during which the new speech of each revolution was first heard and "new persons," new *I*'s were born.

Third came a narrative or historical phase in which the new persons founded and maintained new institutions, as *we*.

Fourth, and finally, there was an objective phase in which the new imperative, speech, persons, and institutions became commonplace, not only in the nation of their birth but all over the planet. The new persons became *they*.

Of course, that four-phase sequence recapitulates the order of any significant personal or social human experience, as shown on the Cross of Reality: *thou (you), I, we,* and *they*. And it recapitulates the four basic kinds of speech: imperative, subjective, narrative, and objective.

The Clock's Spring

Out of Revolution tells the history of the West in the past millennium as one continuous story, the story of five closely related "secular" revolutions, all of which arose in response to what he calls "the Papal Revolution." When Pope Gregory VII, in 1076, asserted the power of the church over Europe's kings and emperors, he began the first revolution intended to change the whole world. Until the Papal Revolution, the human story had been told in terms of separate warring tribes and empires. Now, for the first time, there emerged a powerful, unifying planetary institution. The Catholic Church was concerned not just with Europe; it aimed at converting and emancipating the whole human race.

There was an incredible dynamism in that first world revolution. The Crusades, the cathedrals, the universities, the beginning of science, all resulted from the creative energy of the High Middle Ages. From the 11th to the 16th centuries, for almost half of this past millennium, the Pope presided over a rapidly expanding Christendom. This was the beginning of what we now call "world history."

Rosenstock-Huessy's perspective on this past millennium can be encapsulated by the image of a clock's spring. We can think of the

Papal Revolution as if it were the winding-up of this spring, drawing on all the energy of Christianity's first millennium. This winding motion, this storage of kinetic energy, created a powerful church that dominated the West and had begun to dominate the world. But when the clock's spring had been fully wound, the Reformation reversed its motion, and the energy that had been stored was released in the form of five great secular revolutions. All five were planetary in their ambitions; all were replies to the Papal Revolution, and they retained its messianic impulses. Even though they had secular goals, they came to life within the orbit of Christianity and served the larger purposes of Christianity.

What were those five? First came the Reformation of 1517, which Rosenstock-Huessy called "the German Revolution." Next came the British Parliamentary Revolution of 1649; then the "twin revolutions": the American War of Independence in 1776 and the French Revolution of 1789; and finally, the Russian Revolution of 1917. The achievements of each left unfinished business, leading on to the next. The progressive achievements of these revolutions tell not only a story of the human spirit, but also a story of how the Holy Spirit acts in history. That is, the Holy Spirit that acts as our gift of speech, and more specifically as our gift of the high speech that calls us to a new future.

What were the accomplishments of each great revolution?

The Papal Revolution (1076)

Instead of having to storm a Bastille, Pope Gregory VII managed to start the Papal Revolution simply by sitting in his study and writing *Dictatus Papae*, a document that asserted his dominion over all the royalty of Europe.

His revolution's imperative was to realize the kingdom of God on earth by emancipating all humankind. It sought to establish Christendom not only over kings and emperors but over the whole planet. The church would become our first *transnational* institution.

This revolution's new speech had two prongs. On the one hand, it was the argumentation of theology, which organized the various sciences and made itself their queen. On the other hand, it was prayer, via plainchant and ever more elaborate worship. The new persons created by this speech were the Crusaders, the Franciscans, the Dominicans, the members of the craft guilds, the university professors; and eventually there were those who discovered that we lived on a globe: the captains of the sailing ships in the Age of Exploration.

The Papal Revolution's new institutions, of course, were those in which its new persons worked: religious orders, universities, and guilds. Other new institutions were the governments that dispatched the sailing ships.

Finally, its planetary result, achieved over a period of 400 years, was the successful establishment of Christendom, not only in Western Europe but in outposts all over the planet.

In retrospect, we can see how this revolution's messianic ambitions had an orientation toward the future, which is indicated by the right-pointing arrow on the Cross of Reality.

Rosenstock-Huessy described the universality of this revolution:

> The Papal Revolution, by asking the Roman monarch to give back his right of investiture to the universal church of Peter and Paul, expressed the idea of a new sovereign co-existing with every king and emperor in every parish. . . . The idea of a trans-local organization, a corporation was realized. The Catholic Church is not at all international. It would be bad taste to call her so.

The German Reformation (1517)

After many years of planetary progress, by the 16th century Gregory's dictatorship of the Pope was no longer a great source for renewal. The excessive power of the church had led, in the end, to the tortures of the Spanish Inquisition and the selling of indulgences, that form of salvation for pay that so enraged Martin Luther.

The German Reformation of 1517, led by that good monk, had the imperative goal of bringing Christianity to renewed life in the secular world, making the individual believer free from the dictates of Rome. Its goal was freedom of conscience.

In terms of the Cross of Reality, its orientation is the upward arrow, the subjective, emphasizing precisely our inner conscience.

Its resulting new speech was secular literature, music and art, plus the Bible—translated into the vernacular and available in every home. Before the Reformation, almost all high art in every civilization had a religious character. Of course, science too was freed from church authority—and began to experiment.

The German writers of the 16th-century Reformation hymns prepared the way for the 18th- and 19th-century composers of oratorios and symphonies, from Bach to Beethoven. Its new persons included those musicians, artists, civil servants, public school teachers, scientists, and academics. Equally important were the conscientious laymen, who served as secular priests and felt equal to their pastors.

These new persons administered the Reformation's new institutions, including public schools, the civil service, and academies.

The planet-wide achievements of this revolution have included the universal acceptance of public education and scientific investigation. They have also included the inevitable bureaucracies that support a secular civil society. Rosenstock-Huessy speaks highly of the civil servant:

> To understand the real inner justification for the strict discipline of a civil service, we must turn to the German revolution; for it alone gave the civil servant a religious position in his country. In the German revolution the drab, grey life of the average bureaucrat was suddenly transformed, as if by a great volcanic eruption. Graft, bribery, the spoils-system, stain the character of the civil servant in every country which has not been touched by this great revolution.

The British Parliamentary Revolution (1649–1688)

Although the Reformation had established a secular civil society, in Germany and beyond, during its first century that civil society was still ruled by kings and princes. It remained for Oliver Cromwell to lead the English Parliamentary Revolution of 1649–1688, which toppled King Charles I and then King James II.

Cromwell's Puritans had the imperative goal of freeing the civil society from the dictates of kings and princes—and to free or "purify" the church from lingering royal and Catholic influence. In brief, its imperative was *political freedom*.

This revolution's resulting new speech was that of law, debate, and argument. Such was the speech of its new persons: aristocratic gentlemen, lawyers, and parliamentarians.

Its corresponding new institutions, of course, were parliaments and courts.

With its emphasis on law and tradition, its cross orientation was the left-pointing arrow, toward the past.

On the scale of the planet, its results were parliamentary democracies, states under the rule of law, and reliable legal systems. Rosenstock-Huessy extols the British Commonwealth:

> The word "Common," which appears in the phrases Common Prayer, House of Commons, common sense, reached its climax in the enthronement of "Commonwealth." The word communicates the thrill of pride over the fact that Church and State were now united into a Commonwealth, whilst formerly the Chancellor had to alternate, so to speak, between the two.

The French Revolution (1789)

Despite its rule of law, England remained a society ruled by aristocrats after 1688. The landed gentry and the Lords remained decidedly more important than the lowly man in the street. And the continent still had its kings. It remained for Voltaire and Rousseau, as theorists, and then Robespierre as executioner, to launch the French Revolution, which would elevate that bourgeois citizen to power.

This revolution had the imperatives of *liberté, egalité, fraternité.* It sought freedom not only from the power of the church (be it Catholic or Protestant), and from kings, but also from preening aristocrats. Now the bourgeois entrepreneur would be king, and Reason would be enthroned with him.

Its new speech was expressed in a flowering of national literatures and arts, plus journalism. And its new persons, besides the entrepreneur, were novelists, newspapermen, and increasingly objective and experimental scientists.

These new types held forth in such new institutions as corporations, independent newspapers, and institutes of technology.

Finally, the French Revolution's planetary results include capitalism, competitive markets, free enterprise, and a free press.

By comparison with its predecessors, this revolution was focused on life's outer front—where rationalism and objectivity are dominant, and it corresponds to the downward-pointing arrow on the cross.

As Rosenstock-Huessy describes this revolution:

> Once in a long while it happens that a great question is brought up and discussed and fought through once for all. The equal right of every human being is a fruit of the French Revolution which was conquered once for all for Moujiks and Jews, blacks and yellows, men and women.

The American Revolution (1776)

This brings us to the American Revolution. In Rosenstock-Huessy's view, this revolution's imperatives were drawn from both the English and the French revolutions. Though it preceded the French by 13 years, it was inspired by the same anti-royalist and egalitarian sentiments, ones that were being widely expressed on both sides of the Atlantic by the 1770s. Rosenstock-Huessy saw the Americans as successfully combining the Christian-inspired achievements of the English Revolution with the anti-Christian Enlightenment's achievements, as codified by the French.

Thus, the American Revolution's new speech and persons are already noted in the preceding descriptions of the French and English revolutions.

In terms of the Cross of Reality, it combined French rationalist and objective enlightenment with British respect for past tradition.

This synthesizing role of the American Revolution has turned its ongoing life into a primary source of what Rosenstock-Huessy called the "Planetary Revolution," described below.

To capture the dream of the American Revolution, Rosenstock-Huessy pointed to the word united in United States:

> The new unity was a unity not in being but in becoming. It was not a togetherness of possessions but the potentiality of an unfolding, ever widening system. As Thomas Paine shouted: "We have it in our power to begin the world over again. . . ." He was much less interested in the constitution of 1776 or 1787 than in the concept of a world in space and time, destined "to begin all over again."

The Russian Revolution (1917)

The 19th century's new speech and institutions, born of the French and American Revolutions, indeed led to a "century of progress." But its industrial revolution, led by the new bourgeois entrepreneurs, also saw dreadful exploitation of labor. Not only men, but children and women, were treated with utter inhumanity. In response, socialism, and later communism, expressed a new imperative, one that came to be embodied, however imperfectly, in the Russian Revolution of 1917. That imperative was *freedom from economic exploitation.* "Workers of the world, unite! You have nothing to lose but your chains!"

Its new kind of speech was *quantitative:* economic statistics, minimum wages, value added by labor, and gross national products. The related new person, the new *I*, was the proletarian worker who replied to the new imperative by marching with red and yellow banners in Leningrad—or joining the United Auto Workers in Detroit.

In the Union of Soviet Socialist Republics (USSR), and many other countries, its new institution was a *dictatorship*, nominally of the proletariat, but actually of a Communist Party elite. In Western democracies, its new institutions were government agencies, which sought to control national economies and prevent exploitation of labor.

The Russian Revolution's direct result was the emergence of a great industrialized nation in a formerly backward land. Eighty percent of Russians were illiterate in 1890. Indirectly, its worldwide result, when expressed as social democracy, managed to tame the excesses of laissez-faire capitalism in both Europe and the United States. The US New Deal, with Social Security, the CCC, and all those other alphabet agencies, would never have come into existence without the field of force created by the Russian Revolution.

One can see this revolution as recapturing the Papal Revolution's messianic belief in our glorious future. At the same time, it spoke the French Revolution's new rationalist and objective language. In Rosenstock-Huessy's words:

A Bolshevik dictionary might contain: Quantity: The Masses. Quality: The Bolshevik Party. Society:. . . Class situation is explained in figures and statistics. Changes in human history become visible in statistical changes, as in the key of distribution. This is provoking language.

In the beginning pages of *Out of Revolution*, Rosenstock-Huessy makes a statement that helps us see how the negative sides of all those revolutions were related to their positive achievements:

> All great revolutions re-create public law, public order, public spirit and public opinion; they all reform private manners and private feelings. They themselves must therefore live in a third dimension, beyond the reach of public law and private conviction. They live in the unprotected, unexplored and unorganized space which is hated by every civilization like hellfire itself—and which probably lies near hellfire. But it lies near heaven too. Heaven and hell are the only words left to us for this character of openness and immediacy.

The Planetary Revolution (1945 forward)

After the Second World War, Rosenstock-Huessy had more to say about the great revolutions. In *The Christian Future*, he wrote that we would continue for centuries to live in their fields of force. He saw the two World Wars as a final revolution, a planetary revolution in which the thousand-year period of Christendom had come to an end. The positive aspect of this Planetary Revolution, however, was that it drew together the separate strands of the revolutions that had formed Western man—including the Russian Revolution. And from these strands it was weaving the new material of a global society, a Great Society, which would now emerge on the face of the planet. As he puts it:

> The two world wars were the form of world revolution in which this new future reached into everybody's life; the nationalist and communist ideologies with their dreams of revolution were checkmated and are mere foam around the real transformation. The real transformation was made by the wars and it made the Great Society final. She is the heiress of State and Church.

If we admit that the World Wars were the negative side of today's planetary revolution, and that this revolution's *positive* side is its role as heir of all the others, we can go on to describe its imperatives. It will certainly be enough, in the first centuries of the third millennium, to work toward the emancipation of all humankind by achieving freedom of conscience, political freedom, freedom of individual enterprise, and freedom from economic exploitation.

Rosenstock-Huessy vs. the Idealists

When *Out of Revolution* was published in 1938, one of its prominent reviewers was Crane Brinton, a Yale professor who himself had just written a book on the great revolutions. In his review, Brinton suggested that Rosenstock-Huessy belonged in the tradition of German idealism. This was certainly not the case.

How is it that Rosenstock-Huessy should not be confused with his idealist opponents? German idealism, as it came to a head in Hegel, imagines that there is a *transcendental* reality, which he called "Absolute Spirit" or "World Spirit." This Spirit is gradually advancing and revealing itself throughout history, inspiring this drab world here below. That's not the story told in *Out of Revolution*. Here we learn about a human spirit that moves through and in us, not above and beyond us. Rosenstock-Huessy's presentation is rooted in the down-to-earth events, persons, freedoms, and institutions of which we know at first hand. If God is present in this history, as Rosenstock-Huessy believed he is, then he must be what Bonhoeffer imagined: "a suffering God."

The Spirit and the Revolutions in 2008

Out of Revolution shows us how the Holy Spirit, as future-creating imperative speech, is at work in history. When we look back at the great, all-embracing revolutions of the past millennium, we can indeed see that they were revolutions of the spirit. In biblical language, they envisioned "a new heaven and a new earth."

Out of Revolution is convincing because it appeals to our own memory, even our own experience, of the events it describes. The Enlightenment and the Russian Revolution are still swirling through our lives today. One still hears commentators emphasize our issues with "communist China."

Then the Reformation's separation of Church and State, expanded and confirmed by the British, French, and American revolutions, is newly threatened in the United States of 2008, as represented by the forces of religious fundamentalism.

The Spirit and the Third Millennium

One of Rosenstock-Huessy's students, the legal scholar Harold Berman, wrote a widely acclaimed book, *Law and Revolution*. In it, Berman describes how the Western legal tradition has been formed by the great revolutions. Of course, Berman credited Rosenstock-Huessy as the source for this idea. Elsewhere Berman has written about the Holy Spirit as "the God of History":

> The historical challenge of the third millennium of the Christian era, Rosenstock-Huessy taught, is to create out of the many peoples of the world a single community; and in seeking to accomplish that goal, the emphasis of the Christian faith must be on the third person of the triune God, the Holy Spirit, who prophesies unity and, taking many forms, inspires people of diverse belief systems and loyalties to listen to each other, to learn each other's languages, and to overcome their mutual hostilities.
>
> In Rosenstock-Huessy's words: "The story of salvation on earth is the advance of the singular against the plural. Salvation came into a world of many gods, many lands, many peoples. Over against these it sets up a singular: one God, one world, one humankind."

Christianity Is Not a Religion

When we recognize that all the peoples of this planet live today in the fields of force created by the Papal Revolution and its successors, we realize that Christianity is much more than a religion. Christianity has been the motor for most of the progress, in every portion of the globe, throughout a millennium. In the first half of the millennium, it used religious language; however, since the Reformation, it has increasingly expressed itself in secular terms.

That explains why Rosenstock-Huessy declared that "Christianity is not a religion." By *religion* he meant the kind of closed cult that claims to offer unique advantages to its devotees and often disparages the religions of others. He also meant a system of belief that concentrates on its origins in the past—and thus tends to resist change. Christianity, by contrast, when seen in the light of its total revolutionary history, has been absolutely focused on bringing about change. It has been engaged in constant renewal, with opening us up to each other, with freeing all the captives—from the powers of kings and emperors, popes, nobles, aristocrats, and finally, in just the last century, from robber-baron capitalists. Thus, Christianity's impact on society in the last millennium was vastly more important beyond the church than within it.

Far from being other-worldly, Christianity created today's one world, our global society. A dramatic example is China. As Rosenstock-Huessy put it, "The China after 1911 is a part of the Christian era. . . . If you have a son of Heaven in Peking, that meant that they had a special heaven, a special world." The Christian Sun Yat-Sen led the 1911 revolution that ended the empire of the Son of Heaven, and prepared for Mao Zedong's importation of the Russian revolution. It was actually a Congregational minister who baptized Sun, when he was a young man in Hong Kong, using the baptismal name Rixin, meaning "daily renewal."

A Messenger for Out of Revolution

Out of Revolution has been in print and in distribution for almost 70 years. Now we will travel back in time to the first decade of those years, when I packed two copies of the book into my bag as I prepared to go to Paris early in 1948.

6 GOD IS LIKE A WHOLE HUMANITY

Russian creative religious thought has introduced the idea of Divine Humanity. As in Jesus-Christ, the God-man, there occurred an individual incarnation of God in man, so similarly in humanity there should occur a collective incarnation of God.

—Nikolai Berdyaev

IN NOVEMBER OF 1947, as I was finishing my studies at Dartmouth, Eugen gave me a letter of introduction to Nikolai Berdyaev. I had hoped to meet him when I went to Paris, where I'd be doing graduate work on Russian history at the Sorbonne. Indeed, I had hoped Berdyaev would provide some guidance for the paper I planned to write there. When I wrote to him in November, asking if I might meet him, I attached Eugen's letter as well as an outline of my proposed paper.

PARIS – APRIL 11, 1948 – Of all the roles I might play in life, my present one seems about the least likely. By now I could have become a graduate student in New York, or maybe a chicken farmer in Vermont, but never a Russian Orthodox seminarian in Paris. Yet, for the past three weeks, I've been going every Tuesday to the Institute St. Sergius where I'm auditing Father Alexander Schmemann's course on church history. My classmates, all dressed in black, are studying for the priesthood.

Unfortunately for me, Schmemann lectures in Russian, and I miss at least a third of what he says. Since I founded the Russian Club at Dartmouth in 1946, I've become fluent in ordinary conversation, but Schmemann's theological vocabulary is often beyond me.

Still, I've gotten the main points. Saint Sergius, after whom this seminary is named, might be called Russia's spiritual father. A 14th-century monk, he built the Trinity Monastery about fifty miles north of Moscow. Eventually, what became known as the Trinity-St. Sergius Monastery also became a sort of Vatican for the Russian

Orthodox Church. It was the first Russian monastery to be conse-
crated to the Trinity, something quite new in Christendom—and a
sign of Orthodoxy's special focus on that image.

Now that I've had three classes, I'm wondering how much longer
I can last. At least I've met one good friend. Igor Spassky, who sits on
my left in class, is 27 years old, comes from a Russian priest's family,
and knew a lot of Orthodox Church history even before studying it.
And unlike some of the more conservative students, Igor is enthusiastic about my hero, Nikolai Berdyaev. In fact, he's begun to write
a book on Berdyaev, basing it on postwar discussion meetings he'd
attended with the "last" great Russian philosopher.

Naturally I told him about my own book on the Cross of Reality.
Igor may be helpful with that; two weeks ago I gave him typescript
copies of the first few chapters to look over, plus some notes for a
chapter that I plan to write here, one that would relate Eugen's way
of thinking about God to Berdyaev's. My new status as a "seminarian" should help with that task.

Tomorrow I'll have my fourth class at St. Sergius and Igor will
be joining me afterward for lunch. Of course, I'm looking forward
to his comments on my book.

Two weeks ago he took me to my first Orthodox service at the
seminary. With its a cappella singing, that service was an overwhelming experience for me. Those voices went not simply into my ears
but into my whole body, creating an inner resonance from head to
toe. Feeling as if I were back in the earliest years of the church, I was
so moved that I joined the congregation in crossing myself. I'd never
made that sign before, and I was astonished to find myself doing it
without embarrassment.

It's quite a ride on the Métro to St. Sergius from my Left Bank
apartment on Boulevard Raspail. My wife Libby and I arrived there in
mid-February. Besides this weekly class at St. Sergius, I'm taking two
courses at the University of Paris, better known as "the Sorbonne."
After this year in Paris, we may go to New York where I'd like to
enter Columbia's Russian Institute and prepare for the sort of career
I've been imagining ever since Buchenwald: becoming a Russia spe-
cialist, and aiming for the State Department.

On the other hand, these peaceful months in Paris could be
interrupted at any moment by a phone call from Berlin, where

East-West tensions are mounting daily. Last December, just as we'd completed plans to come here, an old friend from Camp William James days, Enno Hobbing, got in touch with me and offered me a job. He had been born in Berlin, had graduated from Harvard in 1940—and then, after meeting Eugen, became involved with setting up the camp. Now he's in Berlin again, as editor-in-chief of *Die Neue Zeitung* ("The New Newspaper"), the US government newspaper for the German public. Enno wanted to know if I'd consider joining him in Berlin as deputy editor-in-chief of the paper, which has a staff of 50 Germans. I'd said I was interested indeed, but would have to think about the issue of interrupting my Russian studies.

A Call to Berdyaev

Just over two weeks ago, March 25, I finally telephoned Berdyaev. It was a momentous phone call, one I'd kept postponing until I had my courses well under way at the Sorbonne. I'd been looking forward to making this call since last fall, when he had responded to the letter I had sent.

With my letter I had attached an outline of the project I wanted to pursue in Paris, a paper on the "Russian Idea." The outline started with the origins in the 1840s of Russian philosophy, which is essentially a religious philosophy, via the work of the Slavophiles Ivan Kireevsky and Alexei Khomyakov. The next step was to show how that mid-19th-century philosophy had culminated in Vladimir Solovyov and Berdyaev, and had then been welcomed in the West.

I stopped staring at the phone, picked it up, and dialed Berdyaev's number in the suburb of Clamart. In seconds I'd be hearing his voice, talking to the man who was the real reason I'd come to Paris, this prophet whose work I had been reading since 1940. His housekeeper answered the telephone, and I asked for him. "I'm sorry," she replied, "Nikolai Alexandrovich died just yesterday."

The next day I went to St. Sergius seminary, met Father Schmemann, and enrolled in his weekly history course, on a trial basis. Schmemann was only a few years older than his students but already an impressive man. With Berdyaev gone, I'd want to contact other Russian thinkers in Paris—and St. Sergius seemed a good place to start.

In fact, Schmemann's course on church history has dovetailed nicely with the modern history course I'm taking at the Sorbonne, one that covers Russia's Silver Age. Last week I completed a first sketch of what I plan to write about that amazing period:

Russia's Silver Age

It is widely known that Russia had a 19th-century Golden Age, in literature and other arts, from the time of Pushkin (1799–1837) down to Dostoevsky (1821–1881) and Tolstoy (1828–1910). What is less well known is that, from about 1895 to 1922, there was a similar spiritual ferment, a period now known as The Silver Age. Those years saw an incredible burst of creativity in all of Russia's arts, literature, religion, and philosophy. It was such a powerful burst, indeed, that it continued through the war and past the revolution. Solovyov, who died at age 47 in 1900, is considered the founding father of this period because he inspired its secular writers, poets, and artists as much as its renaissance of religious and philosophical thought. His most admired work was *Lectures on Divine Humanity*, drawn from a series of lectures he delivered from 1878 to 1881. These lectures, which attracted both Dostoevsky and his spiritual opponent, Tolstoy, were a landmark event in Russia's intellectual life.

Nikolai Berdyaev, as a key successor to Solovyov, in 1905 had helped organize "The Religious-Philosophical Vladimir Solovyov Society." This Moscow group was founded by Sergei Bulgakov (1871–1944), the socialist-turned-priest, who later came to Paris and founded the Institute St. Sergius. The Solovyov Society, which brought together many of Russia's leading religious and secular intellectuals, played an important role during the Silver Age; its discussions concentrated on how Russia could integrate Western and Slavophile thinking into a new Russian self-identity. The society's members were so respected that, after the 1917 revolution, Lenin was unsure about what to do with them. Finally, in 1922, he loaded them and their families onto a ship in what was then the port of Petrograd—and sent them to exile in Germany.

One of the few Solovyov Society members who missed that ship was a young priest named Pavel Florensky (1882–1937). A close friend of Bulgakov's, Florensky was not only a priest; he was also an outstanding physical scientist, one whose lectures on electricity at Moscow University seemed so vital to the new Soviet government that they didn't want to interrupt him. Despite the fact that he insisted on lecturing in his black priestly robes! Later he was arrested—and died in the Soviet Gulag. Many now call him a "Russian Leonardo," so wide and innovative was his range of thought.

When one takes the thinkers and writers of Russia's Golden and Silver ages together, one sees how they created a full century of religious, artistic, and philosophical innovation. Most of it occurred either within or on the fringes of the Orthodox Church. Thus, it is not too much to say that this was a period of Orthodox reformation.

Panentheism vs. Theism

April 12, 1948 – As we'd planned, Igor met me for lunch today at Chez Nicole, our favorite bistro, just down the street from St. Sergius. We began our conversation with my book; he was astonished by the degree to which Berdyaev and Rosenstock-Huessy appear to be twins on many themes. More than most philosophers, they're concerned with what the machine age has done to our consciousness, fragmenting our sense of time and our selves. Neither has any use for metaphysical abstraction from concrete experience. Both seek to interpret religious categories, especially the Holy Spirit and the Trinity, in terms that will speak to today's secular minds. And both envision their work as leading beyond philosophy—to take form as a new science, a new discipline.

Igor told me that his own book showed how Berdyaev culminated a stream of Russian philosophical thought that began with Kireevsky and Khomyakov. He described how Russian philosophy had always seen itself based on the principle of the *Logos*, the living word, as opposed to Western philosophy, which grounded itself in *Ratio*, or reason. Khomyakov had been the first Russian to focus on language as a field of study, and his enthusiasm for this subject had stayed alive in his philosophical heirs, particularly Bulgakov and his friend Florensky. Igor said that these two had written meditations on the meaning of our grammatical persons, ones that seemed quite similar to Rosenstock-Huessy's.

As we finished lunch, Igor asked me, "You know, Clint, I've wanted to ask you why you're so committed to Russia. Do you have Russian ancestors?"

I replied that my ancestors were lowland Scots, and explained how my commitment to Russia had begun at Buchenwald. Talking to the Russian prisoners, I found myself being changed from an innocent, optimistic American into a worldly wise "Euro-American," or perhaps a citizen of the planet. I felt as if I'd been sucked into the maelstrom of Russian history; it was no longer "over there," outside me, an object of study. It seemed to become my responsibility. Now that we and the Russians both have hydrogen bombs, our very survival may depend on how well we know each other.

Igor asked if Rosenstock-Huessy shared my interest in Russia.

I described Rosenstock-Huessy's interest in Russian philosophy, which began when Franz Rosenzweig's cousin, Hans Ehrenberg, had introduced both him and Rosenzweig to it. Ehrenberg himself was a convert to Christianity, and had become a Lutheran minister. The fall before I left for Paris, Rosenstock-Huessy had had me translate one of Ehrenberg's most important essays, "The Russification of Europe or the Question of the Trinity." It appears as the epilogue to a highly significant book, *Eastern Christianity*, in which Ehrenberg collected key essays by Russian thinkers, from Pushkin's friend Chaadayev to Solovyov and Berdyaev.

Igor was smiling; he had heard of the book and hoped there would soon be a French edition. Then he asked me if I'd read the selection from Bulgakov about panentheism and Sophia.

I replied that I had, but I wasn't sure I understood how those two concepts were related.

Igor explained that Solovyov and Bulgakov were both trying to get beyond traditional theism, which Berdyaev called "abstract monotheism." *Panentheism*, the term used by Bulgakov to describe his thought, was just a more formal name for what Solovyov meant by *divine humanity* and *Sophia*.

Igor continued to describe how all three of those names relate to the same idea: God's incarnation in all humanity. Theism describes a God who is essentially outside us: the "wholly other." The heresy of pantheism describes a God who is everywhere, just the same as all the forces of nature. But panentheism is not heretical at all. By adding that prepositional "en," it suggests God as in us, and us in God. Berdyaev once captured this understanding of God, in *Spirit and Reality*, by saying that the Holy Spirit is incarnated in human life—and that we might therefore think of God as being "like a whole humanity."

"Of course, Berdyaev's thinking is well ahead of what most of our classmates at St. Sergius would accept," Igor said.

I could suddenly see why Solovyov tried to revive *Sophia* as a name for how God is embodied in humankind. But Ehrenberg had said, in a footnote in *Eastern Christianity* that *Sophia* was an "artificial" and a "gnostic" idea. He said that the "natural" intermediary between God and man, the real source of revelation, was speech, as presented by the "speech thinkers," of whom he mentioned Rosenstock-Huessy, Rosenzweig, Ferdinand Ebner, and himself.

The Russian Idea

May 8, 1948 – I'm soaking up the sun on my favorite bench in the Luxemburg Gardens, a glorious green park that's within easy walking distance of our apartment. I'm thinking about this last month in Paris, our third in this "city of light" where the Goddess of Reason was actually enthroned as a statue soon after the revolution of 1789. My, how her Enlightenment has radiated! Tomorrow will be my seventh Tuesday luncheon with Igor, even though my weakness in theological Russian has forced me to drop out of Schmemann's class.

Besides my classes at the Sorbonne and St. Sergius, I've done some valuable proselytizing for Eugen. He sent me here with two copies of *Out of Revolution*, one for Berdyaev and the other for Emmanuel Mounier, a prominent Catholic writer and editor of the journal *Esprit*. Last week at lunch I made my delivery to Mounier.

Spirit is a good title for his magazine. Mounier's "personalism," like Berdyaev's "religious existentialism," goes in the same direction as Eugen's thought. I sometimes wonder if Eugen—or his students—shouldn't package his work as another "-ism," but I know he hates the idea. He says that all "-isms" are "frozen" ways of thinking. By the same token, he probably wouldn't like his thought to be described as panentheistic. However, I think it's excusable; he's certainly more panentheistic than theistic. And he's certainly not far from joining Berdyaev as a Christian existentialist.

During lunch with Mounier, we had a good discussion of

Eugen's thought. Then we turned to Berdyaev. I told him about my having wanted to talk to Berdyaev about my "Russian Idea" paper. I explained that I had identified four key elements in that idea:

1. Solovyov's "Divine Humanity," the collective incarnation of God in man, as first presented in his 1878 lecture.
2. Berdyaev's "Trinitarian thinking," in which he emphasizes how Orthodoxy sees the Trinity in our daily experience.
3. Khomyakov's *sobornost*, often translated as "conciliarity," but more appropriately understood as a voluntary "freedom-in-unity" *(l'unité libre)*.
4. Kireevsky's *tselnost* (wholeness) and its related *tselnoye znaniye*, (integral knowledge).

Mounier pressed me for a further explanation of what Kireevsky meant by those terms.

"He meant integrating everything we know," I said, "including both religion and science. He had an intuition that the Orthodox tradition, when updated, could provide us with *tselnoye znaniye*, integral knowledge."

I went on to explain how Kireevsky, who's considered the founder of Russian philosophy, said that we can achieve integral knowledge only when we take four different approaches to the truth. Objective, rational thought is just one of those four. Reading him, I sensed that he had an early intuition of Rosenstock-Huessy's Cross of Reality. Kireevsky's thought could be called "supra-rational," a term I'd also use to describe Rosenstock-Huessy's thinking. I added that these Russians were not ivory tower thinkers; they all had social goals.

Mounier offered to consider a short version of my "Russian Idea" paper for publication in *Esprit*. Its core readers are Catholic socialists.

Rosenstock-Huessy at Dartmouth

I got up from the bench and went to a nearby bistro for some tea. When I returned to the bench, I took from my briefcase Rosenstock-Huessy's *The Christian Future*, which I brought with me to Paris, to re-read. Published in 1946, it is certainly the most accessible of his books; yet, like *Out of Revolution*, it has never taken off. Those who have attended Rosenstock-Huessy's courses do not find him a difficult thinker at all, but his fellow faculty members at Dartmouth are puzzled by him, as are most academics. He refuses to speak their cold, objective, disengaged language, so they have nothing to do with him. It is almost as if he sought their rejection, preferring for us, the next generation, to be the ones who would give life to his thought.

But here there is another problem. The circle of his devoted students is often too devoted. Some seem inclined toward a closed cult that focuses only on what Rosenstock-Huessy says, overlooking the fact that it is really up to them to say it *differently*. My parents, who are now among Eugen and his wife Margrit's best friends, have helped me avoid this trap, as has Libby. One of our unspoken marriage vows was that I would not be a Rosenstock-Huessy cultist.

These thoughts took me back to the Dartmouth campus of two years ago. I decided to major in philosophy, partly because I wanted to take all four courses that Rosenstock-Huessy taught. And partly because I knew that this would lead me to reading his own sources of inspiration, such challengers of conventional wisdom as Søren Kierkegaard (1813–1855), Ludwig Feuerbach (1804–1872), and Friedrich Nietzsche (1844–1900)—and challengers of his own understanding of language, his contemporaries Martin Heidegger and Ludwig Wittgenstein. The problem with Heidegger, I concluded, is that he *mystifies* speech. Identifying language with "being," he implies that "being" *itself* speaks, almost independently of us. The problem with Wittgenstein is that he sees language as something to be analyzed, treating it objectively as a game, not recognizing it as our deadly serious means of survival.

Nietzsche, with his "God is dead," is assumed to be an opponent by many Christians, but Rosenstock-Huessy agreed with him. He said that exclamation "was a true accusation of. . . . the clergy of our departmentalized religion." He added, "Probably no one between 1870 and 1917 did more than Nietzsche to resuscitate God in the hearts of men."

The Tasks of the Three Millennia

May 10, 1948 – Rosenstock-Huessy and Berdyaev both concentrated on understanding the meaning of spirit. Indeed, they imagined that the third millennium should be born under the sign of a new understanding of the spirit. Thus, they were both attracted to Friedrich Schelling's description of the three millennia of the Christian era.

Inspired partly by Schelling (1755–1854), Rosenstock-Huessy developed his own interpretation of the tasks of the three millennia.

The first millennium was devoted to a full realization of how *we were made in the image of God: to the Son.* This was accomplished through the establishment of the Christian church and the recognition of Christ as the center point of history.

The second millennium was devoted to a full realization of how *the planet Earth was created as our common home: to the Father.* This was accomplished through the establishment of science as our means of understanding creation, the natural world.

It remains for the third millennium to be devoted to a full realization of how *we create a peaceful global society: to the Spirit.* This will be accomplished as we establish new, unheard-of institutions. They may well be small groups of intersocietal pioneers, people who will teach us to speak the one language of humankind.

May 16, 1948 – My conversations with Igor have replaced my classes at St. Sergius—and have given me new insights on Berdyaev. I've now read his *Spirit and Reality*, and have been mulling over the section where he wrote about God as being "like a whole humanity." Of course, he's building on Solovyov's conception of divine humanity.

God Is Like a Whole Humanity

Toward the end of *Spirit and Reality*, Berdyaev makes a remarkable statement: "Spirit—the Holy Spirit—is incarnated in human life, but it assumes the form of a whole humanity rather than of authority. . . . God is like a whole humanity rather than like nature, society, or concept."

In those concise words, Berdyaev suggests how we can get beyond our anthropomorphic and theistic idea of God as a supreme being. "Whole humanity" evidently includes all creation, the earth and universe, since humanity could certainly not exist without this physical setting, this *space*. Similarly, "whole humanity" includes all *time*, since we are not whole unless we include our beginnings and our end. And "whole" also points to what makes us whole: in religious terms, the spirit. Berdyaev's proposal is in the tradition of Eastern Christianity, which has always been more panentheistic than theistic, imagining us in God and God *in* us.

To relate Rosenstock-Huessy's thought with Berdyaev's, we became human beings as we learned to speak. It is living speech, the dialogue that human beings have with each other, that moved us, over the millennia of evolution, from being inhuman mammals to finally becoming *members of whole humanity*. We might say that we became cells in God's body. And we might think of those cells as "sentences." *We are each a sentence in the story of whole humanity, a humanity that becomes holy because speech makes it whole.*

If God is like a whole humanity, then he is not aloof from our suffering. Such a God would be involved in the experience of war and revolution, which we have had in the last century, indeed in the last millennium.

Perhaps we could even say that God knows himself only in us, enjoys himself only in us, and has no other being than his life in us.

Finally, I should answer the objection that "whole humanity" may sound impersonal, something like Comte's lifeless "great being." But God imagined in this way still addresses us personally. That is, all the generations that have gone before us, all over the world, down to our own parents, have spoken the Word that addresses us now, summoning us as *thou*, moving us to respond as *I*.

The Trinity and the Cross of Reality

May 24, 1948 – This afternoon I had one of those moments when there's a click—and things seem to fall in place.

As I was walking around the central fountain in the Luxemburg Gardens, I was thinking about those two great icons that had formed in my mind: the Trinity and the Cross of Reality. Both seemed universal, pertaining to *all* of reality, yet one was completely religious and the other completely secular. How could I relate them to each other?

First, I thought about how differently the Trinity is imagined in the Eastern Church from how it is imagined in the West. Orthodoxy sees the Trinity in much more intimate and personal terms than the Western churches do. Father, Son, and Spirit are not distant divine objects but persons whom we represent at every moment of our lives. That Eastern *experienced* Trinity contrasts with the Western more distant and formal one. Thomas Aquinas said "that God is threefold and one is solely an item of belief and it can in no way be demonstrated."

With that difference in mind, I began to think about how I could relate the Eastern version of the Trinity, the *experienced one*, to the Cross of Reality. And then it came to me.

It is the Holy Spirit that inspires us in the imperative, calling us to the future. That is *revelation*. We hear ourselves addressed as *thou (you)*.

The Son is our subjective and personal reply, as *I*. Subjective speech makes us aware of our personal responsibility for bringing our inspirations down to earth—and thus redeeming the world.

Next, we represent the Father as we take creative action. When we make ourselves heard in the narrative of history, we participate in the Father's *creation*. As in marriage, we must act with others, thereby forming a *we*.

Finally, when our listening, speaking, and acting are completed and visible in the day-to-day world, others can speak about us-objectively. They can see how some part of the world was redeemed by our actions. They now describe us as *he, she,* or *they*.

On the Cross of Reality, these relationships appear as follows:

Son – Redemption
The inner space of the person
Subjective speech
I

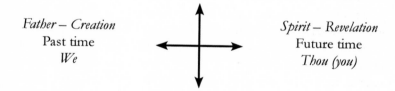

Father – Creation	*Spirit – Revelation*
Past time	Future time
We	*Thou (you)*

Redemption of the World
The outer space of the world
He, she, they

Reflecting on these relationships, we might say that the name *God* does not refer to "a being who exists" somewhere outside us, but instead to the trinity of powers that we assume as we speak our times and spaces into a whole. We represent and complete the

Trinity's actions as we bring these divine powers down to the earth of the objective world, the world of times and spaces. The three divine Persons, which were once known to us as items of belief, can now be recognized as categories of being and of becoming fully human. We represent them whenever we speak beyond the limited frame of our natural body as the mammal *homo sapiens*.

To put it more succinctly, the name God might not refer to the *object* of our religious thought; it might refer to the *subject* of our lives. That is, it can refer to what we are capable of representing when we bring reality to full expression in the world. In that case, God does not simply exist; instead, he speaks, and he speaks primarily in us.

The Trinity in All Religions

Of course, it is not only Christians who bear this Trinitarian image within themselves. All members of our race were born with it, and possess it, whether they are religious or not. We sin when we distort or destroy that image in ourselves.

This image of the Trinity is found not only in all persons; it seems to be present in almost all religions. God is generally perceived as both a father-like Creator and a source of Spirit, the Word of truth. Then there is usually a Son, a third vital Person, often a human being, who is either the religion's founder or a major figure in its story.

For example, Hinduism has its Krishna, a mythological figure who is still imagined as having lived on earth. The Upanishads and the Bhagavad-Gita are like emanations of the Spirit, the holy Word. And Brahman is the God-head, the Creator, the ground of the divine.

Islam has Mohammed as the Son; while he is certainly not worshiped, he is central to the faith. As he heard Allah's Word and dictated the Koran, that was clearly an action of the Spirit in him.

Buddhism has the Buddha; while he thought of himself only as a spiritual teacher, many of his followers tend to worship him and give him god-like attributes. His teachings are treated as divinely inspired Word. (Admittedly, the Creator God is only inferred in Buddhism.)

Judaism has Moses and anticipates a Messiah. The Torah is read as God's Word.

Christianity has Jesus, God's Son, as the Messiah, the Word become flesh. The Bible is read as God's Word, written by men inspired by the Spirit.

Thus, in those five major religions we have, in various degrees, a trinity of Creator Father, faithful Son, and Spirit.

Rosenstock-Huessy described the Son in even more universal terms. He said that we recognize the Son whenever we see how the spoken word comes to be embodied in a person's life. Of course, he meant the spoken word of high speech, speech that seeks to tell the truth, establishes relations with others, and makes peace. Such vital words come to us as vocatives and imperatives, commands, and prophecies. We live the life of the Son when we hear those prophecies and make promises to fulfill them. That has been the goal of all high speech and ritual from the beginning of history.

Rosenstock-Huessy managed to link the Trinity with the Cross of Reality, without saying that he was doing so.

— The spoken word, commands, and prophecies are how we hear the *Spirit's* imperatives toward the future.
— Promises to fulfill those prophecies are our subjective, inward replies as *Son*.
— Ritual refers to the ceremonies through which we tell the narrative of the *Father's* past creation.
— And the word embodied in a person's life is how the three persons of the Trinity are present in our daily lives—in the *world*.

This secular interpretation of the Trinity is not a Gnostic rationalization of the mysteries. In fact, it emphasizes why any religion's Trinity will always remain a mystery, even when we understand it in a non-religious sense. Berdyaev put it well: "The life of man and of the world is an inner moment of the mystery of the Trinity."

The mystery remains in the sense that it describes an active process, and one cannot predict the outcome of such a process. At any time, between any two or three persons, in any group, new inspiration may take an unexpected turn. It remains the mystery of interpreting the strange past, experiencing the creative present, and having faith in the unknown future. It is our participation in this process that separates us from the natural world, the one we know objectively.

June 20, 1948 – This noon I had my farewell lunch with Igor. I'd told him two weeks ago that I had accepted Enno's offer of the managing editor job in Berlin and would be leaving Paris on June 24. The Russians are about to seal off the city from the West. What

Walter Lippmann has begun to call the "Cold War" is about to see its first battle. And George Kennan's containment policy is about to get its first test.

Of course, Igor and I plunged into our usual topics, ignoring the fact that we might never see each other again. I told him that I'd made great progress on my article for *Esprit*. I was planning to title it, "Between East and West: Rediscovering the Gifts of the Russian Spirit." In fact, I was now thinking of expanding the article into a book that would make clear how the *Logos*-word thinking of Russian philosophy was not only ripe for discovery in the West, but had already been welcomed by the Western dialogical thinkers, particularly by Rosenstock-Huessy and Hans Ehrenberg.

I also told Igor that our discussion of Berdyaev's ideas in *Spirit and Reality* had enabled me to finish my chapter on religion in my book about the Cross of Reality.

As we discussed that cross and Eugen's metanomics, Igor said that these subjects seemed a far cry from what had brought us together: Schmemann's lectures on St. Sergius and his Trinity Monastery.

I replied that I disagreed with him. My decision to attend St. Sergius certainly was inspired by Eugen. I wanted to know more than the *objective facts* about Russia. I wanted to be immersed in the *narrative of her past* and to catch her *subjective inner spirit*. Armed with those perspectives, in the course of my writings, I expected to show that Russia's *future* may well have as much to do with St. Sergius as it does with Lenin. Perhaps more. Someday Lenin's revolution will subside, and a new generation will want to reconnect with the past that he and Stalin obliterated. I told Igor that I would like to speak to that new generation.

"So would I," Igor said. "Let's promise to meet again in Moscow one day—and get our books published there. They'll need Berdyaev when they get over Stalin, and they'll need Bulgakov, Solovyov, and all the rest. Right down to your beloved Kireevsky."

"Yes, we should meet again in Moscow," I replied. "Or even better at the Trinity-St. Sergius Monastery. Then we might find the Trinity Cathedral where St. Sergius lies buried. . . and stand together at his tomb. Or perhaps even kneel."

7 FROM THEISM TO PANENTHEISM

God is a universal presence undergirding all of life.

—John Shelby Spong

God is not a supreme being or a supreme person. The divine mystery revealed in the New Testament is a dimension of human life: God is present to human life as its orientation and its source of newness and expansion.

—Gregory Baum

NORWICH, VERMONT – JUNE 20, 2006 – Looking back on those five months in Paris from the perspective of June 2006, exactly 58 years later, I realize how privileged I was to have that time within the world of Eastern Christianity. Most of my friends today are only dimly aware of the Eastern Church.

One Westerner who was *quite* aware of that Church—and who realized that it had preserved certain teachings that were missing in the West—was Pope John Paul II. Not long before he died, the Pope told the church historian Jaroslav Pelikan that ever since the schism of 1054 (when the Eastern and Western churches split), "Western Christendom has been breathing on one lung."

What is it that is missing in the West? What does our other lung contain? Obviously many things, but high among them is the East's panentheistic understanding of God. To me that has seemed a valuable corrective to the West's tendency to be excessively theistic, with God imagined as a supernatural being, an independent intelligent entity who decided to create the universe.

Bishop Kallistos (Timothy Ware) is a prominent contemporary Orthodox theologian who says that we should move away from that theistic way of describing God. In a recent book on panentheism, he writes: "Among all too many Christian thinkers. . . there has been. . . a widespread tendency to speak as if God the creator were somehow external to the creation. . . . All such imagery is sadly defective."

Thus, we have a paradox. Arguably the most traditional church

111

in Christendom is one of our best resources as we consider how to get beyond theism.

Two Bishops in Revolt

Among Protestant churches, the Anglican Communion is the closest in spirit and tradition to the Orthodox Church. Therefore, it is not surprising that two bishops of that church have been leaders in the efforts to move beyond traditional theism. What is particularly intriguing is how one of these bishops, John A. T. Robinson, turned to Berdyaev when he sought to express just what he meant by panentheism.

Robinson, whom I mentioned in the Prologue and who was Bishop of Woolwich in England, published his remarkable book, *Honest to God*, in 1963. However, it was not until 1967, in his follow-up book, *Exploration into God*, that Robinson became quite specific about the fact that he was working to articulate panentheism. In that book's prologue he describes how, as a student, he began to read Berdyaev. Then, toward the end, he said, "Berdyaev, in fact, probably comes as near as anyone to the theological synthesis we are seeking." He went on to quote that same Berdyaev line that Igor had pointed out to me: "God is like a whole humanity rather than like nature, society, or concept." Finding that Bishop Robinson zeroed in on those same words, and had such a deep respect for Berdyaev, gave me a sense of vindication: There was now someone in the limelight who had also seen the value of this critically important Russian guide.

Bishop Robinson died in 1983, but his work has been taken up by his friend and colleague Bishop John Spong. In his *Why Christianity Must Change or Die*, Spong describes how Alfred North Whitehead and others have contributed to panentheism. He then expounds on Tillich's panentheistic image of God as the "ground of being" and asks, "Is it possible that we bear God's image because we are part of who God is?"

Of course, the answer is yes.

Two Catholic Theologians in Revolt

Thus far I have cited only Orthodox and Protestant thinkers in support of panentheism. There are two prominent Catholic theologians, both from Canada, who should be included in this list.

One evening in August 1970 Eugen showed me a letter he had received from Gregory Baum, a teacher at St. Michael's College at the University of Toronto. Baum said that a good friend had just given him a collection of Eugen's books in German, and he was now looking forward to a study of Eugen's work.

I never learned if Baum went ahead with that pursuit, but it has always been clear to me that Baum and his associate Leslie Dewart at St. Michael's were pursuing a path remarkably like Eugen's. I first came upon their books, and met Baum, in the mid-1960s when I was leading the ecumenical discussion groups I had set up at the Norwich Congregational Church. Dewart's *The Future of Belief* and Baum's *Man Becoming* are both quite panentheistic. Both books address overcoming our Greek philosophical inheritance that assumes that, to be real, God must be conceived as *existing*—either as a supreme being or as some other outside power. To many in our discussion group Baum and Dewart appeared as radical, as daring, and as promising as Bishop Robinson or Harvey Cox.

Baum concludes *Man Becoming* with these words:

> God is not a supreme being or a supreme person. The divine mystery revealed in the New Testament is a dimension of human life: God is present to human life as its orientation and its source of newness and expansion. The traditional doctrine of the Trinity has enabled us to discern an empirical basis for speaking of God's presence to man: God is present as summons and gift, in the conversation and communion by which men enter into their humanity.

Inspired by the work of the French philosopher Maurice Blondel, who died in 1949, Baum declared that "God is redemptively present to the whole of human history," and that "every sentence about God can be translated into a declaration about human life." It follows that "as we speak about human life in all its dimensions, we are in fact also speaking about God." Baum contrasted the universality of this approach with the exclusivity of Karl Barth's theology, in which we know of God only through Jesus Christ.

One line from Baum's *Faith and Doctrine* astonished me when I happened on it: "To believe that God is Father is to believe that I am Son." Here was a Catholic *peritus*, one of the "experts" at Vatican II, describing our role as Son, our subjective *I*, just as Rosenstock-Huessy might have. The Son as a category of being and becoming more fully human, rather than as an object of belief in a system of religion. The Son as one of the three ways that God is present to us.

I have no idea if Rosenstock-Huessy and Blondel, who wrote many of their new insights at about the same time, were familiar with each other's work. As Baum presents Blondel, there are striking similarities. Take Blondel's most basic premise: that revelation "is not the addition of new knowledge to human life, introduced from another world," but rather the discovery of "the hidden. . . dynamism present in human life everywhere." Blondel made the actions of men in the world the core of his theology. "We must transport the centre of philosophy to action, for there we also find the center of life. . . . To will all that we will is to place the being and action of God within us." Baum expanded on these words of Blondel when he wrote that he understood "divine transcendence as referring to a dimension of history (and possibly the cosmos) which is the source of overcoming the present and bringing forth the radically new." He contrasted his new idea of transcendence with the old idea that transcendence "referred to the existence of God above time in eternity, independent of man and his history."

Baum believed that, among Catholic theologians, this new panentheistic understanding of God had become so widespread in the 1960s that it might be called a "consensus." Transcendence had come to be associated with "the critical and constructive process, by which man assumes responsibility for this future, personal and social." In other words: "God is present to man in the action that constitutes his history, and creates an experience that is, properly speaking, supernatural."

The panentheistic note in Dewart's work is just as clear. His *The Future of Belief* in 1966 created as much of a stir among Catholics as Cox's *Secular City* had among Protestants the year before. And Dewart was quite familiar with Rosenstock-Huessy, acknowledging him as "among the first (1945) to suggest that 'languages are not means by which we represent the truth after it is perceived, but. . . means to discover hitherto ignored truth.'"

In *The Future of Belief* Dewart pointed to a fascinating fact: in the first millennium of the church, *before* the birth of theology, God *was* understood as a Trinity of actions in the world. *It was Scholastic theology that destroyed this understanding.* After Thomas Aquinas, Dewart writes:

> The Christian concept of God no longer "begins with the three Persons"; it begins. . . with an Aristotelian unmoved Mover and First Cause, or with Subsisting Being Itself. . . . The concept of a "trinitarian" God personally involved in human events out of the abundance of his reality was. . . gradually subordinated to that of a monotheistic Supreme Being eternally contemplating himself in heaven.

This notion of God, with its origins in the abstractions of Greek philosophy, became so entrenched in theology that we lost the notion of God's threefold presence *in* us as Father, Son, and Spirit. Instead, we have been given the idea that a single supreme being has various degrees of immanence or transcendence. To overcome this Greek form of theism, Dewart in effect asks us to return to the first millennium's understanding of God. He proposes that theology in the future would conceive God in the category of presence rather than in the traditional category of *being.*

A Catholic priest in our discussion group thought "presence" wouldn't do; it was not substantial or specific enough. At the time I did not feel it was suitable to suggest a way out of his dilemma. If I had, I would have tried to describe God's presence in terms of the Cross of Reality, and how we made God present in us whenever we spoke as representatives of the *whole* race and of *all* creation. That would be whenever we spoke from the beginning and the end of times, and from our inmost selves to all of the world. Then our speech attempts to include the whole of creation—and is, therefore, *holy.* When Hitler perverted speech by asserting the superiority of the Aryan "master race" over any others, he sinned against the Holy Spirit.

So God's presence in us is as *his* powers, but today we can recognize that those powers are *our* creative powers of speech. God's presence in us as speech frames and includes all of our actions, making us the historical animal. Christianity, as we have seen, should not make us feel more religious in the sense of dependence on some distant God. It should make us feel *less* religious! That is because the church teaches that God became man, not in some theoretical sense but *in actuality*, right inside history. After Christ we understood that we too were capable of receiving God's powers.

Yahweh *and the* Elohim

Many people understand these things more easily in metaphor or art. That is why one of Rosenstock-Huessy's most effective statements about God's powers—and how we receive them—is made in an illustration printed near the end of *Out of Revolution*. It is Michelangelo's Sistine Chapel painting of God creating Adam. There we see both *Yahweh*, the one God, and the *Elohim*, representing God's powers. Rosenstock-Huessy interpreted the painting as follows:

> Michelangelo shows God creating Adam, and keeping in the folds of his immense robe a score of angels or spirits. Thus at the beginning of the world all the divine powers were on God's side; man was stark naked. We might conceive of a pendant to this picture; the end of creation, in which all the spirits that had accompanied the Creator should have left him and descended to man, helping, strengthening, enlarging his being into the divine. In this picture God would be alone, while Adam would have all the Elohim around him as companions.

In *The Christian Future*, Rosenstock-Huessy wrote about how the Church Fathers had described this process of making man like God:

> They called it "anthropurgy": as metallurgy refines metal from its ore, anthropurgy wins the true stuff of Man out of his coarse physical substance. Christ, in the center of history, enables us to participate consciously in this manmaking process and to study its laws.

Among the man-making laws we can study are the laws of language, and the history of their discovery is the topic of the next chapter.

8 A BRIEF HISTORY OF
DIALOGICAL THINKING

Two extremes: to exclude reason, to admit reason only.

—Blaise Pascal

For me the question is not so much What is reason? as What is language?
—Johann Georg Hamann (1730–1788)

IN THE FIRST FOUR CHAPTERS we met the originators of dialogical thinking in the West: Rosenstock-Huessy, Rosenzweig, and Buber. All three were pioneers in the movement away from theism and toward panentheism. All three described, in various ways, how God was in the process of enlarging man's being into the divine.

Their allies in the movement toward panentheism cut across three Christian denominations: the Orthodox—Berdyaev, Bulgakov, and Solovyov; the Anglican—Robinson and Spong; and the Catholic—Baum and Dewart.

Before moving forward, a brief history of dialogical thinking is in order—one that will show certain fascinating links between the forerunners of the Protestant and Jewish dialogical thinkers and their Eastern Orthodox allies. All of these forerunners were reacting to the Enlightenment's enthronement of rationalism—and its related dismissal of religion.

Just who were the forerunners of Rosenstock-Huessy, Rosenzweig, and Buber? Three of the most important were fellow Germans: Johann Georg Hamann, Friedrich von Schlegel (1772–1829), and Ludwig Feuerbach.

It is instructive to begin with Feuerbach, who started out as a Hegelian idealist but then turned on his master. (For more background on Feuerbach and others in this chapter, see the Biographical Notes; those are particularly relevant here.)

Buber acknowledges the origins of his *I and Thou* in Feuerbach: "I myself in my youth was given a decisive impetus by Feuerbach. . . .

Never before has a philosophical anthropology been so emphatically demanded."

Rosenzweig wrote of his speech-thinking that "Ludwig Feuerbach was the first to discover it."

And Rosenstock-Huessy began *Speech and Reality* with the statement: "Ludwig Feuerbach, one hundred years ago, was the first to state a grammatical philosophy of man. He was misunderstood by his contemporaries, especially by Karl Marx."

Hans Ehrenberg saw Feuerbach as such a critical source for the new language-based thinking that he took the trouble, in 1922, to republish Feuerbach's 1843 *Principles of the Philosophy of the Future*. The key statement that Feuerbach made in that book was his Principle No. 59:

> The single man for himself possesses the essence of man neither in himself as a moral being nor in himself as a thinking being. The essence of man is contained only in the community and unity of man with man; it is a unity, however, which rests only on the reality of the distinction between I and thou.

Here, and in similar statements, Feuerbach began thinking in terms of how language, through grammar, molds us into different persons. He elaborated on speech itself when he said:

> A divine impulse this—a divine power, the power of words. . . . The word guides to all truth, unfolds all mysteries, reveals the unseen, makes present the past and the future, defines the infinite, perpetuates the transient. . . . The Word of God is supposed to be distinguished from the human word in that it is no transient breath, but an imparted being. But does not the word of man also contain the being of man, his imparted self,—at least when it is a true word?

Before he published his *Principles*, Feuerbach had created a sensation, in Germany and beyond, with his *The Essence of Christianity*. This book, published in 1841, called for a "higher anthropology," a science of man *based on Christianity*—but on Christianity in a non-supernatural sense. He described his goal as leading philosophy and religion "from the realm of departed souls back into the realm of embodied and living souls"; that is, pulling them "down from the divine self-sufficient bliss in the realm of ideas into human misery."

So Feuerbach and the dialogical thinkers who succeeded him were clearly seeking a higher humanism, one based on our greatest gifts of the word and the spirit, not the reductionist humanism and materialism with which Feuerbach's name is usually associated.

Moving back now to Feuerbach's own predecessors, we come to Friedrich von Schlegel and Hamann. Although Rosenstock-Huessy's interpretation of language was as different from Hamann's as a car is from a horse and buggy, his eccentric 18th-century intellectual ancestor certainly played a key role in showing that language is a more central category than reason. Isaiah Berlin's *The Magus of the North: J. G. Hamann and the Origins of Modern Irrationalism*, published in 1994, dealt with just that issue.

First, Berlin established the 18th-century Hamann as the spiritual father of the 18th- and 19th-century German Romantics—from his student Johann Gottfried Herder (1774–1803), to Herder's friend Johann Wolfgang von Goethe (1749–1832), to Goethe's friend Friedrich Schelling (1775–1854), and to Goethe's admirer, Friedrich von Schlegel.

While Berlin does not get into it, since Schelling and Schlegel were critical inspirations for Ivan Kireevsky and the flourishing of Russian philosophy that grew from his work, Hamann became a spiritual father of these Eastern thinkers as well. Kireevsky went to Germany in 1830, and made a point of going to hear Schelling's lectures.

Following in Kireevsky's trail, Solovyov, Florensky, Bulgakov, and Berdyaev—all of them—found vital inspiration in the German Romantics, those rebels against the arid rationalism of the French Enlightenment.

Second, the title of Berlin's book contains the word "irrationalism" in its title. That alarms me because I have been trying to present my intellectual heroes as perfectly reasonable. Kireevsky and Rosenstock-Huessy in particular have been described here as "suprarational," since they quite deliberately said that reason (logical and objective language) was *essential—but not exclusive*—in understanding anything. Was Isaiah Berlin wrong?

In 1959, the University of Münster gave Rosenstock-Huessy an honorary degree, hailing him as "the Hamann of the 20th century." Unfortunately, being recognized as the "new Hamann" was not entirely a blessing. The old Hamann was decidedly eccentric. He liked to call himself an "ignoramus," with "a mind like blotting paper," and a writing style characterized by "fragments, leaps, and hints." Still, as a critical inspiration for thinkers from Goethe to Schelling and beyond, he has an undeniable status, one that Berlin fully accords him.

Berlin called Hamann "the most passionate, consistent, extreme and implacable enemy of the Enlightenment and, in particular, all forms of rationalism of his time." He said that "Goethe saw Hamann as a great awakener, the first champion of the unity of man—the union of all his faculties, mental, emotional, physical, in his greatest creations." And he concluded, "It is doubtful whether without Hamann's revolt. . . the worlds of Herder, Friedrich Schlegel, Tieck, Schiller, and indeed of Goethe too, would have come into being."

Whereas Rosenstock-Huessy and Rosenzweig, like Berdyaev, drew on Schelling for the idea that we were now about to embark on a third period in history, the age of the spirit, and whereas they saw Goethe as the first citizen of this new age, Rosenstock-Huessy cites Friedrich Schlegel as a more specific source of inspiration. Schlegel provided Rosenstock-Huessy with certain key ideas—seeds, you might say—that blossomed into *Out of Revolution*, as well as into his writings on language.

First, in *Out of Revolution*, Rosenstock-Huessy says that his "history of the inspirations of mankind" was "first conceived by Friedrich Schlegel," a thinker who "foresaw our own attempt to deal with the continuous process of creation in mankind itself."

Second, in his 1935 essay, "The Uni-versity of Logic, Language and Literature," Rosenstock-Huessy pointed to Schlegel as a "predecessor" in disclosing that "language, logic, and literature are various forms of crystallization in one process."

After reading that in Rosenstock-Huessy's essay, I looked up Schlegel's writings and found what indeed seemed to be the seeds of Rosenstock-Huessy's understandings of speech and the Cross of Reality. That cross seems prefigured in Schlegel's 1847 book on language:

The first truth then that psychology arrives at is the internal discord within our fourfold and divided consciousness. . . . It is only in the highest creations of artistic genius, manifesting itself either in poetry or some other form of language. . . that we meet with the perfect harmony of a complete and united consciousness, in which all its faculties work together in combined and living action.

Now Schlegel's perception that we have a "fourfold consciousness" not only seems to prefigure the Cross of Reality; it also anticipates what Kireevsky said about integral knowledge in his "New Principles for Philosophy."

This brings us back to my conversation with Emmanuel Mounier, in which I said that Rosenstock-Huessy's cross seems to have been anticipated by Kireevsky. Now it appears that we know why. It seems quite likely that both men derived their approach to integral knowledge from a single source: Friedrich von Schlegel.

That Kireevsky was probably influenced by Schlegel is confirmed by Andrzej Walicki, a notable historian of Russian philosophy at the University of Notre Dame in Indiana. Abbot Gleason's biography of Kireevsky reports the details as follows:

Walicki regards Kireevsky's "integralism" as part and parcel of a sweeping critique of revolutionary rationalism, almost all the elements of which were taken from German romantic and counterrevolutionary thought. Walicki. . . stressed the similarities between Kireevsky's "integralism". . . and that of Friedrich Schlegel. What Kireevsky called the "union of all the forces of the soul" seems to have been essentially what Schlegel meant by *"die Einheit des Bewußtseins."* (the unity of consciousness).

Isaiah Berlin's label of "irrationalism" for Hamann appears now to have been an understandable, but not accurate, description. Hamann's anti-Enlightenment and anti-rational ideas, not to mention his eccentric habits, could certainly lead one to use the term "irrationalism"—especially because it also has shock value in a culture that prizes rational thought. But when excerpts from

Berlin's book were printed in the October 21, 1993, *New York Review of Books*, Hamann scholar James O'Flaherty wrote a letter to the *Review* (November 18, 1993), protesting Berlin's "irrational" label. O'Flaherty pointed out that there was now a consensus among Hamann scholars that he was *not* irrational but should be thought of as introducing "intuitive reason."

Berlin replied that this term seemed meaningless to him. It is, however, clear that something resembling "intuitive reason" is more on the side of the rational than the irrational. That is why the term "supra-rational" is perhaps closer to the mark. That is also why it is important to highlight Pascal's recognition of the limits of reason. I like to think that our French friend would have welcomed Hamann and his German successors.

To link what's been said in this chapter to the next three chapters, all based in Russia, let us return briefly to Rosenstock-Huessy's enigmatic statement about Feuerbach: "He was misunderstood by his contemporaries, especially by Karl Marx." What Rosenstock-Huessy might have meant is that Marx derived much of his materialist philosophy from Feuerbach, never realizing that Feuerbach, in his *The Essence of Christianity* and *Principles of the Philosophy of the Future*, was exploring a way beyond both materialism and idealism.

Marx, Lenin, and the communist thinkers who followed in their wake, all marching under the banner of materialism, helped prepare the way for that brutal dictatorship that still gripped the USSR in December 1983, when a small group of Americans went there to launch a project called US-USSR Bridges for Peace.

PART II

THE RUSSIAN
PROVING GROUND

TRANSITION TO PART II

Argonautic vs. Academic

One of Rosenstock-Huessy's recurring themes was that the academic mind, with its objectivity and detachment, needs to be replaced by a mind that is engaged with the times of history and its own time. Thus he coined the term "argonautic." This term suggests the character of the new thinking—and the new action—we will need in the third millennium. It was no accident that I chose the name "Argo Books" for the publishing house that Freya von Moltke and I founded to keep his books in print.

In Rosenstock-Huessy's *Soziologie*, he describes the two great intellectual projects of the past millennium: (1) The "scholastic," beginning with Anselm of Canterbury and Pierre Abélard in the 11th century; and (2) the "academic," dating from Copernicus and Galileo in the 16th century and from Descartes in the 17th century. The scholastics gave us theology as the "queen of the sciences"; the academics have given us natural science, with its triumphant achievements in physics.

Their needed successor, in our time, is a third great intellectual project, a truly social science that would be neither scholastic nor academic in character. Rather, it would be "argonautic." Undoubtedly, Rosenstock-Huessy hoped that this new discipline, his metanomics, would be founded by his students and readers, perhaps even by some defectors from academe. We latter-day Argonauts would be happy to jettison academe's lack of passion, and its cold, objective, disengaged language. Like Jason and his crew on the Argo, we would contend with winds that change. No longer in the shelter of Plato's grove—quietly contemplating the good, the true, and the beautiful—we would be like scouts, taking risks. Unlike the academics, we would not equivocate, finding two sides to every question. We would recognize that, unless we steer our ship with a sense of purpose and direction, it will crash into the rock of Scylla or be sucked into the whirlpool of Charybdis.

Rosenstock-Huessy spoke as a prophet of argonautic in the 1940s and 1950s. By the 1960s his prophecy had begun to be fulfilled. The academic who looked out from an ivory tower or wandered in Plato's grove was no longer much admired. Today overseas service, as much as local service, has been integrated into thousands of academic programs. Still, Page Smith was moved, in 1990, to write his *Killing the Spirit: Higher Education in America*. There he wrote of "academic fundamentalism," by which he meant "the stubborn refusal of the academy to acknowledge any truth that does not conform to professorial dogmas."

Synchronizing Distemporaries

In the spirit of argonautic, metanomics would definitely admit that it has a purpose: to establish peace between persons, groups, or nations. Rosenstock-Huessy coined a mouthful of a name for this task: "synchronizing antagonistic distemporaries." One finds that expression at the end of his important short essay, "In Defense of the Grammatical Method." Here he describes the new "concrete field" of metanomics as "society (time)." He pits metanomics against the old field of natural science, which was "nature (space)" and the even older field of theology, which was "values (gods)."

Why did Rosenstock-Huessy see our new task as synchronizing disconnected groups or people, these distemporaries? He meant that the global society of the third millennium would have a unified economy, but that it would be made up of many peoples who are estranged from each other or who are out of synch with each other. Such people can be called distemporaries because they live in civilizations that have vastly different experiences of time and history. One obvious example of such a civilizational divide is that between Russia and the West, the heirs of Eastern and Western Christianity. Another divide, so poignant today, is that between the countries of the Middle East and the West.

A project that dealt with that first divide, US-USSR Bridges for Peace, is about to be described in Chapter 9, while a similar project that currently addresses the second divide, Building Bridges: Middle East-US, is described at our website:

www.BuildingBridgesMEUS.org

The Norwich Center

US-USSR Bridges for Peace was launched through the efforts of a few friends who first gathered together under the auspices of a nonprofit organization, the Norwich Center. That organization had been formed in 1977 to implement a vision of voluntary service dedicated to peace-building projects.

In view of the Norwich Center's purpose, it was not surprising that our initial board included Frank Davidson, who had been a seminal participant in Camp William James. It also included Freya von Moltke and Hans Huessy. With an office located next door to the Norwich Congregational Church, whose minister, Jim Todhunter, was quite enthusiastic about our purpose, it was easy for us to co-opt members of that church to help us launch US-USSR Bridges for Peace. It was that project that put all the principles of dialogical thinking to the test.

The Russian Connection

It will help prepare us for Part II if we turn to what Rosenstock-Huessy wrote in *The Christian Future* about Eastern Christianity—and particularly about Dostoevsky, Solovyov, and Berdyaev:

> Who were the most provoking Christians of the nineteenth century? Was it not Leo Tolstoi, and the author of the *Brothers Karamazov* and *The Great Inquisitor*, Fyodor Dostoevsky? And was it not the Russian Solovyov, who wrote *The Antichrist* in 1890, and dreamed of the reunion of East and West more fervently than even Archbishop Söderblom of Sweden? Was it not Berdyaev, the Eastern Christian, who convinced many Westerners of the New Middle Ages?

That quotation reminds us that Rosenstock-Huessy saw these 19th-century Russians as vital contributors to the Christian future, indeed prophets of the new Christian paradigm that he was presenting in his book. Thus, the Russian connection we are about to make in Part II is no departure from our exploration of that paradigm.

9 BRIDGES FOR PEACE

One thing is certain: we have no hope for abolishing war until we accept the framework of a universal planetary method of crossing borders between all peoples and all countries.

—Eugen Rosenstock-Huessy

LENINGRAD – DECEMBER 2, 1983 – There were ten of *us* this morning, our group from New England, lined up facing more than 3,000 of *them*, Russians from Leningrad. Our delegation represented nine New England churches, and we stood before a golden icon screen at the front of the high nave in St. Nicholas Cathedral.

I stood next to Metropolitan Anthony, who was the celebrant at this Sunday service. Tall, bearded, and gaunt, resplendent in golden robes and wearing a bejeweled crown, he is one of the Russian Orthodox Church's five "princes," ranking just below the Patriarch. Watching him, smelling sweet incense, and hearing the soaring voices of the congregation, I was transported back to the chapel at St. Sergius in Paris.

As the long service drew to a close, Metropolitan Anthony turned to me and asked, in perfectly clear English:

"Now would you like to greet the congregation?"

I was completely unprepared for this. Then I recalled that I had a notecard in my pocket with a Russian greeting I had planned to use at lunch with the metropolitan and his priests after the service. I pulled it out.

"Dear brothers and sisters in Christ," I said in Russian, and continued on:

I bring you greetings from nine churches in New England. We have come on an unusual mission, and we seek your help. We invite you to join us in building bridges of understanding between the US and USSR, bridges of peace that will remove the enemy images that have arisen between us.

Since our diplomats seem unable to establish a dialogue between our nations, we hope to begin a dialogue between our peoples, a sort of "citizen diplomacy" that will try to end the Cold War between our countries.

Therefore, we are here today to invite members of your church, and other churches across your land, to join us in founding US-USSR Bridges for Peace. We invite you to visit our country, as we are visiting yours. We want you to meet the governors of our states and the leaders of our churches. And we want the public in both our countries to know that this citizen dialogue is taking place, that we are tearing down the walls of mutual hate and suspicion.

By such simple acts as talking with each other, as I am talking with you now, we hope to achieve our goals. In the name of our Lord, who asked us to be peacemakers, amen.

I looked into the eyes of the people closest to me, and I could tell they'd understood. A recessional hymn concluded the service, and our group headed to lunch in the cathedral.

Our Russian guide for this visit to St. Nicholas Cathedral was Father Jonathan, a man of perhaps 35, with bright blond hair and a buoyant personality. He had met us the day before, when we arrived at the Hotel Moskva, all quite exhausted after an overnight train trip from Helsinki. He sat with me at lunch, and after some wine, our conversation became more personal. Jonathan told me he had graduated in physics from Leningrad University, and although he had begun to teach it, he found his subject boring. He stopped teaching and took up seminary studies. He asked what I had done and I told him about attending St. Sergius and how I might have become a diplomat or a Russian history professor, but finally ended up in business.

"But now I've begun a new career," I said, and proceeded to tell him about the Norwich Center. I explained how the center's first project was US-USSR Bridges for Peace.

Our conversation was interrupted when Bishop Agafangel stood and asked me to tell him and the other priests about our project.

I then described how this visit to St. Nicholas was part of the first bridge, which for us Americans was a two-week stay in the

Soviet Union. Besides Leningrad, we would spend several days in Volgograd, and the rest of our time in Moscow. Actually, this was the *second half* of a two-way exchange. A ten-person delegation from the Soviet Peace Committee, including Bishop Anthony, Orthodox Bishop of Stavropol, had begun the first step on this bridge-exchange last April, when we had hosted them for two weeks in New England.

Bishop Agafangel then added that Bishop Anthony had recounted that visit to the United States at the summer meeting of bishops, noting how hospitable he found New Englanders.

"He's most enthusiastic about this project and extends his greetings to you," Bishop Agafangel said.

"Well, Bishop Anthony was a star during last spring's visit," I replied, and explained how the Bennington, Vermont, school board had rescinded its initial invitation for Bishop Anthony to address a school assembly, simply because a letter to the local paper said that that he wouldn't be a real bishop, but a KBG agent in priestly clothing. *The New York Times* picked up this tidbit, and the next thing we knew, the national television host, Ted Koppel, wanted to cover the whole exchange on his *Nightline* show, and to interview Bishop Anthony. Thus, one angry letter gave us more than five minutes on national television, a level of publicity that would have cost us millions of dollars to buy.

I asked Bishop Agafangel if Bishop Anthony had told the other bishops about this.

Agafangel said he had, and that "on the television show, some 'expert' on the Soviet Union, actually a defector from our country, had strongly implied that Anthony was an agent dressed in priest's clothing."

I mentioned that the American public still was convinced that religion no longer existed in the USSR. But when Bishop Anthony appeared at public meetings, he immediately shattered American stereotypes. That was a primary goal of our "Bridges" project. As a result of last April's visit, we were now discussing the idea of annual exchanges with the Peace Committee and the Soviet Women's Committee. In fact, we also hoped to begin such exchanges with the Russian Orthodox Church.

Bishop Agafangel said he believed the church's External Relations Department would be sympathetic to our proposal.

After another half hour of discussion among all of us about these plans, we went on a bus for a city tour. Father Jonathan was my seatmate. We discussed the origins of my interest in Russia, how I'd read *The Brothers Karamazov* in 1940, then Berdyaev and Solovyov in 1941, and how, after the war, Rosenstock-Huessy had encouraged me to follow up on them. My friends had begun to call me a Slavophile.

"Don't you ever regret dropping your love for Russia, our writers, and our philosophers, in favor of going into business?" Father Jonathan asked.

"Actually, as the owner of a small business, I was master of my own time. I could continue to read and write about Berdyaev and Solovyov, just as I've managed to write almost every day about Rosenstock-Huessy."

We spoke about a book I had written two years earlier, *Letters to the Third Millennium: An Experiment in East-West Communication*, which introduced Rosenstock-Huessy's ideas in the context of helping to overcome the East-West ideological divide. That book was followed by a much shorter one, *Between East and West: Rediscovering the Gifts of the Russian Spirit*. It made some of the same points as my *Letters* book, but concentrated on how Russian thinkers, from Kireevsky and Khomyakov to Berdyaev, were moving in the same direction as Rosenstock-Huessy and Franz Rosenzweig.

Father Jonathan wanted to know what "the same direction" meant. I explained that both my German and my Russian intellectual heroes sought to overcome today's sense that there are *two* orders of reality, the worldly secular one and the other-worldly religious one. They challenged the idea that the only real world is the one described to us by natural science, while religion must be consigned to the realm of faith and morals. For them, spirit is as real as matter—and God is not a supernatural being, but a power alive in each of us. From that perspective, they all sought to reconcile science with religion.

"I think they've disclosed a down-to-earth spirituality," I said, "one that could reach Kireevsky's goal of *tselnoye znaniye*, integral knowledge."

"Certainly all true Russian philosophers seek such knowledge," said Jonathan, adding that he thought Western thinkers had given up on that.

When we returned to the Moskva Hotel, I went up to my room and brought down a spiral-bound notebook containing a copy of my typescript for *Between East and West*. It was in that format that I had given other copies to the Peace Committee during their visit to the United States earlier in the year.

As I handed my notebook to Jonathan, a member of our delegation interrupted us with an emergency about her passport. Jonathan was still there in the lobby 15 minutes later when I returned. He had read enough to see that he agreed with my presentation of the Russian Idea. That is, four of its key components were Divine Humanity, Trinitarian thinking, *sobornost*, and integral knowledge. He had also noticed my acknowledgment of how Kireevsky had foreseen Rosenstock-Huessy's Cross of Reality.

Father Jonathan at the Moskva

DECEMBER 3, 1983 – After a day spent seeing the St. Peter and Paul Fortress, then meeting various Peace Committee leaders, our delegation had a quick supper and went to the ballet. I'd arranged to leave them so that I could have a one-on-one supper with Father Jonathan, the physics professor-turned-priest.

It took us some searching to find a booth in the hotel restaurant where we could talk. Just beyond the booths, there was a dance floor lit up with blue and red flashing lights that half-revealed and half-concealed practically nude dancers waving huge feathery fans. It seemed as if General Secretary Yuri Andropov's Russia was undergoing some sort of identity crisis.

Finally, we found a corner booth and ordered supper and some wine. Jonathan had read my whole American *samizdat* edition of *Between East and West*—and reconfirmed his approval.

I wondered aloud if there were any new Berdyaevs on the horizon in the Soviet Union.

Jonathan mentioned a Sergei Averintsev, an instructor at the Gorky Institute whose work appears as literary criticism, but was "full of unusual religious insight." He also mentioned Mikhail Bakhtin, whose understanding of language he described as "highly spiritual." In fact, his presentation of dialogue seemed remarkably like Rosenstock-Huessy's. His best-known book was *Problems of Dostoevsky's Poetics*. He had died in 1975.

"He's all the rage in academic life today," Father Jonathan said. "Not only here but in France and your country."

Bakhtin had been arrested and exiled in 1929 for participating in a religious discussion group. But today, Jonathan went on, scholars were publishing his work quite freely.

I asked Jonathan if he could tell me what Bakhtin had written about Dostoevsky.

He replied that Bakhtin had described Dostoevsky as the first to write "polyphonic novels." By that he meant novels in which the author gives full expression to the voice and view of each character—and does not seek to make the author's own viewpoint dominant. Thus, one hears Ivan Karamazov's voice and views as clearly as one hears Alyosha's.

I wanted to know if Dostoevsky's work was available in stores, and he said it had become easy to find in just the last decade. He thought I might like to contact the critic Yuri Karyakin, who was now considered the leading Dostoevsky scholar.

I then asked if there were any Western religious thinkers whose works one could buy in the USSR.

"Certainly not in our bookstores," he replied. "But last year our Leningrad Theological Seminary was able to get copies of Dietrich Bonhoeffer's *Letters and Papers from Prison*. I teach a course there on Protestant thought, and now I include that book."

Father Jonathan had noticed that I had compared Bonhoeffer's understanding of God with Solovyov's, and observed that both of them were more panentheistic than theistic.

Actually, I said, I thought Bonhoeffer might have been influenced by Solovyov and Berdyaev. Eberhard Bethge's biography of Bonhoeffer mentioned that he had been attracted to these thinkers by reading Hans Ehrenberg's *Eastern Christianity*—just as I had been.

We then discussed the fledgling interest in panentheism in the United States. I mentioned the recent publication of *Original Blessing*, by a Dominican scholar named Matthew Fox. That book advocated a "panentheistic spirituality" and cited Berdyaev in support of it.

After that we turned to Bonhoeffer's theme of a "religionless Christianity." Father Jonathan said that had been a difficult concept for his seminary students and wondered how I understood it.

I replied that Camp William James, to which I'd referred in *Between East and West*, had been recognized as one of the inspirations for the American Peace Corps. Then US-USSR Bridges for Peace had been inspired by both those projects. Alone and together, they were acts of religionless Christianity, because volunteers had taken time out of their lives to meet the needs of a planetary society.

Father Jonathan agreed with my point and said that he would try it out on his seminary students.

The wine bottle was empty, it was approaching 11 p.m., and the fan dancers had finished their last number. As the bill was being settled, we discussed the rather small opposition to the "Bridges" project. The only vociferous opposition was from Natalya Solzhenitsyn, now living in Vermont with her husband, the exiled Nobel laureate Alexander Solzhenitsyn. She had written a letter to our newspaper in which she said, "Speaking for myself and my husband, you are building a bridge that will never reach the other side."

Father Jonathan said he hoped Mrs. Solzhenitsyn was wrong, but added that, given the current rhetoric between our governments, the outlook wasn't promising. He wondered whether "citizen diplomacy" could really make a difference.

I replied that groups like ours often took heart from the words of the anthropologist Margaret Mead: *"Never doubt that a small group of thoughtful, committed citizens can change the world. Indeed, it is the only thing that ever has."*

Yuri Zamoshkin at the Institute

MOSCOW – DECEMBER 13, 1983 – We returned from Volgograd two days ago. Then yesterday we had a meeting at the Office for External Relations of the Orthodox Church. There, as Father Agafangel had predicted, we were able to make plans for exchange visits between Russian and American clergy. At the same time, some of the women in our group met with the head of the Soviet Women's Committee and made plans for exchange visits that would bring Soviet women writers, educators, and other professionals into contact with their American counterparts.

With that productive morning behind us, this afternoon we had what was the most productive meeting of our whole visit. We were the guests of Yuri Zamoshkin at his Institute for the Study of the USA and Canada. When Zamoshkin had led the Russians to New England last April, on the first leg of this exchange, I'd found him to be the perfect man for that role. Trained as a sociologist, he was head of the section on US politics at this institute, a think tank whose output commands respectful attention in the Kremlin.

In his late 50s, with graying hair and a white moustache, Zamoshkin is alert and handsome. Add his tweed jacket, and he could easily have defected to the Dartmouth Sociology Department.

At 2 p.m. we entered Yuri's lair. Our group filed into a large meeting room in the Institute's 18th-century building. He welcomed us and introduced the several scholars who'd be joining us in the afternoon's workshop discussions. We then broke into small groups that met in different corners of the room.

I joined a group led by Sergei Filatov, who heads an Institute section that studies religion in the United States. We discussed the role of Protestant individualism in forming the American psyche, and how Orthodox *sobornost* (a "conciliarity" which gives priority to the community) forms the Russian psyche. The illness of the American psyche, we all agreed, is an excessive preoccupation with oneself, the almighty *I*, whereas the illness of the Russian psyche is a too-centralized and authoritarian version of *sobornost*. Tsarism, of course, offered the Russians no voluntary sobornost, and Communism has provided even less. That is, it has put all the emphasis on "the glorious future" of *all* and given only lip-service to the genuine, *freely formed* community of *we* (which was the vision of *sobornost* put forward by Khomyakov).

Groups in the other corners of the room discussed environmental issues, arms control, and cultural questions. After the first hour, we each rotated to a different group. I chose the one on arms control, where a young man named Andrei Kokoshin was the Russian discussant. We quickly became less interested in the details of various treaties than in the ideological dynamics behind the military confrontation. I said that the US ideologues are essentially "monological"; they shun dialogue as if it were a sign of weakness. In *both* countries, we and Kokoshin agreed, there are plenty of such people; they are the hawks who drive the arms race. In the United States, détente has been in trouble since 1977 when Paul Nitze and his Committee on the Present Danger led a most successful effort to revive the Cold War. With hard-line ideologues like Richard Perle, the Assistant Secretary of Defense for international security policy, feeding their propaganda, their superhawk line was that the Soviet Union was about to launch and "win" a nuclear war.

"We believe that the Nitze committee played an important role in leading to the brinkmanship we experience today," Kokoshin commented. "You can be sure they've awakened an equally ideological constituency here."

I said that the American Committee on US-Soviet Relations, the honorary chair of which is George Kennan, with its leadership made up of distinguished like-minded figures, provides an effective counterpoint to the Nitze group's hard line. That is, it regularly engages in dialogue with prominent Soviet visitors and sends its members to the USSR for similar discussions. In fact, Kennan had recently written an article in the *New York Times* in which he said he objected "to people who talk about war as though it were perfectly natural that if you could go to war, you would. Normally, people have gone to war for a purpose, and if they didn't have a purpose, they wouldn't do it. And I don't see the purpose from the point of view of the Soviet government."

Kokoshin said he hoped that the American and Soviet Kennans would prevail over our respective ideologues.

Later, over tea, Yuri told me that his institute would be glad to cooperate with us on "Bridges" future exchanges. He said that the Institute's head, Georgy Arbatov, had been impressed that William Sloane Coffin, the chaplain at Yale University, had addressed the Soviet "Bridges" delegation to the United States in Russian. I told him that this morning we had confirmed plans to begin annual exchanges with both the Russian Orthodox Church and the Soviet Women's Committee.

Yuri then thanked me again for the copy of *Between East and West*, which I had given him in the United States. He added that he had limited knowledge of the Russian or Western thinkers discussed in it. However, he had a good friend at the Institute of Philosophy to whom he had given his copy.

While he had colleagues at that institute who disagreed with him, he doubted if Russia would ever seek to reconnect with the spiritual creativity of her Silver Age, as I had suggested she might in

Between East and West. Like Western Europe, only about 10 percent of the Soviet population could be considered religious believers. As he put it, the USSR was "no longer the country of Dostoevsky and Solovyov. They're essentially pre-modern."

I replied that I thought both of those "has-been" writers actually belonged to the future. In a country that still recited Alexander Pushkin's "The Prophet" in school, as I had been told, I believed Dostoevsky and Solovyov would remain prophets. I could imagine many Russians becoming re-committed to their heritage.

Yuri smiled at my defense of my Russian heroes. As we parted, I told him that our group was headed the next day to Zagorsk, to the Trinity-St. Sergius Monastery. "That's about as pre-modern as you can get!" I said, as my parting shot.

Yuri admitted that he had never been there.

At the Trinity Cathedral

MOSCOW – DECEMBER 14, 1983 – As I had hoped, today's visit to the Trinity-St. Sergius Monastery, 43 miles northeast of Moscow, turned out to be the high point of our trip. Within those great crenellated 14th-century walls, one could feel the heartbeat of Russia—and of the Eastern Church.

From listening to sonorous chant, to viewing golden onion domes, to praying before an icon screen, to smelling incense, to hearing the seminary dean tell us of their program here, to sitting at lunch with the priests, our ears and eyes, lips and noses, minds, mouths and stomachs, hands, and feet had made our bodies full participants in the mystery of that place.

At lunch I told the dean I hoped he would come to the United States on one of the yearly exchange visits we'd now agreed to begin with the Russian Orthodox Church.

At the end of our visit, as the others in our group took the path back to our bus, I lingered at the entrance to Trinity Cathedral. Then I stepped inside once more, went quickly to St. Sergius's sarcophagus in the dimly lit interior, crossed myself, and knelt.

Open Christianity

LENINGRAD – SEPTEMBER 19, 1990 – This is my ninth visit to Peter the Great's city on the marsh. When Natalya Solzhenitsyn said that our bridges would "never reach the other side," she must have thought we'd never get beyond the facades of the Potemkin villages the Soviet system would erect. Perhaps she would have been right if we hadn't learned the language and didn't know the history. "Bridges" had hired an Executive Director in 1985, Richard Hough-Ross, who'd been pastor of the United Church of Christ church in Peacham, Vermont. He soon became more fluent in Russian than I.

I think I should write Natalya when I get back. She used to be a regular customer at Shopping International, my Norwich mail-order and retail business. I'm sure she would be surprised to learn about the full scope of the progress that "Bridges" has made over the past seven years. We have had regular exchanges with the Orthodox Church, the Peace Committee, the Women's Committee, and several academic institutes. And now we've established offices in all the New England states, with their governors often welcoming the Soviet delegations.

However, our greatest achievement has been to serve as a sort of catalyst and model for many other similar groups. In fact, our idea of citizen diplomacy has spread like wildfire—so that now there is a national network of more than a hundred cooperating groups, at least one in almost every state. The network has sent more than 50,000 Americans to the USSR and brought similar thousands of Soviets to the United States. The organization, and the concept, have now spanned two American presidencies. Since all our exchanges seek television and press coverage, millions in each country have learned about what we're doing. In the USSR, we've found many groups glad to participate, not only in Moscow but in at least 20 other cities, from Tallinn in Estonia to Baku in Azerbaijan.

We've even been invited to meet Premier Mikhail Gorbachev in the Kremlin. In February 1987, he had invited 700 people from outside the USSR to come to a three-day conference in Moscow, one that ended with a Kremlin reception to meet him and the rest of the Politburo. Incredibly, Andrei Sakharov, the physicist who had built their hydrogen bomb and had later become their most famous dissident, was at this "coming-out party." Even more incredibly, I had had a long conversation with Sakharov about our "Bridges" project, something of which he heartily approved.

I've never been one for seeking autographs, but I asked Sakharov for his; I wanted a memento of our unlikely meeting.

The "Bridges" project has led to something else, as well. For the last three days here I've been meeting with Konstantin Ivanov, the president of a new organization called Open Christianity. Their ambitious goal is to start a school and college that will make Christian education a core part of their curriculum. Tony Ugolnik, a "Bridges" activist, had put me in touch with them, thinking that we might be able to help them. The first step in their plans is to acquire a two-story, block-long building just off Nevsky Prospekt, Leningrad's most celebrated street—the equivalent of the Champs-Elysées in Paris.

Yesterday Konstantin and I toured that large but decrepit building, and then discussed their plans over lunch.

Before we began to discuss the building, Konstantin said he'd heard from Tony that I had had a lifelong interest in Solovyov and Berdyaev, and mentioned that the college would be teaching their work, along with that of other Silver Age thinkers.

I gave him a copy of *Between East and West*, which he said he would have a friend translate for him and for some of the others at Open Christianity.

He then went on to describe how the Leningrad City Council had received their request to acquire the building, and had indicated they might make a positive response. However, they were concerned that Open Christianity might not have the funds to make even the minimum repairs necessary. Konstantin said that, if Bridges for Peace could give him a letter indicating that we'd help them secure financing, he thought that would clinch the deal.

"Bridges" has no cash reserves, and survives only because volunteers give us their time, I told him. Still, I could write a letter saying that "Bridges" would make every effort to raise $50,000 toward repairs of the building, without committing the organization. The Peace Committee office could type it up on our letterhead, which showed distinguished academics on our Advisory Council. Konstantin thought that would be perfect.

I left him and went back to the second part of my agenda here, leading a group of New England businessmen who plan to teach business management to budding Soviet entrepreneurs next spring.

Among them is Tony Neidecker, an old friend from my Exeter days. "Bridges" is launching that program under the name "The Transnational Institute," and we have a prominent Soviet economist, Nikolai Shmelev, as our Russian president.

I drafted the letter last night, took it to the Peace Committee this morning, and then delivered it to Konstantin at noon at the Moskva. He was immediately captivated. The fact that the money was by no means in hand was irrelevant. The old myth that US streets are paved with gold gave the document its clout.

With the building matter behind us, over lunch I told Konstantin how "Bridges" was seeking Russian partners to launch a program that would be concerned with the renewal of Russian spiritual life. We were thinking of kicking off the program with a fall 1991 conference, hopefully with its first sessions for three days in Leningrad and its concluding sessions for three days in Moscow. I explained that we'd already found Moscow partners in the Institute of Philosophy and a little organization called Put, and asked him if Open Christianity might be the sponsor of the Leningrad sessions.

Konstantin readily assented. For participants he had in mind friends in Leningrad University and also in the theological academy, and was certain Open Christianity could sponsor the Leningrad sessions. He asked who would be invited from the United States.

I said that a friend of mine in Dartmouth's Russian Department, Lev Loseff, had suggested we try to get George Kline from Bryn Mawr College, James Scanlan from Ohio State University, Bernice Rosenthal from Fordham University, Caryl Emerson from Princeton University, and Andrzej Walicki from the University of Notre Dame. If some of those scholars agreed to come, their own colleagues would take our conference seriously.

I then went on to explain that we weren't planning to launch this project under the name "Bridges for Peace." We hoped that the initial conference sponsors—Open Christianity and the Institute of Philosophy—would also want to help us form a new and more appropriate sponsoring organization.

"We're thinking about reconstituting the Vladimir Solovyov Society," I said.

Konstantin was immediately enthusiastic. We discussed how the original Solovyov society had been founded in 1905 by Sergei

Bulgakov and Berdyaev. By re-founding the society in Moscow, we could establish it as a transnational organization, with secretariats in Moscow, Leningrad, the United States, and in other countries.

Konstantin said the timing for such a society was perfect. A new interest in Berdyaev and Solovyov was sweeping the country since Gorbachev's *glasnost*, and a venture like this would certainly find support.

"The timing is perfect." I certainly hope so. For more than 40 years I've been dreaming of this moment. What will the 1990s bring? A normal Russia? One interested in recovering her pre-communist heritage?

Almost a year ago, on November 9, 1989, Gorbachev had let the Berlin Wall be torn down, thereby ending the Cold War. Libby and I were soldiers in Berlin when that war began. Others are already claiming *they* ended it single-handedly. The Reaganites say their Star Wars missile defense system forced the "Reds" to throw in the towel. We citizen diplomats say we certainly *helped* to end it, by dissipating the mutual enemy images.

Maybe Reagan and *we* together did play a role, but I still think Gorbachev deserves more of the credit. He did not so much capitulate to superior military power as acknowledge the rot within. It was the challenge from Andrei Sakharov's mere existence, and the millions who agreed with him, that brought the system to collapse. Russians were simply no longer willing to live for an empty ideal.

I wonder what my Open Christianity friends will think of *Between East and West*, bound in true *samizdat* form, when they learn more about its contents. Will they share my enthusiasm for Rosenstock-Huessy, Bonhoeffer, and religionless Christianity? Will they understand why I found the Russian philosophers to be allies? After all, the name "Open Christianity" suggests Christianity beyond the church.

NORWICH, VERMONT – DECEMBER 11, 1990 – This morning, out of the blue, I have received a fax from Open Christianity. They plan to publish my *samizdat*; in fact, they've already translated it. Amazed and delighted, I've faxed them back to give them my OK.

FEBRUARY 5, 1991 – Nikolai Shmelev faxed me a copy of the letter he's just sent to his friend, Leningrad Mayor Anatoly Sobchak, endorsing Open Christianity and supporting its application to the

Leningrad City Council for acquiring the building off Nevsky Prospekt.

MARCH 26, 1991 – Another fax from Open Christianity. My letter plus Shmelev's did the trick. They have their building.

10 THE SOLOVYOV SOCIETY

Man is created in the image of God. In his personal consciousness man possesses the image of the divine persons; as a member of the human race he possesses the image of the union of the three persons, he is conscious of himself not only as I, *but as* thou *and as* we.

—Sergei Bulgakov

ST. PETERSBURG – SEPTEMBER 7, 1991 – We certainly live in a global society. My translator this morning was Elena Reshetnikova, a bouncy young blonde in a Bates College t-shirt, acquired during a year in Maine, attending classes there. Wide-eyed and chatty, she told me she finds Premier Boris Yeltsin "too Western."

Open Christianity has come through, not only by finding Elena but with all the other arrangements. This conference, the one that Konstantin Ivanov and I had only dreamed about a year ago, couldn't have had a better start. It is attended by more than a hundred people, including professors from Leningrad University.

When Konstantin greeted me and introduced Elena, he told me how delighted he was that George Kline and Andrzej Walicki, two of the world's leading scholars on Russian philosophy, were among the ten Americans I had managed to recruit. Konstantin also said that he would have supper with me tomorrow, to let me know about progress on renovating their building and on publishing my book.

The hall we met in could hardly have been more elegant: a great two-story-high ballroom in an ornate 18th-century mansion, now home to the Institute for the Study of Art. It was a fine venue for what we'd billed as "The First US-USSR Conference on the Recovery of the Russian Philosophical Tradition." As planned with Konstantin last fall, Part 1 of the conference would be three days here; Part 2 would be three days in Moscow.

Moscow. What will that be like in these end days of the communist dream? Only three weeks ago, on August 19, I had turned on the television, and became incredulous at hearing a grim, grey

143

Communist Party coup leader, Vice President Gennady Yanayev, his hand trembling, announce that Gorbachev was out and his group was taking over. For 24 hours, even President Bush seemed to accept it as a done deal. But then that burly Siberian, Boris Nikolayevich Yeltsin, had clambered up on a tank in front of his parliament's "White House"—and the army had refused to attack him. Not surprisingly, when Mikhail Sergeyevich Gorbachev returned from his vacation house arrest, he ended Communist Party rule. For three weeks now the public has been gleefully dismantling all the Lenin statues in Moscow and Leningrad. Two years ago, Bush and Gorbachev declared the end of the Cold War; now communism itself, at least in Russia, has finally collapsed.

Our visit here during these cataclysmic events feels like 1917 in reverse: the revolution unraveling right before our eyes. Yesterday, in fact, Leningrad changed its name back to St. Petersburg.

Since I'd arrived almost an hour early for the conference, Elena had been able to read my paper "The Promise of Russian Philosophy," and clarify the few questions she had. Then she helped me draw a large diagram of the Cross of Reality on a blackboard, with the key words in Russian. She finished that just in time for me to launch into my paper:

The Promise of Russian Philosophy

According to Alexei Losev (1893–1988), Russian philosophy, which first emerged in the early 19th century, has concentrated on questions of the spirit, man's destiny, and his relation to God. It is based on the *Logos* or word, as opposed to the Western reliance on *ratio* or reason. With that distinction in mind, I think it is possible to discern a thread that runs from Alexei Khomyakov (1804–1860) to Mikhail Bakhtin (1895–1975), a focus on the powers of the spirit made manifest as speech, as the living Word. Let me briefly trace that thread.

Khomyakov might be called Russia's first "lover of the word" in that he nurtured the infant science of philology. He built on the research of Wilhelm von Humboldt (1767–1835), the German who first described humankind as living in a cosmos of speech. However, Khomyakov believed that the Slavs could develop a higher and livelier interpretation of the word than the Germans. "The word of truth," he said, contains "in itself a character of universal activity, ennobling the moral being of its disciples."

Khomyakov's friend Ivan Kireevsky (1806–1856), in his "The Possibility and Necessity of New Principles in Philosophy" (1856), wrote that four different "faculties" give us access to the whole truth. I'll comment later in this paper on those faculties, which seem related to four different kinds of language.

Drawing on his two Slavophile predecessors, Vladimir Solovyov (1853–1900) suggested that the word worked in man to make him a partner of God. In his 1878–1881 "Lectures on Divine Humanity," Solovyov said that the *Logos*, the word, was "the active unifying principle" in establishing the great human society, to which he gave the name *Sophia*.

Nikolai Berdyaev (1874–1948) welcomed Solovyov's interpretation of "Divine Humanity," but perceived the word and man's relation to God in a less idealistic and more conditional way. He saw the word made manifest as *spirit*, "the divine principle" which we carry within ourselves "creatively and actively." He anticipated a post-theological and post-scientific "third age" of the spirit when "a new anthropology will be made known and the religious meaning of human creativity will be recognized."

When Pavel Florensky (1882–1937) wrote his famous *The Pillar and Foundation of Truth*, it was received with reservations by Berdyaev, who called it "stylized Orthodoxy." However, Florensky seems to be going beyond dogmatism when he describes the word in terms of a "dialogic action," one that changes us into different grammatical persons. The word of love, addressed to each of us as *thou*, he says, moves us to realize ourselves as a subject, *I*, then later to recognize ourselves objectively as *he*. He said that this action of the word, in and through us, could be seen as reflecting the three persons of the Trinity.

Florensky's friend Sergei Bulgakov (1871–1944) made a similar formulation, relating our grammatical persons to the persons of the Trinity: "As a member of the human race [man] possesses the image of the union of the three persons, he is conscious of himself not only as *I*, but as *thou* and as *we*."

As a young man, Bakhtin not only read Florensky but also formed much of his own thinking in discussion groups that pursued Florensky's goal of synthesizing all human experience, including the religious. Undoubtedly his early concern with religion and philosophy explains why Bakhtin's literary criticism always serves the larger purpose of articulating a philosophy based on the word, specifically on the principle of dialogue. For him "life by its very nature is dialogic."

Bakhtin says that, to get beyond the narrow analytical concerns of contemporary linguistics, we need a new discipline, one that would be animated by the dialogical principle. His proposed "metalinguistics" would interpret the life of the word as it moves through history, society, and each one of us. He described us as living at the center of a "chronotope" of two different times, past and future, and two different "spaces," an inner and an outer. (His "chronotope" is from the Greek *chronos* for time and *topos* for space.)

The Spirit as the Creative Word

In retrospect, we can see that what had been relatively abstract and idealistic understandings of spirit and word in the earlier Russian philosophers had become, in Bakhtin, quite concrete. There is a progressive development, an increasing appeal to our ordinary experience of speech, as we move from Khomyakov's "word of truth," to Kireevsky's "four faculties," to Solovyov's "active unifying principle" of *Logos*, to Berdyaev's "divine principle" of spirit, to Florensky's "dialogic action," and finally to Bakhtin's "dialogical principle."

That progress, I think, can be described as an increasing realization that what the church, in the first millennium, had described as the Holy Spirit can be recognized today as a *universal creative principle*, the action of spirit in all persons.

And this spirit, which once had seemed expressed as a divine
Logos can now be recognized as *the creative word, the flow of life-
giving speech between individuals and from generation to generation.*

*(The next section of the paper described how the Western dialogical think-
ers, and particularly Rosenstock-Huessy, were working toward a dialogical
method. I then took up Kireevsky's work.)*

Kireevsky's Integral Knowledge

Among Eastern thinkers, Ivan Kireevsky, in particular,
can be seen as an early prophet of a dialogical method, one
that would address human concerns.

In his "The Possibility and Necessity of New Principles
in Philosophy" (1856), he wrote that there are *four* "faculties" through which we apprehend the truth. Besides our
"abstract logical capacity," there are "the promptings of
aesthetic thought," "the ruling loves of the heart," and "the
voice of ecstatic feeling." "[Man] should constantly seek,
in the depths of his soul, that inner root of understanding
where all the separate faculties unite in one living whole of
spiritual vision."

Such a vision, Kireevsky said, could lead to "integral
knowledge." Because he supplemented reason's abstract
logic with three other "faculties," I think we can describe
Kireevsky as proposing a "supra-rational" approach to
understanding the truth about anything, be it in the realm
of the spirit or in more mundane matters.

Without too great a stretch of the imagination, one can
see how Bakhtin's chronotope and Rosenstock-Huessy's
Cross of Reality are prefigured in Kireevsky's four faculties.
Our "abstract logical capacity" pertains to how we deal with
the outer world; "the promptings of aesthetic thought"
pertains to the impressions and feelings in our inner self;
"the ruling loves of the heart" pertains to our love for what
we've inherited from the past; and "the voice of ecstatic
feeling" pertains to the future imperatives to which we feel
called to respond.

This paper created a flurry of questions. Among those who came forward to talk with me later was an Orthodox priest, perhaps in his mid-40s. Father Benjamin, whose thin, ascetic face and piercing eyes gave him an appropriately Christlike look, turned out to be the vice rector of the Leningrad Orthodox Theological Academy. In excellent English, he thanked me for my paper and said that he had heard about our plans to refound the Solovyov Society; he would be glad to help with that.

After lunch, I set off on a walk around the spacious St. Isaac's Square in front of our conference building, feeling a great sense of relief. I had finally presented the core of my ideas—40 years in the making—in public.

The scholars who listened to me this morning undoubtedly assumed that my paper was the result of some recent research on Bakhtin, Rosenstock-Huessy, and their predecessors. But I knew it had very different origins. That paper, drawn from the first chapter of *Between East and West*, really summed up ideas I had been nourishing since the 1940s—and especially since St. Sergius in Paris.

ST. PETERSBURG – SEPTEMBER 9, 1991 – Over the next two days some 40 more papers have been presented by scholars from Russia, the United States, and other countries. During my supper with Konstantin yesterday, he thanked me for the $8,000 Tony Ugolnik and I raised for their building last spring. The renovations were going slowly. Similarly, in this collapsing economy, he was not so sure about getting my book out in Petersburg. He hoped my Moscow friends might help them find a publisher.

On a more upbeat note, I told him the MacArthur Foundation had given us $20,000 last January to fund that business management program we were starting with Nikolai Shmelev. In fact, our New England executives had taught the first seminar to 38 student businessmen in the Komi Republic last May.

We had also heard that the MacArthur Foundation is likely to fund a second Solovyov Society conference at Dartmouth, now scheduled for July 8–11, 1992. I hoped Konstantin would accept our invitation to that. He said he'd be delighted to come. He also told me how to contact the Dostoevsky scholar Yuri Karyakin, who we hoped would make a keynote address at Dartmouth.

At noon today we wrapped up this first part of our conference. This evening our US group boards the overnight train to Moscow where we'll have its second part.

Refounding the Solovyov Society

MOSCOW – SEPTEMBER 13, 1991 – The Moscow sessions of our conference have been as successful as St. Petersburg's were. At this afternoon's closing session, I invited everyone to attend one concluding event: We had a bus waiting to take us to Novodevichy Convent. There we'd have a ceremony at Solovyov's grave and commit ourselves to refounding the Vladimir Solovyov Society.

At 5 p.m. some 40 of us piled off the bus, then followed a pebble walk leading to a black marble stone marked simply "Vladimir Solovyov 1853–1900—publicist, philosopher." (The Russian *publicist* means a writer on current issues.) After we had gathered around the low iron fence surrounding his family plot, four of us moved forward to stand by the stone and begin the ceremony: Sergei Horujy, a Moscow mathematician who is becoming well known as a thinker on Russian philosophy; Oleg Genisaretsky, the head of Put; George Kline, and I. We began the proceedings with a short prayer and I read a statement of purpose. Then I called on Sergei, Oleg, and George for brief reflections. We closed with everyone singing the short verses of the Orthodox funeral hymn, *Vechnaya Pamyat*, Eternal Memory, led by the Rev. Robert Slesinski, one of our American scholars group.

The Bakhtin Connection

MOSCOW – APRIL 27, 1992 – As I waited for Marina, my Peace Committee guide, in the hotel lobby this morning, I looked over the letter that had put me in touch with Vitaly Makhlin.

Moscow, December 12, 1991

Dear Mr. Gardner!

Dr. Sergei Horujy, you spoke to him in September in Moscow, told me you are interested in the work of M. M. Bakhtin, in general, and in the "Bakhtinsky Journal," in particular. I am happy to present you with the Journal No. 1, and to begin associating with you.

I am now the head of the Bakhtin Center in Moscow. The center has been organized to work on the Bakhtin heritage and to put essays and books in print. I propose that we cooperate, this way or others.

So, I'd be delighted to cooperate, and to receive any papers on Bakhtin within philosophical discourse. It is really of great significance, and besides, I am sure the "Bakhtin problem" is closely connected with cultural relations between Russia and the West.

So, dear Mr. Gardner, I'd be happy if you respond.

I'm an adjunct professor at the Moscow Pedagogical State University, Dept. of Philosophy. My telephone number is 021–14–39.

Yours sincerely, Vitaly Makhlin

Just as I finished reading over that letter, Marina arrived and we set off for Vitaly's apartment.

When we arrived, Marina excused herself, since my new friend's English was more than adequate.

As I hung up my coat, I glanced at a box under his hall table. It contained a stack of papers that were copies of a book in German: Franz Rosenzweig's *The Star of Redemption!* Vitaly saw me staring dumbfounded at the box. "Yes, I expect to translate that into Russian," he said.

I didn't know anybody in Russia was interested in Rosenzweig. "Now you and I will have to expand our agenda," I said. "First Bakhtin, then Rosenstock-Huessy, then Rosenzweig."

After Vitaly had sent me that letter last December, I had replied with the proposal that we meet this week. And I'd included a copy of the first chapter of *Between East and West*. Of course, that chapter, titled "The Promise of Russian Philosophy," was close to the same text as my September 1991 paper in St. Petersburg, the one that linked Bakhtin's focus on speech with Florensky's and on back to Khomyakov. Besides Horujy's, another introduction to Vitaly had come to me via Caryl Emerson, a leading Bakhtin expert in the Department of Slavic Languages and Literatures at Princeton. Caryl, who is helping us form the Solovyov Society, has told me that Vitaly is her key contact here.

Vitaly invited me into his kitchen where he warmed up some chicken. As we discussed the first chapter of *Between East and West*, Vitaly told me he was fascinated by the way I'd linked Bakhtin with the founders of Russian philosophy and looked forward to reading the rest of the book.

I explained that Open Christianity had translated the whole of it into Russian, and presented him with a copy of their typescript as well as a copy of my spiral-bound *samizdat* English original.

"We Russians love *samizdats*," he said.

I then gave him the short version of my years pursuing Rosenstock-Huessy and Rosenzweig, Berdyaev, and Solovyov—through the war, Paris, Berlin, founding Shopping International, next Argo, and finally Bridges for Peace.

Then Vitaly told me the story of how Bakhtin was "discovered." There were three young scholars at the Gorky Institute who had begun reading some of his work in the late 1950s, but they thought he was no longer alive. When they learned he was, they visited him in Saransk and discussed the idea of republishing his forgotten texts. Soon, one of them, Vadim Kozhinov, managed to publish his *Problems of Dostoevsky's Poetics*. This and other works rang a bell in Russia, one that was soon heard in Europe, the United States—and then around the world.

This story of an unknown scholar suddenly achieving world-wide acclaim was certainly poignant for me. "I can't get over how academia today is so excited by your Mikhail but practically ignores my Eugen," I said.

We then talked about the fact that Rosenstock-Huessy was such an articulate Christian that he was quite unacceptable to the academic mind. Writing on language, he identified speech with the Holy Spirit. And his writings on history and sociology, full of references to Christianity, are equally suspect, applauded only by an Auden or a Niebuhr. He certainly was unwilling to conform to today's professorial dogmas.

Vitaly pointed out that the Soviet regime silenced anyone who took Christianity seriously, as they arrested Bakhtin in 1929. That Western academia would silence writers for the same offense was a sobering thought.

We went on to discuss our current writing efforts: my work on a book about the Cross of Reality, and his writing on Western thinkers whose ideas about language resemble Bakhtin's.

He wondered who else had written about Rosenstock-Huessy. I told him about Harold Stahmer's 1968 book, *"Speak That I May See Thee!": The Religious Significance of Language*, which introduced Rosenstock-Huessy and several other speech-thinkers, as he called them. I also told him about the international conferences on Rosenstock-Huessy's work, the first of which was convened in 1982 by Darrol Bryant, a professor of religious studies at the University of Waterloo in Canada.

Hearing of Canada, Vitaly asked what other countries had developed Rosenstock-Huessy circles. I explained that Germany had the largest group, but that, per capita, Holland is the country where Eugen's work has made the largest impact.

Vitaly and I then discussed the intriguing fact that most of the people who were enthusiastic about Rosenstock-Huessy were in the field of religion, with relatively few in the humanities and social sciences. I told him about how Richard Shaull at Princeton Theological Seminary had once invited me there to speak on Eugen, while the well-known Jesuit scholar Walter Ong had also drawn on Eugen's work.

Next we discussed how Bakhtin circles published a magazine about their hero while the Rosenstock-Huessy Society in Europe published one as well. In the United States, I explained, there was not a society, but the Eugen Rosenstock-Huessy Fund filled the place of one, sponsoring conferences and operating Argo Books; my nephew Mark Huessy directed the fund and book activities. Freya von Moltke, with her sons Helmuth and Konrad, were among the prime movers of the Fund.

We were running out of time to discuss the third man on our agenda, Franz Rosenzweig. Still, I told Vitaly how I once discussed *The Star* with Rosenzweig's son Rafael at his home in Israel in 1970. Like most readers of his father's work, Rafael had found it difficult. It was one of those books that everyone hails but never really understands.

"As I see it," said Vitaly, "*The Star* is misunderstood as a contribution to Jewish thought. It's really meant to introduce new thinking, beyond the frameworks of religion and philosophy. Franz said that himself."

That led me to suggest that a good way of understanding what Rosenstock-Huessy and Rosenzweig were doing is to see how they differed from Karl Barth. Like that great Christian theologian, they wanted to get away from the 19th century's watered-down liberal theology. But, unlike him, they did not do this by simply reasserting the power of the word, as found in the Bible. Instead, they pointed to the power of the word in each generation and in every tradition. Rosenstock-Huessy put his differences with Barth very simply when he wrote: "Karl Barth and the dialectical theologians say that God appeared only once."

We agreed to meet again on May 6.

MAY 6, 1992 – When I arrived at Vitaly's apartment this noon, he was even more animated than when we had met nine days ago. We set up shop in the kitchen and he cooked pork chops while starting in with his thoughts on *Between East and West*. He was delighted with the book, he said, and would comment on the Cross of Reality in an article he was going to write for the Russian journal *Problems of Philosophy*.

He thought that the coincidences between Bakhtin and Rosenstock-Huessy were simply astonishing. It wasn't only that they both conceived of a chronotope, a time-space model that reflects the patterns of speech. Beyond that, both of them described language as a social phenomenon—and distinguished themselves sharply from the school of linguistic analysis that had dominated language studies from the 1930s to the 1950s.

Not least among the coincidences was that both thinkers were great admirers of Søren Kierkegaard, with his devastating critique of theologians as "professors of the crucifixion." That led me to tell Vitaly about two more of Eugen's heroes, both innovators whose thought, like Kierkegaard's, had received little attention in their lifetimes: the Italian historian Giambattista Vico (1668–1744) and the Swiss polymath physician, Paracelsus (1493–1541), whom Eugen saw as a key figure in the rise of science.

Turning back to today, Vitaly agreed to organize a Bakhtin session at the Solovyov Society's third conference here in March 1993.

Finally, I sprang a big question. I asked him if he'd be willing to gather a group of Russian scholars to translate *Out of Revolution*.

Argo would pay for this. Vitaly said he'd have to think about that, but in principle he liked the idea.

This Bakhtin connection is bearing fruit beyond my wildest imagining.

Sergei Averintsev at the Prague

MOSCOW – MARCH 20, 1993 – This morning I called my guide Oksana Klimovskaya to plan the schedule for the day. The main event was a luncheon meeting with the renowned literary scholar Sergei Averintsev at the Prague Restaurant, located in Moscow's bohemian and literary quarter on the Arbat pedestrian street. Before that we would spend the morning cruising bookstores, to see if they still had my *Between East and West: Rediscovering the Gifts of the Russian Spirit* for sale. Its Russian translation, made by Open Christianity (and improved by Vitaly), had finally been published by Nauka, a Russian Academy of Sciences press, in January, in an edition of 3,000 copies.

I had been looking forward to meeting Averintsev ever since 1983—that evening with the fan dancers in Leningrad, when Father Jonathan had told me he knew of only one successor to Berdyaev in Russia today, only one outstanding religious intellectual, and this was Averintsev.

Fortunately, Gorbachev and then Yeltsin have recognized his stature. He is vice chairman of the Russian Cultural Fund and a member of Parliament. But, from my point of view, there are two striking things about him: first, he knew Bakhtin and edited some of his works; and second, despite being quite ill at the time, he had agreed to write the introduction to the Nauka edition of *Between East and West.*

Averintsev's illness had prevented him from attending our Dartmouth conference, and I later learned his health had become much worse. He'd flown to Switzerland for blood transfusions and wouldn't be able to write the introduction after all. Instead, the Russian orientalist, Vladimir Maliavin, had volunteered to write it, and my book appeared on schedule in January.

The three bookstores Oksana and I visited this morning still had copies of my book. Sales were apparently brisk.

At 12:30, after Oksana and I met Averintsev in the Prague's elegant lobby, she excused herself since we didn't need an interpreter.

When our borscht was served, my luncheon companion offered to say grace. Sturgeon followed the borscht, and we began talking about *Between East and West*. He had liked my point that Bakhtin was an heir of Florensky and earlier Russian philosophers.

He said he'd be glad to join the Solovyov Society, and I told him how well last year's conference at Dartmouth had gone. He asked me why it was held there, and I explained how the society grew out of our Vermont-based Bridges for Peace project, which had been supported by Dartmouth's Russian Department.

"I'm pleasantly surprised to learn that a New England college and its surrounding communities would become so interested in our spiritual heritage," he said.

I explained how our society had been fortunate enough to have good people on our advisory council, many of whom helped us obtain foundation support. The council included the former national president of the United Church of Christ, Avery Post, and a member of Dartmouth's Religion Department, Fred Berthold. In fact, I was able to get Professor Berthold to address a seminar on Russia's spiritual renewal, by way of preparation for our conference. That seminar was part of a new adult education program at the college, the Institute for Lifelong Education at Dartmouth. Participants made reports on Dostoevsky, Bakhtin, and Orthodox theology. Professor Berthold had told our group about how the Eastern church differed from the Western church on the matter of original sin and the fall of man.

Averintsev asked if Berthold was Orthodox himself.

I explained that Fred is a Congregationalist, but he admires how the Eastern church has preserved a more integrated view of matter and spirit than has the Western church. He told our seminar that the East followed the teaching of the 2nd-century theologian Irenaeus, with his view that Adam and Eve were innocent children who couldn't have realized what would happen if they ate that apple. From two different interpretations of that ancient myth, two spiritualities arose. In the West, through Augustine and then Calvin, matter—and especially the human body—seemed to be "fallen," while in the East, matter—in nature and the body—was seen as the necessary bearer of spirit, not inherently bad at all. That's a more holistic understanding.

Averintsev nodded his agreement and then asked about the speakers at the Dartmouth conference. I listed Jack Matlock, the former ambassador to the USSR, and Harvey Cox. In fact, a poignant moment at the conference had been when Father Benjamin from Petersburg had challenged Professor Cox. In his talk, Harvey had said that reading Berdyaev's *The Destiny of Man* had been a revelation for him—and he'd become convinced that Russian thought was important for Westerners to grasp.

After his talk, Father Benjamin had stood up and said, "While I appreciate what you say about our tradition, I have one question. Why is it that Russia, with all her *sobornost*, has managed to ruin a fifth of the earth's surface, while America, with all her miserable pragmatism, has created the most successful society the world has ever known?"

Averintsev asked how that question had been answered.

I recalled that I was not impressed by the several answers offered by the audience. If I had made a stab at it, I would have said that Khomyakov presented *sobornost* as a *reforming* principle, one hardly congenial to the top-down autocracy of the Tsars, one that was never really understood beyond intellectual circles—and one never actually realized in Russian society. And William James stood for more than pragmatism.

Averintsev said that he agreed.

We spoke a little more about the Solovyov Society, and its fourth conference, planned for Bergamo, Italy, next June. He said he'd be glad to come to that if his health continued to improve.

Sasha Pigalev in Volgograd

MOSCOW – JULY 1, 1993 – This morning I visited the offices of *Logos* magazine, since friends had suggested they might be interested in reviewing my book. As I started chatting with their editor, Valeri Anashvili, he asked if I'd been in touch with a scholar from Volgograd, Alexander Pigalev. I hadn't. In fact, I had never heard of him.

"Well, just last month he sent us an article about Rosenstock-Huessy. We're thinking of publishing it. Would you like to talk to him? We have his telephone number."

A moment later, Professor Pigalev was on the line. I asked how he had learned about Rosenstock-Huessy.

He said that an article by a German sociologist, Dietmar Kamper, had been his introduction. That was over a year ago. Since then he had been able to get Rosenstock-Huessy's books on microfilm from the Lenin Library in Moscow.

I asked him if there were any Russian thinkers who prepared him for Rosenstock-Huessy. He said he had been reading Sergei Bulgakov for some years.

After that conversation, I wondered why in the world the Lenin Library would have Rosenstock-Huessy's works on microfilm. Might Yuri Zamoshkin have been responsible for that?

And Bulgakov! Now the founder of the first Solovyov Society as well as St. Sergius Institute had come into my life again. Florensky's friend and one of the first to call his work "panentheism"; exiled in 1923, soon after Berdyaev. Amazing that it would be this very man who had prepared Pigalev for Rosenstock-Huessy.

MOSCOW – MARCH 17, 1994 – Six months after that phone conversation with Sasha Pigalev, in January, I received a long letter from him about his success in introducing Rosenstock-Huessy in Moscow. (See Appendix B.) When I finally met him for lunch today, he gave me a copy of the magazine, *Problems of Philosophy*, which Vladimir Solovyov had helped to establish. He had found the editors were glad to print his translation of the last two chapters of *Out of Revolution*—in which Rosenstock-Huessy presents his motto, *Respondeo etsi mutabor*, and envisions the creation of a higher sociology, a metanomics. And they preceded that with an introduction by Sasha. I think that's the first time a prominent national academic magazine, anywhere, has printed a significant excerpt from Rosenstock-Huessy's work.

Sasha also gave me his translation of the long review of my *Between East and West* which had been printed in *Problems of Philosophy* last fall. My Russian had given me only a faint idea of what reviewer Leonid Polyakov had said. Sasha explained that Polyakov was quite enthusiastic, and concluded that, "Gardner makes an unusual and useful linkage between contemporary and traditional Russian philosophy."

An Orthodox Imprimatur

MOSCOW – MARCH 18, 1994 – After lunch with Pigalev yesterday, I met in the afternoon at the Institute of Philosophy with scholars who'll be coming to the Solovyov Society's Bergamo conference in June. One of them is Nelly Motroshilova, head of the Department of the History of Philosophy at the Institute. Nelly, whom I first met in 1992, has recently taken charge of an ambitious project, the publication of a complete new Russian edition of Solovyov's work. She hoped our Society might help with funding that project, and I assured her we'd try. We also agreed to start planning for a major conference in the summer of 2000, one that would mark the 100th anniversary of Solovyov's death.

Then this morning I went to Moscow University Press to see if they'd consider publishing *Out of Revolution* here—since the translation team that Vitaly Makhlin had organized last year was likely to complete the job within a month or so. They agreed. The main reason for their enthusiasm, it turned out, was that they knew the work of Harold Berman, whose well-known book *Law and Revolution* had been translated into Russian, and then published very successfully by Moscow University Press.

A lot of good news for two days. But the best news, which Vitaly gave me today, was that the new Moscow journal, *The Way of Orthodoxy*, has printed my "The Promise of Russian Philosophy," substantially as it appears in Chapter 1 of *Between East and West*.

Since *The Way of Orthodoxy* is published by the Russian Orthodox Church's Moscow Patriarchate, I feel as if I have suddenly acquired an imprimatur. Sometimes I wonder if my ruminations on Christianity might not be heretical, but here's some evidence that they may be Orthodox, with a capital O.

BERGAMO, ITALY – JUNE 29, 1994 – A week ago I came about as close to death as I had fifty years ago in Normandy. The morning of June 22 I stood at the front of a large hall in Bergamo University, along with Nina Kauchishvili, the University's Vice Rector and my partner in organizing this Solovyov Society fourth conference. As she and I welcomed everyone, there were many familiar faces in our audience: Vitaly Makhlin, Vladimir Maliavin, Sergei Horujy, Nelly Motroshilova, George Kline, Caryl Emerson, Robert Slesinski,

Harold Stahmer, Lev Loseff, and Hans Huessy. Shortly after I sat down, I felt strangely tired and short of breath. I whispered to Libby that we'd better see a doctor.

It turned out that I was in the midst of a heart attack, so I've spent the last seven days here in Bergamo Hospital's intensive care room. While I've been recuperating, Vitaly and Caryl have sent me a "get well" note along with a formal invitation to attend the big international Bakhtin conference that Vitaly is organizing for July next year in Moscow.

Now I'm thinking about what I learned from Nelly Motroshilova on June 21, when I greeted her and the other Russians on their arrival from the airport. She took me aside and spoke in a low voice, with great feeling.

"Clint, you remember Yuri Zamoshkin who led that first Bridges for Peace delegation you invited in spring of 1983?"

"Of course, I remember him," I replied. "I've seldom met a scholar with such broad interests and so good at overcoming ideological walls."

"Well, I wanted you to know that he was my husband, and that he passed away three years ago. I recently found your address card among the things he'd saved from many trips abroad."

I felt a surge of emotion and embraced Nelly. Now I knew whom Yuri meant when he told me he had a friend at the Institute of Philosophy, one to whom he had given his copy of *Between East and West*. And *what* he meant by colleagues who disagreed with him about whether Russia would ever become recommitted to her heritage from the Silver Age. What an incredible coincidence, that Andropov's USSR would send the uncommitted Zamoshkin to meet me, only to have me now, eleven years later, cooperating with his committed wife.

"Thank you for telling me about you and Yuri," I said to Nelly. "We'll have to get together when I come to Moscow next year for the Bakhtin conference."

11 Metanomics: A Higher Sociology

Without participation in the life of the word through the ages, we remain ephemeral. Speaking, thinking, learning, teaching, writing, are the processes into which we must be immersed to become beings. They enable us to occupy a present in the midst of flux. Language receives us into its community; speech admits us to the common boat of humanity in its struggle for orientation on its pilgrimage through space and time.

—Eugen Rosenstock-Huessy

Life by its very nature is dialogic. To live means to participate in dialogue: to ask questions, to heed to respond, to agree and so forth. In this dialogue a person participates wholly and throughout his whole life: with his eyes, lips, hands, soul, spirit, with his whole body and deeds. He invests his entire self in discourse, and this discourse enters into the dialogic fabric of human life, into the world symposium.

—Mikhail Bakhtin

MOSCOW – JUNE 26, 1995 – Floodlights blinded my eyes as I sat at the speakers' table this morning and tried to see my audience— more than 150 scholars who had come from every corner of the world to this Seventh International Bakhtin Conference at Moscow State Pedagogical University. We were marking, approximately, the 100th anniversary of our hero's birth (which was actually November 5, 1895). I was the second scheduled speaker, following Vittorio Strada, the first Westerner to discover Bakhtin. My paper's title was quite a mouthful: "Toward a Philosophy for the Third Millennium: Mikhail Bakhtin between East and West."

I had my essential visual aid unfurled and ready. On a nearby easel, Vitaly and I had mounted a three-by-four-foot diagram, one that displayed most of the subjects on my "complete" Cross of Reality. To those I had added some of Bakhtin's terms for his version of the cross, his chronotope.

Strada would be speaking in Russian; Vitaly would be translating for me. My talk unfolded as follows:

Toward a Philosophy for the Third Millennium

In 1977, Dartmouth's President John Kemeny, a distinguished mathematician and inventor of the computer language BASIC, gave a speech in which he said that the great need of our time was for a breakthrough in the social sciences so that they could make progress in the same rapid and effective way as the natural sciences. My thesis here is that the spark needed for that breakthrough is first ignited when we bring together the astonishingly similar work of Bakhtin and Rosenstock-Huessy.

At the end of *Out of Revolution*, Rosenstock-Huessy said that as earlier times had asked, "What is the revealed character of the *true* God?" and then "What is the *true* character of nature?" our time should ask, "What must we do to insure the survival of a *truly* human society?" Today's social sciences, after years of imitating the objective method of the natural sciences, still fail to answer that *third question of truth*. If we really are concerned with our global society's survival, we need a new discipline, a higher and more flexible sociology. Bakhtin has proposed the name "metalinguistics" for such a unifying discipline, whereas Rosenstock-Huessy has proposed "metanomics."

Both men saw language and dialogue in a new key—and envisioned a method for the human sciences based on the patterns of language. Both exhibited astonishing similarities as they put forward such a method, from their basic model of the chronotope or the Cross of Reality to their perception that this model could provide a societal method, one based on the four basic types of speech: imperative, subjective, narrative, and objective.

With that opening statement made, I described how both thinkers said that the four kinds of speech were related to the four different grammatical persons we become in any significant experience. I turned to Rosenstock-Huessy's formulation that we are addressed by another as *thou*, respond as *I* (discovering our subjective inner space), go on to form a *we*, and finally are recognized by others as *he* or *she*. Similarly, Bakhtin says that we are addressed by "*the other for me*," respond as "*I for myself*" (discovering our "subjectum"), then become an "I for others," (a we relation), and finally are seen objectively in the world around us. I emphasized that both men say that this fundamental pattern of speech reveals itself as a *social* process. Speech doesn't simply *describe* the human reality; *it creates it.*

I turned to my cross diagram, pointing out how its horizontal axis represents times, while its vertical axis represents spaces. On those two axes I pointed to the four types of speech that Bakhtin and Rosenstock-Huessy say create and orient us to these times and spaces; the four moods of speech that dominate each time and space; then, finally, the different persons that Bakhtin and Rosenstock-Huessy say we become as these different types of speech form and remake us.

I explained that the Cross of Reality provides a new way of seeing how all the sciences and humanities are connected. There is no pyramid with hard science at its base, as is so widely assumed today. The Cartesian scientific vision of a world revealed to us by mathematics and physics turns out to deal with only one quarter of our reality. Any holistic approach to a problem must start from the center of the cross. For example, politics or economics must always take into account history and psychology. And so must law listen to religion.

It is clear that many academics will be put off by this unifying picture, I said. It challenges today's postmodern consciousness, that contemporary affliction of academe characterized by "the *fragmentation* of knowledge, the absence of moral parameters, and the rejection of any unitary truth." The Cross of Reality allows us to find unitary truth without a system, without any metaphysics. It is an open-ended model of the human reality, and its dialogical method is similarly open-ended.

I provided two examples of that method's application. My first example related to the contemporary crisis in Russia.

I said that President Boris Yeltsin listened too much to the Western ideologues of capitalism, to those who presumed that Adam Smith had introduced some finished economic ideology, a timeless idea that can be applied, ready made, to any situation. This approach ignores the time orientations postulated by the Cross of Reality. It overlooks the past 150 years during which capitalism has been drastically modified and become, where it is most successful, simply one of the main components in economies that Rosenstock-Huessy calls "polyphonic." Today's enlightened market economies nurture *both* social responsibility and free enterprise.

My point was that the Russian oligarchs' and Russian mafia's considerable takeover of the Russian economy could have been avoided by a carefully phased change in which legal, parliamentary, and other social foundations were laid in conjunction with each economic step. What happened in Yeltsin's Russia was objective economics, without history and law.

My second example concerned Vietnam. The best and the brightest, from Secretary of Defense Robert McNamara to President Lyndon Johnson, were obsessed with a dualistic ideological vision of *us* versus *them*. They had boiled down that ideological vision simply to the idea that communists were about to take over all of Asia. Such significant historical details as the animosity between China and Vietnam never figured into their equations. The only American experts who had such nuanced perspectives had been hounded out of the State Department during the McCarthy era. That was politics without history.

In both my Russia and Vietnam examples, simplistic, abstract, ideological thinking ("monological") had trumped the more comprehensive dialogical thinking that would have considered more than Russian economics or Cold War politics. Future imperatives, inner psychologies, and past histories would all have been given equal weight with the obvious objective facts.

I concluded that bringing together Bakhtin's dialogical thought with Rosenstock-Huessy's does, indeed, ignite the spark needed for Kemeny's breakthrough in the social sciences. Rosenstock-Huessy's applications of the dialogical method in the fields of history and society complement Bakhtin's applications in the fields of philosophy, literature, and linguistics.

The fact that two men independently arrived at such similar discoveries suggested the birth of a new science. It enlarged the field and overcame the tendency to build a cult around one innovator.

I ended by offering some visions of how we might come to see the world in the light of the new discipline I had described:

—We get rid of the notion that we live one-dimensional lives in a simply mechanical world. We discover that each of us lives at the center of creation, and that times and spaces are being constantly renewed and remade as we accept the responsibilities of living within the Cross of Reality.

—We grasp that what all religions describe as spirit is not something otherworldly. Instead, it is simply the higher form of the speech spoken by the whole human race and made audible in the words of every good man or woman.

—We replace our ancient story of a divine being who called the world into existence—and our more recent story of meaningless atoms competing in space—with a new story. This third story would tell us of the great body of humankind, united through all time by the sweeping web of speech. We would come to recognize the living word as the spark, the electricity, that flashes throughout this web, animating each of us and uniting us with the whole.

—We realize that, just as the atom was imagined by the Greeks but remained hidden until it was seen as forming electrical fields by Michael Faraday and was turned into atomic power by Niels Bohr, so the *Logos*, the Word, was described by Heraclitus, but really was not seen as the *field* in which we become human until Bakhtin's and Rosenstock-Huessy's discoveries.

My talk over, after lunch I sought a peaceful place where I could get back my bearings, after all the energy that had gone into the morning's task. After a ride north on the metro, I found myself in the dappled sunlight of tree-lined paths on the great expanse of Kolomenskoye Park. I had a destination beyond these woods, for at their edge stands the soaring white, eight-sided spire of the ancient Ascension Church. It came into view, dominating this high site, and I could see the Moscow River below, running in lazy curves toward the now-distant city. The Russians have a soft-sounding name, *umileniye*, for the sense of "holy beauty" that such a setting evokes.

I sat on the grass in the shade of the 16th-century church, which is older than St. Basil's. I took out my notebook, since this sunny Moscow afternoon in 1995 seemed a good time and place to reflect on how Russia had become the proving ground for all the ideas I had been nourishing since the fall of 1940.

Testing the Dialogical Method

From the moment I had arrived in Russia in 1983, I had become immersed in dialogue. Quite unexpectedly, that first conversation I had with Father Jonathan led to my discovering Bakhtin, and eventually led to this morning's conference.

All my other dialogues—with Yuri Zamoshkin, Konstantin Ivanov, Father Benjamin, Nikolai Shmelev, Vitaly Makhlin, Sasha Pigalev, Nelly Motroshilova, and Sergei Averintsev—helped to establish ever-expanding projects: Bridges for Peace, the Transnational Institute, and the Vladimir Solovyov Society. They also gave Rosenstock-Huessy's work a firm toehold in Russia.

Of course, refounding Bulgakov's and Berdyaev's Solovyov Society, though a small project, had a huge significance for all of us involved—so intimately was it related to the narrative of Russia's past, her inner spirit, and her future aspirations. The dream I had shared with Igor in Paris—seeing a new generation of Russians who would want to reconnect with the past that Lenin and Stalin had obliterated—was now becoming reality. Russia's future may well have as much to do with St. Sergius as it does with Lenin, perhaps more.

Like the Solovyov Society, "Bridges" and the Institute succeeded because we thought and acted within the parameters of the Cross of Reality. We and our Russian partners wanted to build a bridge to a common future, one beyond our possible mutual nuclear suicide. We both responded, quite vigorously, to that future imperative, the imperative of peace. As we citizen diplomats engaged in dialogue, within the privacy of our homes, we learned about each other's inner spirit and saw each other as individual persons, as *I*'s; we learned about each other's histories and language, and saw where the other was coming from, as *we*'s; and, finally, we organized ourselves to make our exchanges happen in the real world, and had them publicized through press and television in each country. We became visible on the outer front of life, as *they*'s. Any complete and successful human experience touches all those four bases.

Our efforts within "Bridges" were multiplied many times over. There were only three organizations dedicated to US-USSR exchanges when we started in 1983. And those three served primarily their own members. As noted in Chapter 9, by 1990 our example of an open network had helped, directly or indirectly, with the formation of at least 100 similar projects. The resulting national movement eventually sent more than 100,000 Americans to the USSR and brought at least 50,000 Soviets to the United States.

There is little doubt that all those citizen diplomats, and all the related national publicity, helped to end the Cold War. They demonstrated that there really could be a "universal planetary method of crossing borders" in order to "synchronize antagonistic distemporaries."

So, what else was tested in Russia?

When *Problems of Philosophy*, through Sasha Pigalev's initiative, printed the last two chapters of *Out of Revolution*, with their presentation of Rosenstock-Huessy's motto *Respondeo etsi mutabor* and his call for establishing metanomics, it provided evidence that Rosenstock-Huessy's ideas were not beyond the imagination of some leaders in a nation's academic establishment.

Then *Between East and West: Rediscovering the Gifts of the Russian Spirit*, first conceived in Paris in 1948, matured from a *samizdat* to publication by the Russian Academy of Sciences. When I arrived at this morning's conference, Vitaly told me that its second printing of 3,000 copies was already sold out. Since the present book contains most of that book's text, at least a third of what you have been reading here was already being read in Siberia by 1995!

Metanomics was finally put on the map.

When I finished writing out those reflections, I raised my eyes from my notebook and let them follow the Moscow River to where it merged at the skyline with the buildings of the city. I stood up, bade farewell to the Ascension Church, and headed back to the metro.

NORWICH, VERMONT – JANUARY 1, 2007 – The Russian Proving Ground since 1995 has seen even more progress.

In August 2000, as planned, the Solovyov Society and the Institute of Philosophy put on a large international conference at the Institute—to mark the 100th anniversary of Solovyov's death. It brought together 65 scholars from 21 countries. Sergei Horujy presented the keynote address, while Sasha Pigalev, Sergei Averintsev, Father Benjamin, and Caryl Emerson were among those attending.

In 2001 *Out of Revolution*, translated by Vitaly, Sasha, and some others, finally was published in Moscow. The publisher was St. Andrew's Biblical Theological Institute, a widely respected state-accredited organization that promotes education and dialogue. Under the leadership of Rector Alexei Bodrov, they provide theological training as well as regular conferences on Russian religious philosophy (ones on Berdyaev and Bulgakov, for example). Information is at www.standrews.ru.

It's significant that the St. Andrew's institute was founded to continue the work of Father Alexander Men, a much-admired Moscow Russian Orthodox priest whose challenging sermons, often inspired by Solovyov and his successors, may well have led to his assassination on September 9, 1990. He was called "the apostle to the intellectuals."

The Solovyov Society's current main activity is an Internet discussion group, which has more than 300 members (Solovyov-subscribe@yahoogroups.com).

Appendix C comprises an e-mail from Siberia. It seems to confirm what Sasha Pigalev wrote to me: "the seeds must sprout" (as printed in Appendix B).

Now Part III will return from Russia to the United States, where we'll start out in the state of Georgia.

PART III

THE AMERICAN BATTLEGROUND

TRANSITION TO PART III

Part II has described how, in the last two decades of the 1900s, I was able to have dialogues with Russians about all the ideas in Part I. Those Russian friends enabled me to introduce these ideas into larger circles: avant-garde priests in the Orthodox Church, scholars at the Institute of Philosophy, educators at Open Christianity, scholars at the Gorky Institute, leaders in Bakhtin circles—and eventually to all the readers of *Between East and West.*

In Part III I will report on recent dialogues with American friends about these same ideas. It is not as if Rosenstock-Huessy, Rosenzweig, Berdyaev, Solovyov, and Bakhtin were entirely unknown here. It's just that they have never had the broad impact enjoyed by such thinkers as Buber and Tillich. Rosenstock-Huessy was certainly welcomed by Auden, arguably our time's leading poet in the English language, and by Reinhold Niebuhr, arguably America's leading theologian. But Dartmouth's maverick professor remains largely undiscovered in either academic or theological circles.

Strangely, the current whirlwind of books attacking conventional religion and the very thought of God may provide just the opening needed to change that situation. The Unholy Trinity of atheists Sam Harris, Richard Dawkins, and Daniel Dennett, now joined by Christopher Hitchens, form a loud and querulous quartet that is certain to be joined by more. The kind of supernaturalist religion they attack is what Marcus Borg calls "the earlier paradigm." It's the same one that Bonhoeffer thought we had outgrown, when he said that the time had come to articulate a religionless Christianity, one appropriate to a "world come of age."

The Querulous Quartet (who now call themselves "The Four Horsemen") has certainly raised public consciousness about the question of belief in supernaturalist religion and a supernatural God. This helps clear the decks for us to take a new step, one that the dialogical thinkers had begun to take after World War I: to move *beyond belief* that God exists—to a knowledge of how he lives and speaks in each of us. The time has come to celebrate the God who is already within us, as spirit, as speech, and as *Logos*, all of which I claim are one and the same.

12 TRANSFORMING CHRISTIANITY

*Being Christian is not about meeting requirements for a future reward in
an afterlife, and not very much about believing. Rather, the Christian life is
about a relationship with God that transforms life in the present.*

—Marcus Borg

ST. SIMONS ISLAND, GEORGIA – JANUARY 24, 2007 – I have many
friends who say that "everything happens for a reason" and believe
that remarkable coincidences are acts of God's providence. I don't
agree with them, but my lack of faith in a God who intervenes in our
affairs is sometimes shaken by experiences such as I had last night.

I've been here for a three-day conference on "Emerging
Christianity," a meeting at which some 800 concerned Christians have
heard Marcus Borg and Barbara Brown Taylor address that theme.

It was about 6:00 pm, as Libby and I were standing in line for
supper, when the man ahead of us turned around and greeted us.
Carl Johnson said he was a retired Lutheran minister, who had come
to the conference with his wife and her cousin Ken Wolf, a university professor who was standing just ahead, along with his wife. We
all introduced ourselves and the six of us agreed to sit together. At
the table, I began talking to Ken, who was sitting on my right. He
asked what had brought me here.

I explained that I was writing a book that deals with themes
much like those at this conference. I described how a favorite professor of mine, Eugen Rosenstock-Huessy, who had been a friend
of Martin Buber's, had introduced me to a Russian thinker named
Nikolai Berdyaev. And how, planning to meet Berdyaev, in 1948 I
had gone to Paris where I'd met a colleague of his, a Catholic existentialist thinker named Emmanuel Mounier. Then how I'd begun
an article for Mounier's magazine *Esprit*, a text I had later turned into
a small book that had finally seen the light of day in Russia—and
the substance of which was largely incorporated into the book I was
working on right now.

During the two minutes it took me to provide that background to what had brought me to this conference, Ken kept looking at me with widening eyes and steadily mounting interest. Then he replied that in the 1970s he himself had been planning to write a book that would present Buber, Berdyaev, and Mounier as prophets for today, prophets of religious existentialism. Although that book had never materialized, he said he would send me an article that he had published in an academic journal, describing Buber and Berdyaev in just those terms.

Of course, I was floored at hearing this. It would have been unlikely that two Buber enthusiasts would have chanced upon each other in a cafeteria line, but adding in Berdyaev and Mounier made the odds overwhelmingly improbable. I didn't say so but I thought it: Chalk one up for those who believe that God intervenes.

While that was what I thought last night, this morning I've begun to see last night's meeting with Carl and Ken in a larger frame. No, I don't really think that this was a case of God deciding to intervene in our lives. Instead, I think that this was an example of how we often experience marvelous coincidences as we pursue the paths laid out for us by the Cross of Reality in which we live. Carl, Ken and I were all responding to an imperative in our lives when we decided to come here. Our meeting was a wonderful example of how the spirit works in each of us, linking me and Ken to Buber, Berdyaev, and Mounier—and then impelling us to renew that spirit by coming to hear Borg. This actually was an example of how God is like the spirit that is incarnated in a whole humanity, a God already within us, a God whose grace we find at the center of life, not one who intervenes from outside.

Borg's book, *The Heart of Christianity*, describes just such a God—and a Christianity that reads the Bible metaphorically rather than literally. These are two pillars of Christianity's "emerging paradigm," ones that support all the others.

As regards God, we should start thinking in terms of panentheism, as opposed to supernatural theism. On panentheism, Borg writes: "Rather than imagining God as a personlike being 'out there,' this concept imagines God as *the encompassing Spirit* in whom everything that is, is."

That's close to the image of God I have been concentrating on in this book, seeing Rosenstock-Huessy, Bonhoeffer, Berdyaev, and Solovyov as its exemplars. I have also touched on the question of metaphor and made clear that none of these guides was a literalist. For Rosenstock-Huessy there was no supernatural, no "other world" beyond this one. Life's miracles, like meeting Ken last night, are not ones that are contrary to the laws of nature. Christianity's goal is not to compete with electricity or gravitation.

Getting beyond literalism and beyond theism, two main elements of Christianity's new paradigm, lead to three others: faith without belief, living the Kingdom, and how we are *all* born again.

Faith Without Belief

Of course, explaining how one can have faith without belief is critical for a book titled *Beyond Belief.* Borg notes that the earlier paradigm included believing that Jesus was "born of a virgin; that he died for our sins and that God raised him physically and bodily from the dead; and that he will come again some day." That paradigm is "affirmed by fundamentalists, most conservative-evangelical, and many Pentecostal Christians." How can one have faith without such belief? Borg answers that question by examining four primary meanings of the word "faith," using Latin words to help us understand them:

Faith as *assensus,* or assent, meaning that one gives one's mental assent to a proposition. This meaning is a *matter of the head.* It is the sort of faith held by the fundamentalists and their allies. And it's important to see how it differs from the next three meanings, which are *matters of the heart.* These are:

Faith as *fiducia,* or trust, as radical trust in God.

Faith as *fidelitas,* or fidelity, faithfulness to our relationship with God.

Faith as *visio,* or vision, a way of seeing the whole, a way of seeing "what is."

Borg points out that those last three meanings are "relational." "They see faith as not very much about believing. Instead, faith is about the relationship of the self, at its deepest level, to God."

Rosenstock-Huessy said that faith is not a belief in things of the past but a willingness to commit oneself to the unknown future.

That kind of faith is like *fiducia* and *fidelitas*, rather than like *assensus*. Faith as *visio* reminds me of what I was saying in Chapter 2 about the unity of knowledge, how everything relates.

Thus, both Rosenstock-Huessy and Borg, addressing this idea through different paths and across different times, support the thinking behind this book's challenging title. Like me, they want to get beyond belief.

Living the Kingdom

In his chapter on the Kingdom of God, Borg writes that New Testament scholars in all traditions are practically unanimous in agreeing that the central message of Jesus of Nazareth concerned the coming of the Kingdom of God. He quotes Jesus' first words in Mark, "The time is fulfilled, and the kingdom of God is at hand." He goes on to describe original Christianity as political, as a challenge to the oppressive and unjust secular kingdoms of its time. And he details what it would mean to take the Kingdom of God seriously in the United States today: universal health care, an active concern for the environment, economic justice, and avoiding the misuse of imperial power, as in our optional war in Iraq.

Borg's tone in this chapter reminds me of Rosenstock-Huessy's declaration: "The whole idea of the Christian era is but this: 'Now is the time.'" We are not to postpone living the Kingdom. And Borg reminds me of the social concerns that were shared by Solovyov, Berdyaev, and Bulgakov. Like Rosenstock-Huessy, all three saw our task as living the Kingdom now. As Solovyov put it, the Kingdom of God "comes only in so far as it is realized." The Kingdom is not waiting for us in a heavenly afterlife; the Kingdom of God is at hand.

(Mentioning Bulgakov again reminds me that Rowan Williams, the Archbishop of Canterbury, has been a longtime admirer of Bulgakov's writings—and has published a major anthology of them.)

In the United States today, the ethos of living the Kingdom is widespread in the United Church of Christ and other churches—as it is in such socially concerned Christian organizations as Sojourners.

William Blake spoke for all of us when he wrote:

I will not cease from mental fight,
Nor shall my sword sleep in my hand
Till we have built Jerusalem
In England's green and pleasant land.

We Are All Born Again

At first I was taken aback when I came to Borg's chapter on being born again. I thought he was about to sell out to the fundamentalists. But then I realized that he was on target. He suggests that mainline Christians should reclaim this notion; it might enable us to make peace one day with the literalist-fundamentalist camp.

Borg's own experience of being born again occurred in his early thirties, when he had an intense spiritual experience, one that changed him from being just a scholar of the New Testament to being a committed Christian. I have never described my experience that night of May 29-30, 1941, as one of being born again, but of course it was. That was the night in my dormitory room at Dartmouth College when I decided to quit college and join Camp William James. And to write a book about the Cross of Reality.

Borg concludes that most of us experience being born again. He says that dying to one's old self, and rising to a new self, is at the heart of all the world's enduring religions. Lao Tzu said, "If you want to become full, let yourself be empty; if you want to be reborn, let yourself die." Just as those in other traditions are reborn, so they feel they are "saved."

While I never heard him say so, I think Rosenstock-Huessy believed that the experience we had at Camp William James—leaving the safe life of suburbia and academe to live "all-out" in a new commitment—was a way of giving us the experience of being born again. Thus, the Peace Corps and other volunteer service work offer similar opportunities for rebirth.

The End of Faith?

HANOVER, NEW HAMPSHIRE – APRIL 23, 2007 – Every Monday for the last six weeks I have been attending a course in which we read *The End of Faith*, the book that has made Sam Harris a leading guru of the current attacks on God. Under the title "God and Religion: Can This Marriage be Saved?" the course has been sponsored by the

Institute for Lifelong Education at Dartmouth (ILEAD). Led by Arthur Rosen, a retired businessman, and attended by fifteen men and women from surrounding communities, our course had its final session this morning. As planned, each of us read a short paper describing what we had gleaned from our meetings. Mine was:

The God Beyond Theism—A Third Way of Thinking

This course has been a wake-up call for me, reminding me, quite forcefully, that each of us lives in a private religious, spiritual, or philosophical world of his or her own. Art Rosen has been having an experience like that of my Congregational minister, Doug Moore, who says that leading our congregation is like trying to herd cats.

I remember at our first meeting identifying myself as a long-time member of the United Church of Christ. But then, at our fourth meeting, one member of our group asked me, out of the blue, if I'd ever read the Bible. "Thousands of times," I replied, but, of course, I wondered what prompted her question. I'm pretty sure she asked me that because, at almost every meeting, I've noted that I did not imagine God as a supernatural supreme being, all-powerful, all-knowing, and all-loving, one who was capable of intervening in human affairs.

Instead of that theistic image, I said I thought of God in panentheistic terms. Since none of our class had ever heard of that expression, Art asked me to explain it. I said that panentheism, which had been with us as long as theism, referred to thinking of God as alive in each of us, rather than as an entity living above or beyond us. Apparently, my expression of faith in such a God, rather than the supreme being version, suggested to my classmate that I had not read the Bible. Either you were a theist or an atheist; there was no third way.

When we read Sam Harris' *The End of Faith*, it seemed that he agreed with that proposition. Faithful Christians all believed in God as an intelligence that created the universe. Either you had this belief or you didn't. Harris simply sets aside, as utterly insignificant, the many people of faith who interpret the Bible metaphorically and who see God in ways that are panentheistic rather than theistic. At one of the few points in his book where he pays attention to such Christians, Harris speaks quite positively about the theologian Paul Tillich. He quotes him as attacking the sort of "idolatrous faith" which is "an act of knowledge that has a low degree of evidence." But then he writes Tillich off as "a blameless parish of one," someone who has had next to no influence in the Christian community. Actually, the opposite is true.

I noted that Harris himself skirts dangerously close to idolatrous faith when he expresses great admiration for Buddhist meditation. He goes so far as to say that "meetings between the Dalai Lama and Christian ecclesiastics to mutually honor their religious traditions are like meetings between physicists from Cambridge and the Bushmen of the Kalahari to mutually honor their respective understandings of the physical universe."

I also noted that, for me, the most important words in Harris' book were not ones that he himself had written. Instead, they were the book's endorsement by Joseph C. Hough Jr., president of Union Theological Seminary. Hough wrote:

> Here is a ringing challenge to all Americans who recognize the danger to American democracy posed by the political alliance of right-wing religion and politics and the failure of the tepid and tentative responses by liberal persons of faith. While one might dispute some of the claims and arguments presented by Harris, the need for a wake-up call to religious liberals is right on the mark.

Responding to Hough as well as Harris, I said that we who sit in the pews of mainline churches need to mount a much more effective counter-attack on the overt fundamentalism and quasi-fundamentalism that are so widespread in American Christianity today. Harris was right to say that we were complicit by being passive in the face of their challenge—and Hough was right to call our response thus far too "tepid and tentative." I believe that all in our group agreed. Besides the Harris book, our class considered *The Question of God*, as presented by Armand Nicholi in his book by that name. As he contrasted C. S. Lewis with Sigmund Freud, what struck me was that he assumed the reader had to choose one or the other: either you were with Lewis, as a theistic supernaturalist believer, or you were with Freud as an atheist. Again, there was no third way.

Thus, I was able, in this course, to bring up the widely admired work of Professor Marcus Borg and Bishop John Spong—as evidence that many in mainline churches were, in fact, actively pursuing the third way offered to them by Tillich, and by many others: faith in God without supernaturalist theism or a literal reading of the Bible.

When I had finished reading that paper, Art Rosen asked me how I saw Jesus within the framework of this panentheistic thinking. I replied that I put a lot of emphasis, as Borg does, on the distinction between the pre-crucifixion Jesus and the post-crucifixion Christ. The first was a historical figure. The second, whom Paul and others saw as the resurrected Christ, eventually was described as the Second Person of the Trinity, the Son. That Son represented what Christians felt called upon to embody in their lives. In fact, I looked upon Christ as being embodied in all people of good will, just as the Spirit is embodied in all such persons. I agree with those early Church Fathers who said that there were Christians before Christ. In sum, my vision of panentheism was thoroughly Trinitarian and applied to all humanity—past, present, and future.

When I told a friend about this course, he said our theme reminded him of Don Cupitt, an English Anglican priest whom Spong finds congenial. On the Web I discovered that Cupitt's is a powerful voice against supernaturalist Christianity. He sees us entering a Second Axial Age in which we would give up belief systems in favor of a new "religious humanism." He describes his goal as "democratizing religious thinking"—and finds the Quakers a good example of what that means. Quite an antidote to C. S. Lewis!

The Querulous Quartet

NORWICH, VERMONT – MAY 15, 2007 – That ILEAD course gave me just the opportunity I wanted to engage with the work of Sam Harris and his accomplices. I quickly re-read the Harris book, and set about reading Daniel Dennett's *Breaking the Spell* and Richard Dawkins' *The God Delusion*. Unfortunately for me, my plan to concentrate on the Unholy Trinity had to be expanded a bit when a fourth flaming atheist burst upon the scene: Christopher Hitchens with his *God Is Not Great*.

Both Harris and Dawkins are so shrill with their "blasting rhetoric," as *Wired* magazine calls it, that they leave you gasping. Dennett is much more modulated. Hitchens seems to have read more deeply than I had expected for a *Vanity Fair* writer, offering quotations from Dostoevsky to buttress his arguments.

In any case, I continue to welcome the attacks on supernaturalist religion made by this querulous quartet. Their attacks help us separate mature religion from its many childish forms.

Dennett defines religion this way:

> I propose to define religions as social systems whose participants avow belief in a supernatural agent or agents whose approval is to be sought. . . . For some people, prayer is not literally *talking to God* but, rather, a "symbolic" activity, a way of talking to *oneself* about one's deepest concerns, expressed metaphorically. . . . If what they call God is really not an agent in their eyes, a being that can *answer* prayers, *approve* and *disapprove*, *receive* sacrifices, and *mete out* punishment or forgiveness, then, although they may call this Being God, and stand in awe of *it* (not *Him*), their creed, whatever it is, is not really a religion according to my definition.

In response to Dennett, I think prayer is much more than talking to myself. It includes a listening to all the imperatives that others have given me, in their words and lives, imperatives that combine together as God's singular address to me. However, I don't think that God is a *being* that can answer my prayers in the way that an "*agent*" could. Instead, when I listen to God's address, as I pray, I feel increasingly compelled to be his agent in the world. For me the *supernatural agent* image of God that Dennett is attacking is the same one that Bishop Robinson attacked, back in 1963.

In one chapter, Dennett turns to the views of Rodney Stark, author of the 2001 book, *One True God: Historical Consequences of Monotheism:*

> [Stark] distinguishes two strategies: *God as essence* (such as Tillich's God as the Ground of all Being, entirely nonanthropomorphic. . . .) and God as *conscious supernatural being* (a God who listens to and answers prayers in real time, for instance). "There is no more profound religious difference than that between faiths involving divine beings and those limited to divine essences," he says, and the latter he judges to be hopeless because "only divine beings *do* anything." Supernatural conscious beings are much better sellers because "the supernatural is the only plausible source of many benefits we greatly desire."

It's quite evident that Dennett likes the way Stark presents us with only two real possibilities: Choose the clear-cut *supernatural being* option, or the wishy-washy *essence* option. What Stark and Dennett miss is the possibility of a *third choice*: God not as a supreme being or as a divine essence but as *an experienced reality*. As Rosenstock-Huessy put it, in a typically concise way, God is known to us "as an *event*, never as an essence or a thing." The God we experience daily is "the living God," the one who enables us to speak, who puts words of life on our lips. And that God is very much alive in Daniel Dennett and his atheist allies. That living God is the one who moves them to speak about outdated ways of understanding God. But they themselves are outdated. It is instructive that not one of them has an entry for "panentheism" in his index.

Now we come to Richard Dawkins. Like the other members of the Querulous Quartet, he is quite clear about defining the God he attacks. In *The God Delusion*, he describes what he calls "the God Hypothesis." Believers think that:

> There exists a superhuman, supernatural intelligence who deliberately designed and created the universe and everything in it, including us.

During the conference on "Emerging Christianity," Marcus Borg explained that he welcomed Dawkins' rejection of that God hypothesis. "I don't believe in that God, either," he said.

Last week I checked to see how Dawkins was doing on the Internet. I was soon viewing and listening to an hour-long debate he had with Alistair McGrath, a prominent British theologian and natural scientist—who appears to be a literal reader of the New Testament. Their main concern was whether God *exists* or not. Listening to them, I realized how lucky I was, in my freshman year at Dartmouth, to be introduced to Solovyov, Berdyaev, and Rosenstock-Huessy; all three opened up ways of thinking that made that question seem irrelevant.

From those three, and from my own experience, I learned that whatever is valuable in our existence we could come to recognize as God in us. If we exist as valuable creatures—ones who live inspired, responsible, and creative lives—then Spirit, Son, and Father exist in us. God is present in us, interdependent with us, an action in us—and still in process of creating us. One cannot debate, as Dawkins and McGrath attempted to do, the question of whether such a God exists. If we admit that we exist, then certainly God exists in us, as the very ground of our being, as Tillich put it. However, such a God does *not* exist as a separate entity, outside creation or before creation, a supernatural intelligence who deliberately designed and created the universe and everything in it, including us. There Dawkins is right on.

The problem with Dawkins and his allies is their assumption that thinkers like Berdyaev and Tillich have had little impact within the Christian fold today. Dawkins thinks well of Spong, calling him "a nice example of a liberal bishop whose beliefs are so advanced as to be almost unrecognizable to the majority of those who call themselves Christians." He might be right about "the majority," especially if you throw in Africa; but in New England and many other parts of this country, I think the majority of parishioners and clergy have moved beyond literal interpretation of the Bible—and are beginning to welcome the sort of panentheistic thinking introduced by John A. T. Robinson, John Spong, Marcus Borg, Matthew Fox, Leslie Dewart, Gregory Baum, Teilhard de Chardin—and many others. (I speak with some assurance, since the "Bridges" project gave me opportunities to visit dozens of churches throughout the Northeast. The UCC even made me a "commissioned minister" to further the "Bridges" mission.)

Having briefly engaged the Unholy Trinity of Harris, Dennett, and Dawkins, I finally come to Christopher Hitchens and his *God Is Not Great*. Whereas Hitchens is certainly a lively writer, he attacks the same straw man set up by his allies: The God who is not great is that same all-powerful supreme being that has become a hopelessly outdated image for those who love God with their minds—as well as their hearts and souls.

Hitchens calls C. S. Lewis "dreary and absurd," a statement with which I heartily agree. However, Hitchens himself becomes absurd when he asserts that he is "not choosing a straw man," as he makes his elegant attack on Lewis. He calls Lewis "the main chosen propaganda vehicle for Christianity in our time." If you tend to be a literal reader of the Bible, then Lewis may be your cup of tea. But, as has been made clear in such books as *Christianity for the Rest of Us*, by Diana Butler Bass, mainline churches across America are doing quite well as they move from the literalist Lewis brand and adopt the emerging paradigm described by Borg.

The "original error" of religious faith, in Hitchens's view, is that "it wholly misrepresents the origins of man and the cosmos." Again, it is absurd to imagine that all people who are religious think that the world was created in six days, about 6,000 years ago. He and the others in his quartet are simply attacking fundamentalist religion, which a large portion of Christians find as weird as they do.

Hitchens makes a particularly absurd remark about Abraham Lincoln: "It would also be inaccurate to say that he was a Christian." The evidence for this was that "he never joined any church." It just happens that my great-great-grandfather James Conkling was one of Lincoln's best friends—and, when I asked my grandmother about Lincoln's church connections, she said the family recalled them as quite irregular. But to look at Lincoln's life and words, and declare that he was not a Christian, is totally out of bounds. Hitchens makes a parallel remark about Bonhoeffer, calling his work "an admirable but nebulous humanism."

Unfortunately, Hitchens and his companions get some significant traction by quoting the truly alarming statistics about the US population today. They cite figures such as those Kevin Phillips provides in his recent book, *American Theocracy*. He says polls show that 55% of Americans think that the whole Bible is literally accurate; 60% believe that the story of Noah's Ark is literally true, and that God created the earth in six days. If you ask just Evangelical Protestants about whether the world will end in an Armageddon battle between Jesus Christ and the Antichrist, 71% of them will say yes. Phillips notes that the churches housing these true believers made huge membership gains over the last 40 years, while mainline churches saw memberships in relative decline. Of course, the result has been felt in the White House. Phillips quotes television journalist Bill Moyers: "One of the biggest changes in politics in my lifetime is that the delusional is no longer marginal."

And the rise of delusional Christianity is not limited to the United States. Fundamentalism, with its literal belief, is the main current in Africa, China, South Korea, and those other far-flung parts of the world where Christianity is growing most rapidly.

Thus, the atheist choir of Hitchens and friends serve a useful purpose. They remind us that we mainline Christians have our work cut out for us. We should stop being so passive in the face of fundamentalism—and its vestiges in mainline churches. Delusions are dangerous. Delusional religion can create a delusional philosophy, even a delusional political philosophy, like that of the monological American neo-conservatives of the 21st century, the Richard Perles of the world. They call to mind Rosenstock-Huessy's words in *Out of Revolution*: "A wrong philosophy must necessarily lead us into a wrong society."

MAY 17, 2007 – NORWICH, VERMONT – Last night I went to the second monthly meeting of a theological discussion group that was recently announced in our church bulletin. The meetings are being led by Kenneth Cracknell, a retired Methodist minister who has served as director of interfaith relations for the British Council of Churches. As we broke up, Kenneth suggested that our third meeting, in June, should be on our understanding of the Nicene Creed. That topic has prompted the following thoughts, which I plan to present at the June meeting:

The Creed of the Living God

It was in 1946, when I first read Eugen Rosenstock-Huessy's *The Christian Future*, that it dawned on me that I could think of the Christian creed as an experienced reality. Before that, the creed had seemed to me simply a formula that I was supposed to accept as part of being a Christian. From Rosenstock-Huessy I learned that the Nicene Creed of 325 had been expanded and clarified in the Athanasian Creed, attributed to Athanasius, the 4th-century bishop of Alexandria. Unlike the Nicene Creed, the Athanasian uses the word "Trinity" and expounds on the idea that Father, Son, and Holy Spirit are "co-eternal together and co-equal."

In his interpretation of the creed, Rosenstock-Huessy identifies the Holy Spirit with inspiration, with all human-kind's calling to create a viable *future*; the Son (and Daughter) is our personal and individual response to that calling—through leading a sacrificial and committed life in the *present*; the Father relates to our inheritance from the *past*, to "the unity of creation from the beginning."

Thus, Father, Son, and Spirit can be thought of as categories of being and becoming human. The three persons of the Trinity did not appear for the first time 2,000 years ago; they have lived in us from the dawn of our history. They have lived in all humankind, not simply in Christians. They live today in all persons of good will, in the lives of non-believers just as surely as they do in the lives of believers.

After I met Kenneth at our first meeting, I looked him up on the Internet and learned that he had recently published a book, *In Good and Generous Faith: Christian Responses to Religious Pluralism*. When I got a copy, I was delighted to find that Kenneth turns to Franz Rosenzweig when discussing Christian-Jewish dialogue, and to Martin Buber when he discusses dialogue itself.

In his second chapter, "The Universal Presence of the Word: A Christology for Religious Pluralism," Kenneth echoes Marcus Borg in discussing how a vital part of Christianity's new paradigm is its abandonment of the idea that only Christians are "saved." He cites St. Paul as well as early Church Fathers to describe how Christ, as the *Logos*, is understood as pre-existent before Jesus. For example, one of the earliest Church Fathers, Justin Martyr (100–165), wrote:

> We have been taught that Christ is the first-begotten of God. He is the *Logos* in whom the whole human race shares. Those who have lived in accordance with the *Logos* are Christians, even though they were called godless, such among the Greeks, Socrates and Heraclitus. . . .

In the light of Justin's reflections on the *Logos*, Kenneth goes on to interpret the words attributed to Jesus in John 14:6: "No one comes to the Father except through me." What those words really present is a *universal* message: No one comes to the Father but through the pre-existing Word of *Logos*. The message is not that the followers of Jesus are the only ones to come to the Father; rather, those words should be seen as welcoming to the Father all those who have lived in accordance with the *Logos*.

Rosenstock-Huessy's work can be seen as a secular translation of John's prologue on the *Logos* and an expansion of those lines from Justin. For example, *The Christian Future* opens with this epigraph from Hugo de Sancto Victore (1096–1141):

> The time span of the length of the Church goes from the beginning of the world to its end since the Church originated in her faithful from the start and shall endure until the end. . . . For we basically hold that from the beginning of the world to the end of times, no period exists in which there cannot be found those who trust Christ.

Back to Meister Eckhart

MAY 25, 2007 – NORWICH, VERMONT – At a later meeting of our theological discussion group, I hope to present the work of the 14th-century German theologian Meister Eckhart. Since we have already discussed panentheism, we've prepared the ground. I first read Eckhart in the fall of 1941, when my mother bought a new book of his sermons and sayings. Here are three she underlined:

The Father ceaselessly begets his Son and, what is more, he
begets me as his Son—the self-same Son! Indeed, I assert
that he begets me not only as his Son but as himself and
himself as myself, begetting me in his own nature, his own
being. At that inmost Source, I spring from the Holy Spirit
and there is one life, one being, one action.

When creatures came to be and took on creaturely being,
then God was no longer God as he is in himself, but God
as he is with creatures.

The authorities say that God is a being, an intelligent being
who knows everything. But I say that God is neither a being
nor intelligent and he does not "know" either this or that.

Looking through that Eckhart book today, I am struck by how
my fall 1941 reading of it undoubtedly reinforced what I'd just begun
to read in Solovyov and Berdyaev in the spring of that awful year.
I didn't hear the word "panentheism" until 1948, but Eckhart had
brought me to the heart of it seven years earlier.

The Schwärmerei of the Fundamentalists

The enthusiasm for the new paradigm, which was so evident
in the 1960s, especially through Bishop Robinson and his *Honest to
God*, had lost ground by the 1980s. It never occurred to me that we
might be overcome by what Luther called *Schwärmerei*, that empty,
fanatical religious enthusiasm of the people who refer to Jesus as
"my personal savior." I would not mind if these swarms were on the
periphery, and I suppose that, to teach the illiterate, a simple form
of Christianity might be quite appropriate. But for those with high
school educations, like most Americans, I see no excuse.

The literalists and fundamentalists should start loving God with
their minds as well as their hearts; they should, in St. Paul's words,
grow up and "put away childish things." As I have noted above,
they are now close to taking over Christianity in the United States
and beyond. That's why Spong is right to say that Christianity must
change or die. In educated adults, childish Christianity is decadent
Christianity.

When Bonhoeffer spoke of a religionless Christianity, he meant Christianity without any *Schwärmerei.* Martin Marty wrote that, "By *religion* Bonhoeffer meant hyperindividualism, self-contained inwardness, bad conscience or the sin-sick soul as psychological *a prioris* for Christian experience. . . . or piety." The sin-sick revel in their personal sin because it allows them to be "saved" by their personal savior.

With the rise of the *Schwärmerei* legions, we mainline churchgoers now find ourselves engaged in a war on two fronts. The most dangerous troops advancing on us are our fellow Christians. I see less danger on the second front, where the Querulous Quartet hopes to tear down our walls. If Joseph Hough, who leads the seminary where Bonhoeffer had planned to teach, can say he finds Harris "right on the mark," we can welcome such an eloquent atheist as a temporary ally.

Two Morning Notes

When I ended Chapter 1, I said that that I'd save for later the two morning notes that I wrote down the week before the June 6, 1944, invasion, notes concerning prayer and whether there is a life after death. They belong here because they relate to the task of transforming Christianity—and to the task of our being transformed by our faith. They are among my earliest efforts to express what I had begun to grasp about Christianity's new paradigm:

To Whom Do We Pray?

When we pray to God we do not establish contact with a "being" who "exists" somewhere outside ourselves. Instead, we establish contact with the past, present, and future of ourselves and humankind. Those are God's three tenses—the trinity of Father, Son, and Spirit.

But if God is not a "being" who "exists," then to whom do we pray? Do we pray merely to ourselves? No, we pray to the triune God. He lives in us whenever we are the responsive Son. But he has also lived in all the people and all the creation that has gone before us—our inheritance, our past, the story in which we live. In this sense he is our Father. And we pray also toward the future, to our children, our heirs, to the future generations of the race. As we pray that they too may have life, we pray to the Holy Spirit to give them that life.

We pray to the Father as our origins, the Son as our responsibility, and the Spirit as our destiny.

Life after Death

I do not believe that we have any individual consciousness of ourselves after death but that we can die peacefully if we have lived for what we have loved and what we believed in. Our resurrection and eternal life does not mean our continuing existence as a lonely soul above the clouds. Instead, it means that future generations will be enriched, possibly even inspired, by the word that we incarnated in our lives. We incarnate that word not only in our own bodies but in such larger bodies as the family, church, tribe, or nation.

After we die, we live on in those bodies, and in the lives of all whom we have touched. Salvation is not something reserved for members of a particular church, or religion, but is universal for all men of good will. We are saved—we are resurrected—to the extent that we have been responsible participants in the human story. If we had to choose, knowing that we were about to die, between some ongoing personal consciousness or a knowledge that we would be meaningful for the future of all that was dear to us, would we really prefer a million years of consciousness?

Five years after I wrote that second note, in 1949, I showed it to Lothar Zacek, who was our German Managing Editor at *Die Neue Zeitung* in Berlin. He had read Rosenstock-Huessy's work, and wanted me to make clear that there was not an ounce of fundamentalism in my professor's understanding of the Resurrection. There was no "beyond," no literal life after death. Although there was certainly resurrection, it was in what St. Paul called "a spiritual body." In *The Christian Future* Rosenstock-Huessy writes that St. Francis becomes resurrected whenever we in later generations emulate his style of life, his unassuming simplicity. Rosenstock-Huessy cites Lincoln as an example, recalling how this "Commander-in-Chief of a victorious army walked into Richmond in 1865, on foot, without escort." He sees Jesus resurrected that same way, not only in individuals but also in the church—and in all the secular institutions that Christianity has introduced.

Lothar was a Social Democrat with no interest in the church, but he seemed to like the idea that I would include him among the resurrected.

A final thought on this subject. After Fred Berthold, the retired professor of religion at Dartmouth, had delivered a talk at the Kendal retirement community in Hanover, he was asked whether he believed in an afterlife. He said that he had been raised as a fundamentalist, and his parents described life in heaven as being like going to a great picnic—where one would meet one's parents and grandparents. Later, in college, Fred began to see some flaws in this picture. At the picnic table, his grandparents would have to be meeting their parents, and their parents' parents, and so on back for a million years. The table would be quite crowded. His reply brought down the house.

13 THE NEW TRANSCENDENCE

If God is one, then how can reality be two? If God is the origin of all that is—earth, moon, and stars, as well as spirit, soul, and consciousness, then how can science (which means to tell me the truth about physical reality) and religion (which means to tell me the truth about spiritual reality) be enemies? And why should living my life require me to use two different operating manuals? If God is truly one and truly God of all, then how can truth be divided?
—Barbara Brown Taylor

NORWICH, VERMONT – JUNE 1, 2007 – The new transcendence envisioned (and experienced) by Rosenstock-Huessy and his fellow dialogical thinkers was based on their discovery that speech, a completely natural phenomenon, could also be seen as the only miracle, the "only supernatural." To repeat what Rosenzweig had said, "One knew that the distinction between immanence and transcendence disappears in language."

Both the dialogical thinkers and their Russian counterparts— from Kireevsky to Solovyov, Berdyaev, and Bakhtin—were quite properly reacting to the 18th century Enlightenment's enthronement of Reason as well as to its result: the 19th century's experience of the near-collapse of religion.

My German and Russian heroes have succeeded in giving us a new post-Enlightenment vision of God: He is no longer a transcendent being, external to us, but one in whose life we participate. That panentheistic vision, as we have seen, is one of the main pillars of Christianity's new paradigm.

Now this chapter will continue to explore the movement from theism to panentheism, a movement that offers the promise of reconciling science and religion. We will begin by engaging with two scientists, Stephen Hawking and Albert Einstein, on the meaning of time, and then introduce the American "process theologians," our own quite recent panentheists.

I'll start with Barbara Brown Taylor, who joined Marcus Borg on the platform at that conference in Georgia four months ago. In preparation for that event, I read Taylor's *The Luminous Web: Essays on Science and Religion*, a work that deals quite successfully with the science-religion stand-off. Early on she describes "the dualism that has dogged me all my life. . . . I grew up thinking of reality not as one but two." On the one hand, there was the physical reality that "depends on science and reason." On the other hand, there was the spiritual reality, "beyond sight and touch—which depends entirely on God."

However, she asks, "if God is one, then how can reality be two?"

A Brief History of Time

To explore that question, in the early 1990s, Taylor was led to read some science books, and was particularly engaged by Stephen Hawking's *A Brief History of Time*. People bought an astounding 9 million copies of that book, and Taylor thinks it was "his quest for a 'theory of everything' that caught our attention. . . . Wouldn't it be wonderful to discover the unity at the heart of all diversity?" She quotes the famous physicist's concluding paragraph on this unity:

> If we do discover a complete theory, it should in time be understandable in broad principle by everyone, not just a few scientists. Then we shall all, philosophers, scientists, and just ordinary people, be able to take part in the discussion of the question why it is that we and the universe exist. If we find the answer to that, it would be the ultimate triumph of human reason—for then we would know the mind of God.

Now if I understand Hawking, his complete theory of everything would have to be expressible in a single mathematical equation, one that would be consistent with all that we know about physics and the universe. Presumably that equation would include, along with $E=mc^2$, a good many more factors, ones that related time, space, matter, the speed of light, gravity, and energy (and undoubtedly other factors beyond my ken). Such an equation would certainly take into account Einstein's critical discovery that *time is a fourth dimension of space*. And such an equation would reflect Descartes' fundamental insight that everything we know can be reduced to mathematics. As S. V. Keeling writes in his *Descartes*, "He saw no reason why philosophy itself should not become a Universal Mathematics." That's much like E. O. Wilson's *Consilience*, in which all material and social phenomena "are ultimately reducible. . . to the laws of physics."

Thus, Hawking is talking only about the world of space, the world of matter, the world on the outer front of the Cross of Reality. He is *not* talking about the world of *human time*, where we are certainly able to identify past and future. Hawking stresses that the "time" he is describing in his *Brief History of Time* has no past or future. Specifically, he writes that "the laws of science do not distinguish between the past and the future."

In the 1920s Einstein had a tremendous impact on our understanding of the cosmos when he came up with that remarkable insight that time is a fourth dimension of space. In other words, we live in a space-time continuum. Without mentioning Einstein in this book's opening segment on "The Dimensions of Time," I wanted to hint that his concept of time for physics might not be related to human time. Again, "when applied to human beings. . . the term *future* has quite a different meaning from when it is applied to nature. We commit ourselves to the future as an act of faith. Our life in time is just as real and full as our life in space."

Two Kinds of Time: Kairos *and* Chronos

What I'd like to do now is go beyond hinting. I'd like to make a proposition: *that the kind of time Einstein needed to describe a space-time continuum is not the same kind of time that we experience in our lives and in history.*

Since we're near the end of this book, this is a proposition for which I have neither the space nor the time to develop fully! Still, I'd now like to say enough about it to sow the seeds for its eventual acceptance.

First, it is clear that the kind of time described by the laws of science, specifically physical science, does not have a past or future. Physical time is simply a duration; there is no forward movement. In the *Columbia Encyclopedia*, the entry on "time" says: "In addition to relative time, another aspect of time relevant to physics is how one can distinguish the forward direction in time. . . . According to classical physics. . . when all microscopic motions of individual particles are precisely defined, there is no fundamental distinction between forward and backward in time." It goes on to say that the only way to distinguish a forward direction in the existence of matter is "by the increase of entropy or disorder," as in thermodynamics. Hawking makes exactly that same point about entropy in his book.

Now entropy and disorder are hardly conditions that seem related to the way we perceive the future, or progress, in human time. Thus, we must pose the question: Could it really be that human time is fundamentally different from nature's time? Tillich may be helpful with the answer. He suggested that we should distinguish between the ordinary time of *chronos*, which just measures how the clock ticks on, and our higher experience of time, which we might call *kairos*, as the Greeks did. *Kairos* time we might think of as God's time, the time that cannot be measured. *Kairos* time, human time, can have fullness and ripeness. It can have high moments; the time described by physics cannot.

Rosenstock-Huessy always recognized Tillich as a friend and fellow worker on the new Christian paradigm that began to be visible after the First World War. Still, their contributions to the new paradigm were very different. For example, Tillich attracted many followers with his description of God as "the ground of being," while Rosenstock-Huessy found few concepts more distasteful than that of "being." However, when Tillich began to talk about *kairos* time, Rosenstock-Huessy jumped to his support. He proposed that we might use the term "kaironomy" for a discipline that would educate us to understand the sort of time that is not "natural." "Man's time, unlike space, has no yardstick," Rosenstock-Huessy once exclaimed.

With that as background, I'll rephrase my proposition about the difference between the natural time of science and the times of human experience: *We should come to recognize that there are two kinds of time, the natural time of physics, or* chronos, *and the human time of history, or* kairos.

When we consider the Cross of Reality, it shows us that we live at the high-tension intersection between past and future times. If we live responsibly at that intersection, we are always redeeming the time. At all high moments of our lives, whenever we use or respond to high speech, we participate in the life of the Spirit. At those moments, which can occur almost daily, we live in *kairos* time, not *chronos* time.

In a 1954 lecture, Rosenstock-Huessy addresses this issue. He exclaims: "Gentlemen, you and I don't live in the fourth dimension of space. This is all nonsense. . . . You couldn't breathe for one minute if time was one-dimensional because at that very moment, gentlemen, the future would only be composed of the elements of the past."

Whitehead, Hartshorne, and Process Theology

Toward the end of her *Luminous Web*, Taylor suggests that her readers might do well to read the work of Alfred North Whitehead, particularly his 1929 classic, *Process and Reality: An Essay in Cosmology*. She also recommends his theological heirs, Charles Hartshorne (1897–2000) and John B. Cobb, Jr. (1925–). All three will give you background on the development of panentheistic thought in America. However, read his heirs before Whitehead—unless you are a glutton for dense philosophizing. After plowing through his lengthy tome, I have found only bits and pieces that were readily accessible. One of those bits is worth quoting at length because it is such a devastating critique of theism:

> The notion of God as the "unmoved mover" is derived from Aristotle, at least so far as Western thought is concerned. The notion of God as "eminently real" is a favorite doctrine of Christian theology. The combination of the two into the doctrine of an aboriginal, eminently real, transcendent creator, at whose fiat the world came into being, and whose imposed will it obeys, is the fallacy which has infused tragedy into the histories of Christianity and of Mahometanism.
>
> When the Western world accepted Christianity, Caesar conquered; and the received text of Western theology was edited by his lawyers. The code of Justinian and the theology of Justinian are two volumes expressing one movement of the human spirit. The brief Galilean vision of humility flickered throughout the ages, uncertainly. In the official formulation of the religion it has assumed the trivial form of the mere attribution to the Jews that they cherished a misconception about their Messiah. But the deeper idolatry, of the fashioning of God in the image of the Egyptian,

Persian, and Roman imperial rulers, was retained. The Church gave unto God the attributes which belonged exclusively to Caesar.

I know of no better comment than Whitehead's on how Christianity was distorted by Constantine and the emperors and kings who followed in his wake. The supreme being version of God obviously derives from the rulers who saw themselves as supreme beings, as Tsars, as heirs of the Caesars. Worship him the way you worship me!

Rosenstock-Huessy knew Whitehead at Harvard, but I never heard that he found the cosmologist's work of particular interest. However, I think he would have agreed with that quotation, as he might have approved of some of the final thoughts in *Process and Reality*. There Whitehead writes that "the kingdom of heaven is with us today" and affirms "the everpresent, unfading importance of our immediate actions, which perish and yet live for evermore."

Hartshorne builds on Whitehead. His description of panentheism reminds me of Berdyaev's:

> God orders the universe, according to panentheism, by taking into his own life all the currents of feeling in existence. He is the most irresistible of influences precisely because he is himself the most open to influence. In the depths of their hearts all creatures (even those able to "rebel" against him) defer to God because they sense him as the one who alone is adequately moved by what moves them. He alone not only knows but feels (the only adequate knowledge, where feeling is concerned) how they feel, and he finds his own joy in sharing their lives, lived according to their own free decisions, not fully anticipated by any detailed plan of his own. Yet the extent to which they can be permitted to work out their own plan depends on the extent to which they can echo or imitate on their own level the divine sensitiveness to the needs and precious freedom of all.

Although I liked that formulation when I first read it in the early 1960s, and I still like it, in retrospect it is actually too theistic for me. The quotation implies that God is some sort of knowing entity. Berdyaev, a generation before Hartshorne, came closer to what I'd want to say, when he described the Holy Spirit as becoming incarnate in every human being—and therefore suggested that we think of God as being like a whole humanity.

With Berdyaev and Rosenstock-Huessy pointing the way, let me imagine how we can go a few steps beyond Hartshorne. As whole humanity, God takes into his life all the lives that have been lived, each a sentence in his story. Only God as whole humanity can be adequately moved by what each of us has said and done. Only God as whole humanity can know our shared joy; and feel, with a divine sensitivity, what it is that we all have in common. And only God as whole humanity can remember us when we are gone—and welcome us into our resurrection.

John Cobb, a lively interpreter of both Hartshorne and Whitehead, makes Whitehead quite accessible in his *God and the World*, and adds his own perspective. Today you can hear Cobb on a widely circulated DVD. Along with Borg, Spong, and many others, he has participated in an educational project called "Living the Questions," a program offering outstanding resources for people interested in exploring Christianity's new paradigm.

The panentheism introduced by Whitehead and Hartshorne in their process theology seems to be an American version of the panentheism pioneered by Solovyov, Bulgakov, and Berdyaev. Writers on the new paradigm are likely to hail the importance of all five of these well-known thinkers.

Not surprisingly, I find that Rosenstock-Huessy's still-unrecognized contribution to the new paradigm is just as important.

Five Theses on Reconciling Science and Religion

Let me now sum up Rosenstock-Huessy's contribution, seeing it in relation to the work of others touched on in this chapter.

Chapter 4's "Ten Theses on Language" described how four basic kinds of speech create our consciousness of an inner self, the outer world, future time, and past time. Thus, we live in a Cross of Reality, a model of the human condition that reveals how our souls are formed.

That cross depicts the action of high speech in us, and we can come to see that such speech is the embodiment of what Christians call the Holy Spirit. It follows that the Trinitarian God is not something in which we need to believe; that God is already within us, as the very source of our humanity. God's grace is found at the center of life, at the center of the cross in which we live. Spirit, Son, and Father relate to three kinds of speech and their related grammatical persons: *thou, I,* and *we.* We represent all three persons of the Trinity as we act in the outer world, where we are recognized as *he, she,* or *they.*

That quick summary of the ten theses on language moves from simple secular statements to increasingly religious ones. All ten of them were offered as reinforcements for Christianity's new paradigm, a paradigm that moves away from the distant God of supernaturalist theism and toward the immediately experienced God of panentheism.

To those ten theses, we can now add five more, ones which continue their thrust toward reconciling science and religion:

1. The Holy Spirit as the Human Spirit

Neither natural nor social science should have any objection to the kind of Christianity—or religion generally—that I have presented here. The heart of Christianity—and of all truly inspired religion—is the recognition that God's spirit lives in each of us. Rosenstock-Huessy and his allies, in disclosing the secrets of speech, have been able to describe *just how* it is that God's spirit lives in us. Today we can recognize the Holy Spirit as a *universal creative principle,* the action of spirit in all persons. And this spirit, which once had seemed expressed as a divine *Logos,* can now be recognized as the creative word. Thus, when we explore the mysteries of how speech, the word, works in us, we are simultaneously exploring how the Holy Spirit works in us.

2. The Logos Expressed in All Humanity

If we start by acknowledging that high speech is the body of the spirit, we can go on to realize that the *Logos,* the word that was in the beginning, is the word that was made flesh not only in Jesus Christ but in all the generations before and after him. That is, the generations of our faith extend backward to those who first buried their dead—and spoke or sang some words in their praise. They include all people of good will. They include those who lived in tribes and then in the great empires—the Egyptians, Persians, and Chinese. They include Muslims who see their purpose as peace, just as they include the Buddhists, Taoists, and Confucians—who always tended to be more peaceful than their Christian or Muslim brethren.

3. Anthropurgy or Theosis

Since the Christian tradition has always declared that Father, Son, and Spirit are co-equal and co-eternal in the Godhead, whatever is true of the Spirit is also true of Father and Son. All three persons of the Trinity are powers that work in us—*together*. It follows that, when we come to understand how speech, as Spirit, turns us into valuable persons, we are also learning how God as Father and Son is simultaneously turning us into such persons. This is the process that our Christian Church Fathers described as *anthropurgy*, and the Eastern Church has called *theosis*.

4. From Theism to Panentheism

The panentheistic understanding of God is not something new. Its briefest best expression was in St. Paul, and it came to full flower in Meister Eckhart. Since Irenaeus in the second century, it has been the dominant theme in Eastern Christianity. Through Solovyov, Berdyaev, Bulgakov, and Florensky, it was the characteristic spirituality of Russia's Silver Age. Through Whitehead, Hartshorne, Tillich (and many others), it found a home in the United States. While each expression of it is different, they all suggest that we can and should give up the idea of God as an independent, knowing entity, a supernatural power separate from us, before us, and over us. That theistic conception of an autonomous entity that exists beyond creation is positively damaging—because it stands in the way of our realizing how God's continuing life in us, and the very continuance of any life on earth, is up to us.

5. The New Transcendence

Christianity's new paradigm, as presented in the preceding four theses, offers us a new vision of transcendence. The old vision—be it in Judaism, Christianity, or Islam—was based on imagining that there is a transcendental power, a supernatural power that dwells *outside* the universe, outside creation, outside history, outside evolution, outside human beings. By contrast, Rosenstock-Huessy and his allies have given us convincing evidence that there is a transcendental power that is at work *within* the universe, within the process of creation, within history, working at the leading edge of evolution, always present in human beings. This power, however, is *not* supernatural. It is present in us all the time—and is made manifest whenever we say the word that needs to be spoken. It is the power of speech. It is the Word made flesh in all humanity.

Taking those five new theses together, along with their ten predecessors on language, we have fifteen continuing statements that build upon each other. I contend that, since they start with verifiable statements about speech, and retain that base as they move into the realm of religion, they remain anchored in the verifiable, the rational, and the logical. Thus they should be quite acceptable to minds formed by Descartes and the Enlightenment, to minds that take science as a bedrock given. Of course, the Cross of Reality shows us that the bedrock of physical science lies under what we know only about the outer front, the material world of nature.

Taylor's question about the two realities, the physical and the spiritual—and how, "if God is one, then how can reality be two?"— begged an answer. Those fifteen theses are this book's answer. They tell us that the Cross of Reality *shows the intersection between those two realities*: the physical outer space of the world, which is known by science, and the spiritual inner space of the person, which is known only to our selves.

But then the cross goes further than that, enlarging our vision beyond that dualism. By adding the two dimensions of time, it shows that we live in a four-dimensional reality—and that we live God's life whenever we turn *chronos* into *kairos*.

Since each of us lives at the center of the cross, our lives are crucial, not only for ourselves but for all humankind. At the center of the cross there are not two realities; instead, four realities become one. We no longer need two different operating manuals.

Rosenstock-Huessy and his allies have shown us how everything we know is connected, how everything relates, from the most spiritual to the most material. How is the spiritual connected with the physical? They intersect at the center of the cross, where our bodies that exist in space, like stardust, are crossed by the spirit that exists in time, in *kairos* time.

Finally, one simple premise lies behind all fifteen steps in this book's logic. It's the premise that speech is the body of the spirit. That's the logic of the *Logos*.

ON CEMETERY HILL: IN CONCLUSION

The history of the human race is written on a single theme: How does love become stronger than death? The composition is recomposed in each generation by those whose love overcomes murdering or dying. So history becomes a great song, Augustine's Carmen Humanum; in it each line, perhaps each tone, will be a person's life. As often as the lines rhyme, love has once again become stronger than death. . . . This rhyming, this connecting, is men's function on earth. But that this is our function we have known only since the birth of Christ.

—Eugen Rosenstock-Huessy

NORWICH, VERMONT – JUNE 6, 2007 – This would be the day that I died, just 63 years ago—if I had raised my head only a half inch higher when I looked out of my foxhole on Omaha Beach. I have always been quite clear that it was not by my parents' prayers, but by sheer chance, that my life was spared that day. If an all-powerful God were involved, why would he ignore the prayers from the parents of the thousands who died all about me? That was also the question that haunted me after Buchenwald. How can one speak of God after the Holocaust? This book has tried to answer that question.

And today is close to a second anniversary. It was May 29, 1941, just a bit more than 66 years ago, that I stayed up most of the night in Gile Hall, decided to quit college, join Camp William James, and write a book about the Cross of Reality.

It is because of those two anniversaries that I have come here today, to sit on this stone wall on the north side of the Norwich Hillside Cemetery, just 30 feet from the Gardner plot where Libby and I have reserved some space. And about 150 feet from where Eugen and Margrit Rosenstock-Huessy lie. This is a good place and time to think about those two anniversary dates in the 1940s. Looking across the Connecticut River valley, I can see the hills that surround Hanover and Dartmouth two miles away.

A stand of pines blocks my view of the Norwich Congregational Church. At the end of the nave there is a stained glass window given by Libby's great-great-grandfather, Sylvester Morris (1797–1886). It shows a dove descending as the Spirit, and has these words from Micah: "Do justly, love mercy, and walk humbly with thy God." That's all the Lord requires of us.

I have brought my journal with me, still red-bound, the direct descendant of the one I had in my backpack on D-Day.

Christianity's New Paradigm

I have written this book as a contribution to Christianity's new paradigm, the one that John Robinson, then Spong and Borg, have all so eloquently described. One of my unusual contributions has been to point to Solovyov as a key discloser of that paradigm. His *Lectures on Divine Humanity* laid the foundation for Russia's Silver Age, that period when the Eastern Church, through its lay theologians and several priests, brought this paradigm's panentheism to an early and distinctive expression. I have also pointed to how the new paradigm was given a critical impulse by Bonhoeffer and Tillich in Germany, and articulated in more philosophical terms by Whitehead and Hartshorne in the United States. Of course, my most particular contribution has been to focus on Rosenstock-Huessy's work—and see it in relation to all these others.

The Cross of Reality can provide some important scaffolding for the further growth of the new paradigm. As model and method, that cross opens up a larger perspective than what we get from either *timeless* theology or merely *spatial* natural science. Its integrating perspective gets rid of the two-world picture we have inherited from Plato, the German idealists, and from supernaturalist religion.

This cross is the energizing motor of a new discipline that we might call *metanomics*. As Rosenstock-Huessy presented it in *Out of Revolution*, such a new discipline would smelt together "history and science, law and theology." Rosenzweig anticipated metanomics when he made his outrageous claim that the method of speech would "replace the methods of all earlier philosophies." At the very least, this method is not just another footnote to Plato, as Whitehead famously described all the philosophies of the last two millennia.

Although the Cross of Reality is certainly not interchangeable with the cross of Christ, it provides an image of how the Holy Spirit works in us and how God speaks in us, in real times and in real places. Thus it shows how we can have completely authentic religion without resorting to the supernatural. It is at the heart of what I have called a down-to-earth spirituality, one that takes us beyond belief that God exists, to *knowledge* of how he lives and speaks in each of us. Against E. O. Wilson's assumptions, this spirituality offers us a third world view, a *religious empiricism*, one that takes us beyond religious transcendentalism and scientific empiricism.

It certainly does *not* offer peace of mind. Instead, its crucial perspective suggests that the only way we find peace for our souls is by becoming fully engaged in life.

As I quoted Bonhoeffer in the Prologue, we have reached a time when we should not imagine transcendence as "a 'religious' relationship to the highest, most powerful, and best Being imaginable." Today we should recognize that "the transcendental is not infinite and unattainable tasks, but the neighbor who is within reach in any given situation."

Metanomics has an "action arm," one that reaches out to our neighbors, be they as close as the next town over, or as far away as Moscow or Tehran. The idea of "argonautic" replacing "academic" was born for many of us in our work at Camp William James. And that idea is still a-borning. Dartmouth has especially nurtured it; since the 1960s the college has been a national leader in Peace Corps participation. Exeter, also, continues to promote *Non Sibi*—through a significant program of community service.

Over the past 40 years, projects like the Peace Corps—private, public, and religious, in nations around the globe—have become too numerous to count. And most colleges now include in their curriculum a semester of study abroad (or work in inner cities), typically with a service project as the focus. Doctors Without Borders and similar transnational organizations are providing exactly the sort of intersocietal pioneers, the argonauts, who are needed to build the new institutions of the third millennium.

There has certainly been more progress toward building the action arm of voluntary service than there has been toward *articulation* of the principles that lie behind it, those principles first put forward by Rosenstock-Huessy and William James. Whether metanomics might appear as a higher sociology, a reform of theology, or take form as something else, is in the laps of the gods. Or perhaps it is in the hands of defectors from academe. It may take people who are dubious about what I have called academe's "cold, objective, disengaged language" to appreciate the promise of a new discipline.

Whatever form the new discipline takes, it will be based on a fresh perception of what language is—and how living speech is what moves us, changes our times, and creates peace. Since the 1940s I have been seeking to give a second generation's response to what Rosenstock-Huessy and Rosenzweig had discovered. What they perceived in the patterns of speech, of grammar itself, described a certain, still-unrecognized law of motion of the spirit, a law that describes how speech moves through us and forms our souls. I have pursued their trail ever since, knowing that their discoveries would take at least three generations to introduce.

Here I have simplified their thought by focusing on what seems to be its key. When we realize that speech, a completely natural phenomenon, can also be recognized as the only supernatural, the only miracle, we overcome the barrier that has separated the secular realm from the religious. And we overcome the barrier that has separated science from religion. We undo the damage that has been done to our consciousness over the last 300 years—as religion has retreated to the realm of faith and sentimental attachment, while natural science has become the bedrock of what can be "known."

This book—drawn from a sequence of journals—makes an end-run around academe. As I noted in my conversation with Vitaly Makhlin, the academic resistance to Rosenstock-Huessy has been extreme. So extreme that I sometimes wonder whether I am pursuing a will-o'-the-wisp. Might I have hypnotized myself with this image of the Cross of Reality? Might the small circles pursuing Rosenstock-Huessy's work be wasting their time? Might such people as W. H. Auden, Reinhold Niebuhr, Harvey Cox, Harold Berman, Martin Marty, Marshall Meyer, Page Smith, and Sabine Bonhoeffer have been as deluded as I?

No. I think we're on to something.

And I think the time might at last be ripe, in this first decade of the third millennium, for the project that Eugen Rosenstock and Franz Rosenzweig launched in 1916. The current attacks on supernaturalist religion—by Harris, Dennett, Dawkins, and Hitchens—may help prepare the public, both within and beyond the church, for genuinely new thinking about spirit, transcendence, and God.

Then the time may be ripe in another way. Rosenstock-Huessy's social philosophy has an imperative—and that imperative is peace. Threatened as we are now with the prospect of an unending "war on terror" (a misnomer, if there ever was one), it is clear that the social sciences should give a new priority to establishing peace among the disparate peoples in today's planetary society.

I will conclude with a statement drawn from the last paragraphs of *Between East and West*:

At the Center of the Universe

Let me close with some final thoughts on the future discipline proposed by Bakhtin and Rosenstock-Huessy. It would focus neither on God nor on the natural world, but on man in society. It would tell us how society is kept healthy, and how it makes progress through the life-giving, death-overcoming powers of speech.

And this future discipline would also carry forward Solovyov's and Berdyaev's project. That project might be described as restoring to humankind a vision such as we had in the Middle Ages, when we seemed central to the universe. Indeed, throughout the period of theology's reign, from the 1100s to the 1700s, that vision had been preserved. Only for the "short" time of 300 years, during the age of natural science (with its objective and positivist language), has that vision been lost. Only during this recent time have we come to think of ourselves as quite peripheral in the grand scheme of things: a race of smart monkeys swarming over a tiny planet lost in the space of a billion galaxies. Bakhtin and Rosenstock-Huessy were working not only toward the creation of a new discipline but also toward a new vision of our place in the order of existence. While the stars swim in a sea of matter and space, we human beings swim in something infinitely richer: a sea of speech and time.

If the universe is simply matter, we might indeed be at its edge. Since the universe evidently contains speech, who knows? We might be at its center.

APPENDIX A:
THE COMPLETE CROSS OF REALITY

Language: Subjective speech
Orientation: The inner person ("inner space")
Literature: Lyric
Person & Mood: I – Subjunctive
Fields: Literature, the arts, philosophy, psychology
Religious Aspect: Personal redemption – Son
Stage in experience: Second
Social breakdown: Anarchy

Language:
 Narrative speech
Orientation: Past Time
Literature: Epic
Person & Mood:
 We – narrative
Fields: History, law
Religious Aspect:
 Creation – Father
Stage in experience:
 Third
Social breakdown:
 Decadence

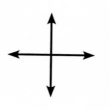

Language:
 Imperative speech
Orientation: Future time
Literature: Dramatic
Person & Mood:
 Thou – imperative
Fields: Politics, religion
Religious Aspect:
 Revelation – Spirit
Stage in experience:
 First
Social breakdown:
 Revolution

Language: Objective speech
Orientation: The outer world (outside space)
Literature: Prosaic
Person & Mood: He, she, they, it – indicative
Fields: Natural science, mathematics, economics
Religious Aspect: The world's redemption
Stage in experience: Fourth
Social Breakdown: War

Appendix B:
A Letter from Volgograd

Volgograd, December 18, 1993

Dear Mr. Clinton C. Gardner,

Recently I have visited Moscow and made the acquaintance of Mr. Vitaly Makhlin. He gave me your address and I decided to write a letter. After our telephone conversation in July, 1993 I was waiting for a letter from you, but unfortunately the post is late.

After our telephone conversation I learned much that was new to me about Professor Eugen Rosenstock-Huessy. My provincial isolation begins to relax and I know now that many people in my country show interest for the speech thinking.

In November, 1993 a scientific conference "Philosophical Tradition, Its Cultural and Existential Dimensions" took place. It was organized by The Russian University for the Humanities in Moscow. I delivered a lecture "The Overcoming of Metaphysics and the Temporal Thinking of Eugen Rosenstock-Huessy." The lecture has received an enthusiastic welcome. As far as I know it was the first detailed presentation of Rosenstock-Huessy's conception in Russia. It seems to me that the seeds must sprout. At the same time I have read your remarkable book "Between East and West." It impressed me deeply.

I decided to write this letter in order to continue our scientific contacts. Your telephone call was a fortune and a real shock for me. After the decades of the Soviet epoch the foreign countries became for us something unreal.

Thanks to your book and to the conversation with Mr. Vitaly Makhlin I know something about you and now I must say some words about myself. I am a professional philosopher and professor at the Volgograd State University. I am the head of the department of culture and art.

My former interests were connected with the history of the Russian philosophy and with the ideas of existentialism. Now I became the ardent adherent of Rosenstock-Huessy's ideas and I cannot live and think as if nothing has happened. It is interesting that the significance of Rosenstock-Huessy's ideas came to light thanks to the conceptions of the Russian religious philosophy (I mean, of course, my own way of thinking).

Mr. Vitaly Makhlin invited me to take part in the translation of Rosenstock-Huessy's work "Out of Revolution." May I ask you to send me this book in order that the translation will speed up?

I am afraid of abusing your generosity, but I would be very thankful for every material concerning Rosenstock-Huessy's life and thought. I am also eager to correspond with everybody who devoted himself to the development of Rosenstock-Huessy's philosophical heritage. Would you mind helping me?

> With kindest regards, Yours,
> Sasha Pigalev

Appendix C:
An E-Mail from Siberia

December 09, 2001

Dear Mr. Gardner,

We are writing you from Tomsk, Russia. In our city the Center of Social Development "Imya" was founded (this month), which was based on E. Rosenstock-Huessy's idea of metanomics ("Imya" means "Name" from Russian). This Center gets together different specialists of Tomsk State University and other institution of our city: psychologists, psychotherapists, philosophers, physicians etc.

The aim of the center's activity is to create and improve the conditions of people joint living. The Center implements different projects in spheres of social therapy, education and consulting.

We edit Almanac of metanomical experience "Imya", which is supposed to include the short (but important) works by ERH, related scholars and texts by contributors of the Center. The first issue of the almanac (from October, 6, 2001) contents "You and Me" and "I Am an Impure Thinker" (translated by I.A. Pigalev).

We are ready to collaborate with you in translating and popularization works by ERH, also in devising his ideas in social practice (first of all to devise the method of metanomics in application to psychotherapy, psychology, social work and education).

At the 1st – 2nd of November 2001, the conference "Existential experience and education" was given by the Center. The theme of metanomics was nearly the main on it.

We hope to meet with you for dialogue on authentic language.

Yours sincerely,
Lukyanov, Oleg,
Center of Social Development "Imya"

APPENDIX D:
CONTINUING ON THE WEB

Following are six ways you can learn more about this book's themes or participate in discussions of them:

1. *Beyond Belief*'s linked websites, www.beyondbeliefgardner.com and www.clintgardner.net, contain many pictures that illustrate events and people described here (see partial listing on page 215).

2. Comments or questions are always welcome at: clinton.c.gardner@valley.net.

3. To join a discussion group about this book and related issues, send an e-mail to: beyondbeliefgardner-subscribe@yahoogroups.com.

   Once you're subscribed, send messages to: beyondbeliefgardner@yahoogroups.com.

   In that group, we expect to start a discussion of Rosenstock-Huessy and Rosenzweig, one in which we can take up Mark Lilla's dismissal of Rosenstock-Huessy as Rosenzweig's "confused young friend." Then we can also engage Lilla via his recent book, *The Stillborn God: Religion, Politics, and the Modern West*, since he makes questionable judgments about Rosenzweig in that acclaimed work.
   Further, our group can take advantage of the fact that Dartmouth will have held a July 2008 conference on the theme "Eugen Rosenstock-Huessy/Franz Rosenzweig: The Dimensions of a Relationship." One of the instigators of that event was Dartmouth professor Susannah Heschel, daughter of Rabbi Abraham Joshua Heschel, whom I quoted at the

beginning of Chapter 2. Among the scheduled speakers at the conference are Wayne Cristaudo, author of a forthcoming work on Rosenstock-Huessy and Rosenzweig; Michael Gormann-Thelen, former head of the Rosenstock-Huessy Society in Germany; and Dartmouth professors Michael Ermarth and Donald Pease.

Finally, our group can expand the Rosenstock-Huessy Web discussion by linking to the new and comprehensive Web article on his work. Written by Wayne Cristaudo, it is at:
http://plato.stanford.edu/entries/rosenstock-huessy.

There one can read about the over 1,000 letters that Margrit Rosenstock received from Franz Rosenzweig while he was writing *The Star of Redemption*. Those letters (in German) are now posted at www.ka-talog.de/eledition.htm.

4. To join a general discussion of Rosenstock-Huessy's work, you can subscribe to a chat list by sending an e-mail to:
erhlist-subscribe-request@bigblue.millikin.edu.
(do not add a subject or any message text.)

Once you're subscribed, send messages to:
erhlist@bigblue.millikin.edu.

5. Some of US-USSR Bridges for Peace history is available at:
www.valley.net/~transnat/transnat.

6. To learn more about the similar organization, Building Bridges: Middle East-US, also founded at the Norwich Congregational Church, go to:
www.buildingbridgesmeus.org.

LIST OF WEBSITE PICTURES

This is a partial listing of pictures on the Web that illustrate people and events described in this book.

Access via: www.beyondbeliefgardner.com.

1. p. 24:   Elie Wiesel and Clint Gardner, November 2002.

2. p. 38:   Clint Gardner's Bible, May 30, 1941.

3. p. 37:   Clint Gardner army photograph, December 1942.

4. p. 38:   Clint Gardner's helmet, June 6, 1944.

5. p. 28:   Eugen Rosenstock-Huessy, late 1940s.

6. p. 135: Yuri Zamoshkin visiting the Norwich, Vermont home of Mary and Peter Teachout, April, 1983.

7. p. 139: Andrei Sakharov's autograph, February 16, 1987.

8. p. 144: The Cross of Reality in Russia, September 1991.

9. p. 149: Refounding the Solovyov Society, September 1991.

10. p. 154: Russian edition of Clint Gardner's book, *Between East and West: Rediscovering the Gifts of the Russian Spirit*, January 1993.

11. p. 156: Ambassador Jack Matlock, Father Benjamin, and Yuri Karyakin, July 1992 at Dartmouth College.

Biographical Notes

All the following notes are from the Internet's Wikipedia, where they are accompanied by in-depth articles. For some of the names, pronunciations have been added in brackets, with the accented syllable shown in italics. Particularly helpful websites are also in brackets. More substantive biographical notes are at this book's web site: www.beyondbeliefgardner.com.

BAKHTIN, MIKHAIL MIKHAILOVICH (November 17, 1895 – March 7, 1975) was a Russian philosopher, literary critic, semiotician and scholar who wrote influential works of literary and rhetorical theory and criticism. . . . Although Bakhtin's career was fraught with difficulties and complications, impeding the publication of many of his manuscripts until after his death, Bakhtin is considered to be a significant thinker of the twentieth century. . . . In the late 1980s, Bakhtin's work experienced a surge of popularity in the West, and he continues today to be regarded as one of the most important theorists of literature and culture.

BERDYAEV, NIKOLAI ALEXANDROVICH [berd*yi*eff] (March 18, 1874 – March 24, 1948) was a Russian religious and political philosopher. Berdyaev decided on an intellectual career and entered the Kiev University in 1894. This was a time of revolutionary fervor among the students and the intelligentsia. Berdyaev became a Marxist and in 1898 was arrested in a student demonstration and expelled from the University. . . . Berdyaev was a believer in orthodox Christianity, but was often critical of the institutional church.
    [Berdyaev websites are at www.berdyaev.com and www.chebucto.ns.ca/Philosophy/Sui-Generis/Berdyaev.]

BUBER, MARTIN (8 February 1878 – 13 June 1965) was an Austrian-Israeli-Jewish philosopher. . . and educator, whose work centered on theistic ideals of religious consciousness, interpersonal relations, and community.
[http://plato.stanford.edu/entries/buber.]

FEUERBACH, LUDWIG ANDREAS VON (July 28, 1804 – September 13, 1872) was a German philosopher and anthropologist. . . . Feuerbach. . . enrolled in the University of Berlin, in order to study under Hegel himself. After two years' discipleship, the Hegelian influence began to slacken. . . . [The aim of his] most important work, *Das Wesen des Christentums* (1841), which was translated into English (*The Essence of Christianity*), by George Eliot, 1853, . . . may be described shortly as an effort to humanize theology.

HAMANN, JOHANN GEORG [*hah*mahn] (August 27, 1730, Königsberg – June 21, 1788, Münster) was an important philosopher of the German (Counter-)Enlightenment and a main proponent of the Sturm und Drang movement. He was Pietist Lutheran, and a friend (while being an intellectual opponent) of the philosopher Immanuel Kant. . . . His distrust of reason and the Enlightenment led him to conclude that faith in God was the only solution to the vexing problems of philosophy.

KHOMYAKOV, ALEKSEY STEPANOVICH [kome*yah*kov] (May 1, 1804 – September 23/25, 1860) was a Russian religious [writer and] poet who co-founded the Slavophile movement along with Ivan Kireevsky, and became one of its most distinguished theoreticians. . . . His writings, printed posthumously by his friends and disciples, exerted profound influence on the Russian Orthodox Church and Russian lay philosophers, such as Fyodor Dostoyevsky, Konstantin Pobedonostsev, and Vladimir Solovyov. . . . Khomyakov's own ideals revolved around the term *sobornost*, being the Slavonic equivalent of catholicity found in the Nicene Creed and loosely translated as "togetherness"or "symphony."
[A fine Berdyaev article on Khomyakov is at www.berdyaev.com.]

KIREEVSKY, IVAN VASILIEVICH [kiriyevskee] (3 April 1806 – 23 June 1856) was a Russian literary critic and philosopher who, together with Aleksey Khomyakov, co-founded the Slavophile movement. . . . He was particularly impressed by the teachings of Schelling, whose representation of the world as a living organism was in tune with Kireevsky's own intense dislike of European rationalism and fragmentedness. . . . After having been refused by his cousin, Kireevsky set out for Europe, where he attended the lectures of Schelling, Schleiermacher, Hegel, and Michelet. During his travels, he perceived the rotten foundations of Western society, based on individualism, which he would later contrast with the integrality (*sobornost*) of Russian society.

ROSENSTOCK-HUESSY, EUGEN [oygen rosenstock hewsee] (b. July 6, 1888, d. February 24, 1973), was a social philosopher who taught at Dartmouth College from 1935 to 1957. Rosenstock-Huessy may be best known as the close friend and correspondent of Franz Rosenzweig. Their exchange of letters is considered by social scholars to be indispensable in the study of the modern encounter of Jews with Christianity. He developed "metanomics," a new approach to characterizing and understanding the social sciences, based on language and on the spoken word, which used grammar as a method to analyze issues in the social sciences.

[www.valley.net/~transnat/erhbio.html.]

ROSENZWEIG, FRANZ (December 25, 1886 – December 10, 1929) was an influential Jewish theologian and philosopher. Rosenzweig's major work is *The Star of Redemption*, in which he expounds his "new philosophy," a description of the relationships among God, humanity, and world as they are connected by creation, revelation, and redemption. In this work he is critical of all Western philosophy that seeks to efface the fear of death and replace actual human existence with an ideal. Hegel's Idealist philosophy is the primary target of such attacks.

SCHELLING, FRIEDRICH WILHELM JOSEPH (January 27, 1775 – August 20, 1854), later VON SCHELLING, was a German philosopher. Standard histories of philosophy make him the mid-point in the development of German Idealism, situating him between Fichte, his mentor prior to 1800, and Hegel, his former university roommate and erstwhile friend.

SCHLEGEL, KARL WILHELM FRIEDRICH (later: VON) (March 10, 1772 – January 12, 1829) was a German poet, critic and scholar. He was the younger brother of August Wilhelm Schlegel. Schlegel was born at Hanover. He studied law at Göttingen and Leipzig, but ultimately devoted himself entirely to literary studies. He published in 1797 *Die Griechen und Römer* (The Greeks and Romans), which was followed by *Geschichte der Poesie der Griechen und Römer* (The History of the Poetry of the Greeks and Romans) (1798).

VLADIMIR SERGEYEVICH SOLOVYOV [so*law*veeoff] (1853 – 1900) was a Russian philosopher, poet, pamphleteer, literary critic, who played a significant role in the development of Russian philosophy and poetry at the end of the 19th century. It is widely held that Solovyov was Dostoevsky's inspiration for the character Alyosha Karamazov from *The Brothers Karamazov*. Solovyov's influence can also be seen in the writings of the Symbolist and Neo-Idealist of the later Russian Soviet era. . . . He influenced the religious philosophy of Nikolai Berdyaev, Sergey Bulgakov, Pavel Florensky, Nikolai Lossky, Semen L. Frank, the ideas of Rudolf Steiner and also the poetry and theory of Russian symbolism.

[www.valley.net/~transnat/solsoc.html.]

Suggestions for
Further Reading

In the age of Google it makes no sense to burden you here with long lists of books. In five minutes on the Web you can learn all you might want to know about the most important works of Rosenstock-Huessy and Rosenzweig, of Berdyaev and Solovyov, or of Bakhtin. For Rosenstock-Huessy, I recommend that you start with *The Christian Future* (Harper, 1966; available from Argo Books) or *I Am an Impure Thinker* (Argo Books, 1970). For Rosenzweig, you might begin with Nahum Glatzer's *Franz Rosenzweig: His Life and Thought* (Hackett Publishing Co., 2000).

To delve more deeply into Rosenstock-Huessy's work, Argo Books has now made *all* of his books, articles, and recorded lectures available on a single reasonably-priced and searchable DVD. Many of his Dartmouth lectures in the 1950s are on that DVD, all faithfully recorded by students Russell Keep, Leon Martel, and a few others. That DVD (and the Rosenstock-Huessy books listed below in the bibliography) can be ordered from Argo Books at 88 Old Pump Rd., Essex, VT 05452-2742; tel. (802) 899-5158; or via Argo's web site at www.argobooks.org.

A special DVD resource for those interested in Camp William James and personal recollections of Rosenstock-Huessy will likely become available by the end of 2008. In April 2008 filmmaker John O'Brien, with David Briggs as interviewer, recorded five hours of such recollections, as elicited from Frank Davidson and me.

SELECTED
BIBLIOGRAPHY

Bakhtin, Mikhail. *Problems of Dostoevsky's Poetics.* Caryl Emerson, ed. & trans. Minneapolis: University of Minnesota Press, 1984.

Berdyaev, Nikolai. *The Destiny of Man.* London: Geoffrey Bles, 1955.

Berdyaev, Nikolai. *The Origin of Russian Communism.* R. M. French, trans. Ann Arbor, MI: University of Michigan Press, 1960.

Berlin, Isaiah. *The Magus of the North: J. G. Hamann and the Origins of Modern Irrationalism.* New York: Farrar, Straus and Giroux, 1993.

Bonhoeffer, Dietrich. *Letters and Papers from Prison.* Eberhard Bethge, ed. & trans. New York: Simon and Schuster, 1997.

Borg, Marcus. *The Heart of Christianity: Rediscovering a Life of Faith.* San Francisco: HarperSanFrancisco, 2003.

Buber, Martin. *I and Thou.* New York: Charles Scribner's Sons, 1958.

Cox, Harvey. *The Secular City.* New York: Macmillan, 1965.

Emerson, Caryl. *The First Hundred Years of Mikhail Bakhtin.* Princeton, NJ: Princeton University Press, 1997.

Fox, Matthew. *Original Blessing.* Santa Fe, NM: Bear & Co., 1983.

Friedman, Maurice. *Martin Buber: The Life of Dialogue.* New York: Harper & Brothers, 1960.

Gardner, Clinton C. *D-Day and Beyond: A Memoir of War, Russia, and Discovery.* Philadelphia: X-Libris, 2004.

Gardner, Clinton C. *Letters to the Third Millennium: An Experiment in East-West Communication.* Norwich, VT: Argo Books, 1981.

Gardner, Clinton C. *Mezhdu Vostokom i Zapadom: Vozrozhdenie darov russkoi dushi.* Moscow: Nauka, 1993. (Russian translation of *Between East and West: Rediscovering the Gifts of the Russian Spirit.*)

Glatzer, Nahum N., ed. *Franz Rosenzweig: His Life and Thought.* Indianapolis, IN: Hackett Publishing Co., 2000.

Holquist, Michael and Katerina Clark. *Mikhail Bakhtin.* Cambridge, MA: Harvard University Press, 1984.

Kline, George L. *Religious and Anti-Religious Thought in Russia (The Weil Lectures).* Chicago: University of Chicago Press, 1968.

Morgan, George. *Speech and Society: The Christian Social Philosophy of Eugen Rosenstock-Huessy.* Gainesville, FL: University of Florida Press, 1987.

Pinker, Steven. *The Language Instinct: How the Mind Creates Language.* New York: William Morrow, 1994.

Preiss, Jack J. *Camp William James.* Norwich, VT: Argo Books, 1978.

Robinson, John A. T. *Exploration into God.* Palo Alto, CA: Stanford University Press, 1967.

Robinson, John A. T. *Honest to God.* Philadelphia: The Westminster Press, 1963.

Rosenstock-Huessy, Eugen. *The Christian Future: Or the Modern Mind Outrun.* New York: Harper, 1966.

Rosenstock-Huessy, Eugen. *Collected Works on DVD.* Essex, VT: Argo Books, 2005.

Rosenstock-Huessy, Eugen. *I Am an Impure Thinker.* Norwich, VT: Argo Books, 1970.

Rosenstock-Huessy, Eugen, ed. *Judaism Despite Christianity.* Tuscaloosa, AL: University of Alabama Press, 1969.

Rosenstock-Huessy, Eugen. *Life Lines: Quotations from the Work of Eugen Rosenstock-Huessy.* Clinton C. Gardner, ed. Norwich, VT: Argo Books, 1988.

Rosenstock-Huessy, Eugen. *The Multiformity of Man*. Norwich, VT: Argo Books, 1973.

Rosenstock-Huessy, Eugen. *Out of Revolution: Autobiography of Western Man*. Providence, RI: Berg, 1993.

Rosenstock-Huessy, Eugen. *Speech and Reality*. Norwich, VT: Argo Books, 1970.

Rosenzweig, Franz. *The Star of Redemption*. William W. Hallo, trans. New York: Holt, Rinehart and Winston, 1970.

Scanlan, James P. *Dostoevsky the Thinker*. Ithaca, NY: Cornell University Press, 2002.

Soloviev, Vladimir. *Politics, Law, and Morality: Essays by V.S. Soloviev.* Vladimir Wozniuk, ed. & trans. New Haven, CT: Yale University Press, 2000.

Solovyov, Vladimir. *Lectures on Divine Humanity*. Boris Jakim, ed., Peter Zouboff, trans. Hudson, NY: Lindisfarne Press, 1995.

Spong, John Shelby. *Why Christianity Must Change or Die: A Bishop Speaks to Believers in Exile*. San Francisco: HarperSanFrancisco, 1998.

Stahmer, Harold. *"Speak That I May See Thee!": The Religious Significance of Language*. New York: Macmillan, 1968.

Sutton, Jonathan. *The Religious Philosophy of Vladimir Solovyov: Toward a Reassessment*. New York: St. Martin's Press, 1988.

Taylor, Barbara Brown. *The Luminous Web: Essays on Science and Religion*. Cambridge, MA: Cowley Publications, 2000.

Walicki, Andrzej. *A History of Russian Thought: From the Enlightenment to Marxism*. Oxford: Oxford University Press, 1980.

Williams, Rowan. *Sergii Bulgakov: Towards a Russian Political Theology*. London: T & T Clark, 2000.

Notes

On this book's website (www.beyondbeliefgardner.com) there will be a more comprehensive bibliography as well as extended versions of many of the notes that follow.

Opening Epigraphs

9 **on our lips:** Eugen Rosenstock-Huessy, *The Christian Future* (New York: Charles Scribner's Sons, 1946; New York: Harper & Row, 1966), p. 94.

9 **No religion:** Eugen Rosenstock-Huessy, *Speech and Reality* (Norwich, VT: Argo Books, 1970), p. 181.

9 **it is a miracle:** Eugen Rosenstock-Huessy, *Der Atem des Geistes* (Frankfurt: Verlag der Frankfurter Hefte, 1951), p. 37.

9 **of the spirit:** Eugen Rosenstock-Huessy, *Practical Knowledge of the Soul* (Norwich, VT: Argo Books, 1988), p. 63.

9 **society, or concept:** Nikolai Berdyaev, *Spirit and Reality*, George Reavey, trans. (London: Bles, 1939), p. 187.

9 **it is realized:** *Collected Works of Vladimir Solovyov* [in Russian], (Brussels: Izdatel'stvo "Zhizn's Bogom," Foyer Oriental Chrétien, 1966), Vol. VI, p. 335.

Prologue

17 **any given situation:** Dietrich Bonhoeffer, *Letters and Papers from Prison*, Eberhard Bethge, ed. (New York: Simon & Schuster, 1997), p. 381.

17 **Letters and Papers from Prison:** Ibid.

17 **"come of age":** Ibid., p. 326.

17 **"religionless Christianity":** Ibid., p. 282.

17 **"in a secular way":** Ibid., p. 280.

17 **"have our being":** Acts 17:28. King James Version.

17 **"in the church":** Marcus Borg, *The Heart of Christianity* (San Francisco: HarperSanFrancisco, 2003), p. 2.

17   **"supernatural theism":** Ibid., pp. 8, 65.

17   **than theistic terms:** Ibid., p. 65.

18   **the natural sciences:** Thomas Kuhn, *The Structure of Scientific Revolutions* (Chicago: University of Chicago Press, 1962),

18   **all-powerful Supreme Being:** Borg, *The Heart of Christianity*, p. 26.

18   **the Christian life:** Ibid., pp. 28-41.

18   **existence for others:** Bonhoeffer, *Letters and Papers from Prison*, p. 381.

18   **"Protestant denominations":** Borg, *The Heart of Christianity*, p. 6.

19   **secular theology:** John A. T. Robinson, *Honest to God* (Philadelphia: Westminster, 1963).

19   **"God must go":** It was in a newspaper article about his book, in March 1963, that Robinson said this. See David L. Edwards, ed., *The Honest to God Debate* (Philadelphia: The Westminster Press, 1963), p. 7.

19   **his own cross:** Rosenstock-Huessy points out that Augustine expressed this idea that the Cross itself has to be crucified. Eugen Rosenstock-Huessy, *Out of Revolution* (New York: William Morrow, 1938; Norwich, VT: Argo Books, 1969), p. 763.

20   **"transformational Christianity":** Borg, *The Heart of Christianity*, pp. 103-148.

20   **Spong has written:** John Shelby Spong, *Why Christianity Must Change or Die* (San Francisco: HarperSanFrancisco), 1998.

20   **"it's like lightning":** Tillich made this remark to a student, Phillip Chamberlin, in 1957, on a beach at Santa Barbara, California.

20   **astonishing coincidences:** Mitch Albom, *Tuesdays with Morrie* (New York: Doubleday, 1997).

21   **Morrie's favorite poet:** Ibid., p. 91.

21   **favorite thinker:** Edward Mendelson, *Later Auden* (New York: Farrar, Straus, & Giroux), p. 260.

21   **list for Mitch:** Albom, *Tuesdays with Morrie*, p. 3.

21   **"other or die":** Ibid, p. 91.

21   **"stronger than death":** Eugen Rosenstock-Huessy, *Soziologie*, Bd. II, *Die Vollzahl der Zeiten* (Stuttgart: Kohlhammer, 1958), p. 759.

22   **Sam Harris:** Sam Harris, *The End of Faith: Religion, Terror, and the Future of Reason* (New York: Norton, 2004).

22 **Richard Dawkins:** Richard Dawkins, *The God Delusion* (Boston, MA: Houghton Mifflin, 2006).

22 **Daniel Dennett:** Daniel C. Dennett, *Breaking the Spell: Religion as a Natural Phenomenon* (New York: Penguin Books, 2006).

22 **Christopher Hitchens:** Christopher Hitchens, *God Is Not Great: How Religion Poisons Everything* (New York: Twelve-Hachette Book Group USA, 2007).

22 **put in command:** I was the Executive Officer of the military government team put in charge of the camp. On May 2, 1945 Captain Peter Ball, commander of our team delegated me to be the acting commander of Buchenwald since he had to be away from the camp more than half the time. This was because he made almost daily trips to Nordhausen and Ohrdruf, two more concentration camps put under our command.

23 **recollection of Buchenwald:** Elie Wiesel, *Night* (New York: Hill & Wang, 1960).

CHAPTER 1: LIVING IN THE CROSS OF REALITY

27 **the Cross of Reality:** Rosenstock-Huessy, *The Christian Future*, pp. 168-169.

28 **Berdyaev's book:** Nikolai Berdyaev, *The Origin of Russian Communism* (London: Geoffrey Bles, 1937; Ann Arbor, MI: University of Michigan Press, 1960).

29 **we should read:** Vladimir Solovyov, *Lectures on Divine Humanity* (Hudson, NY: Lindisfarne Press, 1995).

30 **metanomics:** Rosenstock-Huessy, *Out of Revolution*, p. 757.

31 **"have its way":** William James, "The Moral Equivalent of War" in *The Writings of William James*, John J. McDermott, ed. (New York: Random House, 1967).

31 **wildly different works:** Vladimir Solovyov, *The Spiritual Foundations of Life*, now available as *God, Man and the Church* (Greenwood, SC: The Attic Press, 1974).

32 **at every moment:** Rosenstock-Huessy, *Out of Revolution*, p. 727.

33 **wind and star:** G. K. Chesterton, *The Ballad of the White Horse* (London: Methuen & Co., 1911).

35 **the only text:** Eugen Rosenstock-Huessy, *The Multiformity of Man* (Norwich, VT: Argo Books, 1973).

35   **Stalin and Hitler:** Ibid., p. iv.

35   **"a wrong society":** Rosenstock-Huessy, *Out of Revolution*, p. 744.

CHAPTER 2: RECONCILING SCIENCE AND RELIGION

39   **of natural science:** Rosenstock-Huessy, *The Christian Future*, p. 169.

39   **"to everything else":** Riesman's words are quoted by Nardi Reeder Campion in her *Over the Hill, You Pick Up Speed* (Hanover, NH: University Press of New England, 2006), p. 115.

40   **"and will be":** Abraham Joshua Heschel, *Man Is Not Alone* (New York: Farrar, Straus, & Giroux, 1951), p. 102.

40   **The Unity of Knowledge:** Edward O. Wilson, *Consilience: The Unity of Knowledge* (New York: Knopf, 1998).

40   **"of natural laws":** Ibid., pp. 4-5.

40   **"scientific empiricism":** Ibid., p. 290.

40   **"the laws of physics":** Ibid., p. 291.

40   **"are the same":** Ibid., pp. 292-293.

41   **"I have been changed":** Eugen Rosenstock-Huessy, *I Am an Impure Thinker* (Norwich, VT: Argo Books, 1970), p. viii.

41   **"both men believed. . . . of German Theologians":** Sabine Leibholz, "Eugen Rosenstock-Huessy and Dietrich Bonhoeffer—Two Witnesses to the Change in Our Time," *Universitas* 8, no. 3 (1966).

42   **"Second World War":** George F. Kennan, *Memoirs: 1925–1950* (New York: Little, Brown & Co., 1967), p. 121.

42   **the third millennium:** Cox reported this to me in a conversation in July 1964.

43   **appeal to transcendence:** Martin Marty review of *The Christian Future* in *The Christian Century*, Jan. 4, 1967.

43   **"of the genius":** Martin Marty in an e-mail letter to Norman Fiering, President of the Eugen Rosenstock-Huessy Fund, Dec. 6, 2006.

44   **"casual or boring":** Rosenstock-Huessy, Eugen, *A Classic and a Founder*, 1937, Frances Huessy, annot. (Essex, VT: Argo Books, forthcoming), p. 62. Originally in: *Rosenstock-Huessy Papers, Vol. 1*, Clinton C. Gardner, ed. (Norwich, VT: Argo Books, 1981).

44   **our alloted task:** Wayne Cristaudo, in a 2007 e-mail to Donald Williamson, subsequently shared among members of the Rosenstock-Huessy Internet discussion group on May 23, 2007.

44 **"my tribe increase":** E-mail from Martin Marty to Clinton Gardner, April 15, 2008.

44 **doctoral thesis:** Bruce O. Boston, "I Respond Although I Will Be Changed": The Life and Historical Thought of Eugen Rosenstock-Huessy" (Ph.D. dissertation, Princeton Theological Seminary, 1973).

45 **"united to a spirit":** Anton C. Pegis, ed., *The Wisdom of Catholicism* (New York: Random House, 1949), p. 624.

47 **think or command:** Eugen Rosenstock-Huessy, "Liturgical Thinking," published in the Benedictine journal *Orate Fratres*, Jan. 1950. Also see Rosenstock-Huessy's discussion of this formulation in Eugen Rosenstock-Huessy, ed. *Judaism Despite Christianity* (University, AL: University of Alabama Press), pp. 69-70.

49 **book like Carl Jung's:** Carl Jung, *Memories, Dreams, Reflections*, Aniela Jaffe, ed. (New York: Random House, 1961).

49 **"inspiriting" of matter:** Pierre Teilhard de Chardin, *The Phenomenon of Man* (New York: Harper & Brothers, 1959).

50 **as a "noosphere":** Ibid., pp. 180-183.

50 **"abortion upon itself":** Ibid., p. 276.

50 **"of human society":** Rosenstock-Huessy, *Speech and Reality*, p. 42.

50 **"an open future":** Rosenstock-Huessy, *The Christian Future*, p. 123.

51 **"the only supernatural":** Rosenstock-Huessy, *Der Atem des Geistes*, p. 37.

51 **"the uphill animal":** Rosenstock-Huessy, *A Classic and a Founder*, 1937, Frances Huessy, annot., p. 65.

51 **"like a whole humanity":** Berdyaev, *Spirit and Reality*, p. 187.

51 **I will be changed:** Rosenstock-Huessy, *Out of Revolution*, p. 751.

53 **no evidence for them:** Sam Harris, *The End of Faith*, p. 23. Harris states here his ongoing argument: "Every religion preaches the truth of propositions for which it has no evidence."

53 **of social research:** Rosenstock-Huessy, "The Uni-versity of Logic, Language, and Literature," in *Speech and Reality*, p. 10.

CHAPTER 3: THE SPIRIT AS SPEECH

55 **called the Spirit:** Eugen Rosenstock-Huessy, *Die Sprache des Menschengeschlechts*, Bd. I (Heidelberg: Verlag Lambert Schneider, 1963), p. 573.

55 **the Holy Spirit:** Rosenstock-Huessy, "Der Geist des Menschen ist der heilige Geist" [The spirit of man is the Holy Spirit]. Letter

to Franz Rosenzweig (Zweiströmland: 1926; reprinted Dordrecht: Martinus Nijhoff, 1984, p. 214).

55   **disappears in language:** Franz Rosenzweig, *The Star of Redemption*, William W. Hallo, trans. (New York: Holt, Rinehart & Winston, 1970), p. 199.

55   **"ages to come":** Hans Joachim Schoeps, *The Jewish-Christian Argument: A History of Theologies in Conflict*, David E. Green, trans. (London: Faber & Faber, 1963), pp. 129-130.

55   **understanding of language:** Rosenstock-Huessy, ed., *Judaism Despite Christianity*, pp. 169-170.

55   **Practical Knowledge of the Soul:** Eugen Rosenstock, *Angewandte Seelenkunde: Eine programmatische Übersetzung* (Darmstadt: Rother-Verlag, 1924). In English, Rosenstock-Huessy, *Practical Knowledge of the Soul*, Mark Huessy and Freya von Moltke, trans. (Norwich, VT: Argo Books, 1988).

56   **one-time biblical events:** Franz Rosenzweig, *The Star of Redemption*, William W. Hallo, trans. (New York: Holt, Rinehart & Winston, 1970). Book One of this work deals with creation, Book Two with revelation, and Book Three with redemption.

56   **"he first spoke":** Rosenzweig, *The Star of Redemption*, p. 110.

56   **"disappears in language":** Rosenzweig, *The Star of Redemption*, p. 199.

56   **"the main influence":** Franz Rosenzweig, *Kleinere Schriften* (Berlin: Schocken, 1937), p. 388.

56   **for example:** Rosenstock-Huessy, *Speech and Reality*, p. 22. Rosenstock-Huessy here is discussing Rosenzweig's statement on death (see note below). In *Out of Revolution*, p. 508, Rosenstock-Huessy writes: "Oswald Spengler says in one of his deepest remarks that every civilization sets out with a new experience of death." In *The Christian Future*, p. 101, Rosenstock-Huessy writes: "The Living God comes to us in the midst of living, after death has come upon us, in the form of some crucial experience."

56   **"its poisonous sting":** Rosenzweig, *The Star of Redemption*, p. 3. The translation I provide here is one that was given to me by Rosenstock-Huessy; I find it more successful than the Hallo translation.

56   **"The New Thinking":** Franz Rosenzweig, "Das neue Denken," in Nahum Glatzer, ed., *Franz Rosenzweig: His Life and Thought* (New York: Schocken Books, 1961).

56   **"all earlier philosophies":** Ibid., p. 198.

57　**eleven recent books:** Mark Lilla, "A Battle for Religion," *The New York Review of Books*, Vol. 49, No. 19, December 5, 2002.

57　**"confused young friend":** Ibid.

57　**motion of the spirit:** The expression "law of motion of the spirit" is my formulation, not one presented by Rosenstock-Huessy. However, in numerous writings, Rosenstock-Huessy emphasizes the order of speech as 1. Imperative 2. Subjective 3. Narrative 4. Objective. Since he also equates speech with spirit, his writings led me to propose this expression.

58　**secrets of language:** Rosenstock, *Practical Knowledge of the Soul*, p. 15.

59　**"Revelation is orientation":** Eugen Rosenstock-Huessy, *Ja und Nein* (Heidelberg: Lambert Schneider, 1968), p. 21.

60　**kinds of speech:** Eugen Rosenstock-Huessy, *The Origin of Speech* (Norwich, VT: Argo Books, 1981), pp. 1-2.

60　**"bury one's father":** Ibid., pp. 1-2.

60　**"a man the direction. . . . animal sounds":** Ibid., p. 1.

60　**"nourished by time":** Franz Rosenzweig, *Kleinere Schriften* (Berlin: Schocken, 1937), p. 209.

61　**"storage room for speech":** Eugen Rosenstock-Huessy, "Comparative Religion" Dartmouth Lecture–1954, Vol. 8, Lecture 21.

61　**a good example:** Garry Trudeau's *Doonesbury* is a syndicated comic strip that often deals with contemporary issues.

61　**laughing animal:** Vladimir Solovyov, "Lecture on January 14, 1875," *Collected Works of Vladimir Solovyov*, Vol. 12, p. 526.

61　**"The Survival Value of Humour":** Title of Chapter XIX, Rosenstock-Huessy, *Out of Revolution*.

62　**"simply is immature":** Ibid., p. 754.

64　**the faithful Alyosha:** The reference is to two of the brothers in Dostoevsky's *The Brothers Karamazov*.

65　**narrative speech:** While there are only three formal moods in English (imperative, subjunctive, and indicative), Rosenstock-Huessy treated the "narrative" as if it were a fourth mood, one that intended to "perpetuate reality," as he put it in his essay "The Uni-versity of Logic, Language, Literature," (See *Speech and Reality*, p. 84).

66　**weight of antiquity:** Vladimir Solovyov, "The Secret of Progress," as printed in S. L. Frank, ed., *A Solovyov Anthology* (London: SCM Press, 1950), p. 225.

67   **a new phase:** Rosenstock-Huessy, *I Am an Impure Thinker*, pp. 58-59.

68   **four ways of speaking:** Rosenstock-Huessy, *Speech and Reality*, pp. 84-97.

68   **four moods:** See preceding note on narrative mood, p. 65.

68   **"a here and there":** Rosenstock-Huessy, *Soziologie,* Bd. I, *Die Übermacht der Raüme* (Stuttgart: Kohlhammer, 1956), p. 158.

69   **of that term:** James is quoted on this by Rosenstock-Huessy in *I Am an Impure Thinker*, p. 22.

70   **of his own:** Philip Wheelwright, *Heraclitus* (New York: Atheneum, 1964, p. 19.

70   **"dwelt among us":** John 1:1, 1:14. King James Version.

70   **"because he speaks":** Rosenstock-Huessy, *Speech and Reality*, p. 181.

71   **secular translation:** Rosenstock-Huessy, *The Christian Future*, p. 165.

72   **LEST YE DIE!:** W. H. Auden, "Aubade," *The Atlantic*, July 1973.

CHAPTER 4: THE DIALOGICAL METHOD

73   **from natural science:** Rosenstock-Huessy, *Speech and Reality*, p. 10.

73   **turned to Buber's:** Martin Buber, *I and Thou* (New York: Charles Scribner's Sons, 1958).

73   **accomplished for Buber:** Maurice Friedman, *Martin Buber: The Life of Dialogue* (New York: Harper & Brothers, 1960).

73   **"third Copernican revolution":** Ibid., p. 164.

73   **"social conception of knowledge":** Ibid., p. 164.

73   **feral child:** Ibid., p. 164.

73   **generously acknowledged:** Ibid., p. 162.

74   **"I say thou":** Ibid., p. 164.

74   **"as an Ego":** Rosenstock-Huessy, *Out of Revolution*, p. 746.

74   **with his "method":** Eugen Rosenstock-Huessy, *Das Geheimnis der Universität—Wider den Verfall von Zeitsinn und Sprachkraft*, Georg Müller, ed. (Stuttgart: Kohlhammer, 1958), p. 149.

74   **"as a thou":** Rosenstock-Huessy, *Speech and Reality*, p. 106.

75   **him has done:** Martin Buber, in *Philosophical Interrogations*, Sydney and Beatrice Rome, eds. (New York: Holt, Rinehart & Winston), p. 33.

75   **recounted a story:** Marshall Meyer told this story in a talk at a conference on Rosenstock-Huessy's work held at Dartmouth College in 1988.

75 **"the Grammatical Method":** Rosenstock-Huessy, *Speech and Reality*, pp. 9-44.

75 **"of all science":** Clinton C. Gardner, Introduction to *Speech and Reality*, p. 3.

76 **the social sciences:** John Macquarrie, *Commonweal*, March 27, 1970.

77 **"away as pathology":** Hans Huessy, "Contributions to Psychiatry from the Writings of Eugen Rosenstock-Huessy" in *Eugen Rosenstock-Huessy: Studies in His Life and Thought*, M. Darrol Bryant and Hans R. Huessy, eds. (Lewiston, NY: The Edwin Mellen Press, 1986), p. 149. All other quotations from Hans Huessy are found on pp. 150-167.

79 **speech-related threats:** Rosenstock-Huessy, *Speech and Reality*, pp. 11-16.

80 **reception of speech:** Rosenstock-Huessy, *I Am an Impure Thinker*, pp. 53-64.

80 **"of the soul":** Gary Zukav, *The Seat of the Soul* (New York: Simon & Schuster, 1989).

80 **built into us:** Noam Chomsky, *Language and Mind* (New York: Harcourt Brace Jovanovich, 1972).

80 **of our thought:** Steven Pinker, *The Language Instinct: How the Mind Creates Language* (New York: William Morrow, 1994).

CHAPTER 5: THE REVOLUTIONS OF THE CHRISTIAN ERA

83 **they complete it:** Rosenstock-Huessy, *Out of Revolution*, p. 716.

83 **reform the finite:** Ibid., p. 473.

83 **with his book:** Harvey Cox, *The Secular City* (New York: Macmillan, 1965).

84 **comparison with it:** Reinhold Niebuhr statement provided to Argo Books and printed on the cover of *Out of Revolution*.

84 **"of our time":** Page Smith, Introduction to *Out of Revolution*, p. xiii.

84 **"deeply right":** Stewart Brand, ed., *The Whole Earth Catalog* (San Francisco: The Whole Earth Catalog, 1974).

84 **scientist Karl Deutsch:** Another prominent social critic who thought highly of Rosenstock-Huessy's work was the sociologist and Lutheran theologian Peter Berger.

86 **royalty of Europe:** Rosenstock-Huessy, *Out of Revolution*, pp. 537-539.

87 **call her so:** Ibid., p. 543.

88 **this great revolution:** Ibid., p. 362.

89	**between the two:** Ibid., p. 291.

90	**men and women:** Ibid., p. 75.

90	**all over again:** Ibid., p. 672.

91	**"but your chains":** Karl Marx and Friedrich Engels, "The Communist Manifesto." Currently available on the Web via Wikipedia, the actual correct quotation is "the proletarians have nothing to lose but their chains."

91	**provoking language:** Rosenstock-Huessy, *Out of Revolution*, p. 69.

92	**openness and immediacy:** Ibid., p. 468.

92	**of State and Church:** Rosenstock-Huessy, *The Christian Future*, p. 5.

93	**the great revolutions:** Crane Brinton, *The Anatomy of Revolutions* (New York: Prentice Hall, 1938). On p. 294 Brinton writes on *Out of Revolution*: "Written in what to an American seems the German cloud-cuckoo-land of beautiful and inexact ideas."

93	**"a suffering God":** Bonhoeffer, *Letters and Papers from Prison*, p. 361.

94	**"one humankind":** Harold J. Berman, "The Tri-une God of History." *The Living Pulpit*. April–June, 1999: 19. Rosenstock-Huessy, *The Christian Future*, p. 114.

94	**"is not a religion":** Rosenstock-Huessy, "Comparative Religion" Dartmouth Lecture–1954, Vol. 8, Lecture 28. Available in Rosenstock-Huessy, *Collected Works on DVD* (Essex, VT: Argo Books, 2005).

95	**"a special world":** Rosenstock-Huessy, "Universal History" Dartmouth Lecture–1954, Vol. 12, Lecture 3, Feb. 18, 1954. Available in Rosenstock-Huessy, *Collected Works on DVD*.

95	**meaning "daily renewal":** Wikipedia article on Sun Yat-sen, p. 3.

CHAPTER 6: GOD IS LIKE A WHOLE HUMANITY

96	**incarnation of God:** Berdyaev, *The Origin of Russian Communism*, p. 180.

98	**"Russian Idea":** Solovyov and others have written various interpretations of the "Russian Idea." My particular approach to this theme was to identify four important elements of Russian thought that seemed uniquely derived from Eastern Christianity (see p. 103). I should note that these four were not chosen to exemplify the four orientations on the Cross of Reality.

99	**a series of lectures:** Solovyov, *Lectures on Divine Humanity*.

99	**"Vladimir Solovyov Society":** A history of that society, which notes the society's reestablishment in 1991, is found in: Kristiane

Burchardi, Die Moskauer *"Religios-Philosophische Vladimir-Solov'ev-Gesellschaft" (1905–1918)* (Wiesbaden: Harrassowitz Verlag, 1998). A résumé is available at: www.valley.net/~transnat/burchardi.html.

100 **and our selves:** Nikolai Berdyaev, *The Fate of Man in the Modern World* (London: SCM Press; Milwaukee: Morehouse, 1935).

100 **a new discipline:** Berdyaev writes of "a new anthropology" in *The Divine and the Human*, R.M. French, trans. (London: Bles, 1949, pp. 221-224.

100 **focus on language:** A. Gratieux, A.S. *Khomiakov et le Mouvement Slavophile, Vol. I, Les Doctrines* (Paris: Les Éditions du Cerf, 1939), pp. 98-101.

100 **had written meditations:** See these meditations quoted on p. 143 for Bulgakov and p. 145 for Florensky.

101 **collected key essays:** Hans Ehrenberg and Nicolai Bubnoff, *Oestliches Christentum* (Munich: Oscar Beck, Band I, 1923, Band II, 1925.

101 **"abstract monotheism":** Nikolai Berdyaev, *Freedom and the Spirit*, Oliver Fielding Clarke, trans. (New York: Scribners, 1935), p. 139.

101 **divine humanity and Sophia:** Solovyov, *Lectures on Divine Humanity*, pp. 107-108.

102 **"a whole humanity":** Berdyaev, *Spirit and Reality*, p. 187.

102 **"gnostic idea".... "natural intermediary":** Ehrenberg, *Oestliches Christentum*, Bd. I, p. 205.

102 **"frozen" ways of thinking:** The expression "frozen" used for –isms is one I heard in Rosenstock-Huessy lectures. One of his many attacks on -isms is found in Rosenstock-Huessy, ed., *Judaism Despite Christianity*.

103 **"Trinitarian thinking":** Berdyaev emphasized the Trinity in many of his works. A typical expression is found in his *Freedom and the Spirit*, where he writes of "the life of God as a divine Trinity," p. 139.

103 **l'unité libre:** Alexei Khomyakov, *Complete Works*, Vol. 2 (Moscow, 1891), p. 18.

103 **four different approaches:** Kireevsky, "The Possibility and Necessity of New Principles in Philosophy," in *The Complete Works* [Polnoe sobranie sochinenii] (Moscow: 1911), p. 238.

103 **called "supra-rational":** This term is my own coinage, not one found in Kireevsky or Rosenstock-Huessy.

104 **"being" itself speaks:** Heidegger would not agree with my interpretation in Chapter 3 of *Logos* as word or speech. Instead, he says: "*Logos* is the steady gathering, the intrinsic togetherness of the essent, i.e. being. . . . There can be true speaking and hearing only if they are directed in advance toward being, the *Logos*." Martin Heidegger, *An Introduction to Metaphysics* (New York: Doubleday & Co., 1961), p. 106.

104 **as a game:** Wittgenstein's interpretation of language games is nicely presented at a website maintained by "Postmodern Therapies NEWS." See "Wittgenstein's Concept of a Language Game" at www.california.com/~rathbone/word.htm.

104 **"hearts of men":** Rosenstock-Huessy, *The Christian Future*, p. 92.

105 **his own interpretation:** I first heard Rosenstock-Huessy describe the tasks of the three millennia in 1947 when I took his Dartmouth course on Universal History. His written presentation of this theme is in *Soziologie II, Die Vollzahl der Zeiten* (Stuttgart: Kohlhammer, 1958), pp. 286-314.

105 **"society, or concept":** Berdyaev, *Spirit and Reality*, p. 187.

106 **"great being":** Auguste Comte described humanity as "the great being" in his four-volume *Système de Politique Positive* (1851–1854).

106 **"way be demonstrated":** *The Pocket Aquinas* (New York: Washington Square Press, 1962), p. 291.

109 **beginning of history:** Rosenstock-Huessy spoke of the Son in these terms during Dartmouth lectures in 1946–1947. In 1954 he enlarged on this theme when he wrote his *The Fruit of Lips or Why Four Gospels* (Pittsburgh, PA: The Pickwick Press, 1978), p. 125.

109 **"mystery of the Trinity":** Berdyaev, *Freedom and the Spirit*, p. 20.

110 **the "Cold War":** The newspaper columnist Walter Lippmann is credited with popularizing the term "Cold War" in a book by that name (1947) and in his columns for the *New York Herald Tribune*.

110 **containment policy:** As Wikipedia reports it, in February 1946, George Kennan sent a message from Moscow to President Harry S. Truman (the "Long Telegram"), outlining the weaknesses of the Soviet government. The message presented his thinking about what was later to be articulated as the "containment policy" toward the Soviet Union, in a 1947 *Foreign Affairs* article called "The sources of Soviet conduct." Kennan later said the US had gone too far with his containment policy, and had become confrontational.

CHAPTER 7: FROM THEISM TO PANENTHEISM

111 **undergirding all of life:** Spong, *Why Christianity Must Change or Die*, p. 226.

111 **newness and expansion:** Gregory Baum, *Man Becoming* (New York: Herder & Herder, 1970), p. 283.

111 **"breathing on one lung":** Jaroslav Pelikan, "The Great Unifier," *New York Times*, April 4, 2005.

111 **"is sadly defective":** Philip Clayton and Arthur Peacocke, eds., *In Whom We Live and Move and Have Our Being: Panentheistic Reflections on God's Presence in a Scientific World* (Grand Rapids, MI: William B. Eerdmans, 2004), p. 159.

112 **to articulate panentheism:** John A. T. Robinson, *Exploration into God*, (Palo Alto, CA: Stanford University Press, 1967), pp. 86-89.

112 **"we are seeking":** Ibid., p. 134.

112 **"society or concept":** Ibid., p. 160.

112 **"who God is?":** Spong, *Why Christianity Must Change or Die*, p. 69.

113 **into their humanity:** Baum, *Man Becoming*, p. 283.

113 **"redemptively present". . . . "about human life":** Ibid., pp. 162, 181.

113 **"speaking about God":** Ibid., p. 182.

113 **Jesus Christ:** Ibid., p. 177.

114 **"I am Son":** Gregory Baum, *Faith and Doctrine* (New York: Newman Press, 1969), p. 18.

114 **"human life everywhere":** Ibid., pp. 56-57.

114 **"God within us":** Quoted in John Macquarrie, *Twentieth Century Religious Thought* (New York: Harper & Row, 1963), pp. 173-174.

114 **"the radically new":** Gregory Baum, "Toward a New Catholic Theism," *The Ecumenist*, May-June 1970, p. 59.

114 **"and his history":** Ibid., p. 59

114 **called a "consensus":** Ibid., p. 59.

114 **"personal and social":** Ibid., p. 59.

114 **"properly speaking, supernatural":** Baum, *Man Becoming*, p. 21.

114 **"hitherto ignored truth":** Leslie Dewart, *Religion, Language and Truth* (New York: Herder & Herder, 1970), p. 41.

115 **himself in heaven:** Leslie Dewart, *The Future of Belief* (New York: Herder & Herder, 1966), pp. 145-146.

115 **category of being:** Ibid., pp. 727-728.

116 **him as companions:** Rosenstock-Huessy, *Out of Revolution*, pp. 727-728.

116 **study its laws:** Rosenstock-Huessy, *The Christian Future*, p. 108.

CHAPTER 8: A BRIEF HISTORY OF DIALOGICAL THINKING

117 **admit reason only:** Blaise Pascal, *Pascal's Pensées* (New York: E.P. Dutton & Co.: 1958), p. 74

117 **What is language?:** Ronald Gregor Smith, *J.G. Hamann: A Study in Christian Existentialism* (New York: Harper & Brothers, 1960), p. 249.

118 **"so emphatically demanded":** Martin Buber, *Between Man and Man* (New York: Macmillan, 1978), p. 147.

118 **"first to discover it":** Glatzer, *Franz Rosenzweig: His Life and Thought*, p. 203.

118 **"by Karl Marx":** Rosenstock-Huessy, *Speech and Reality*, p. 1.

118 **republish Feurbach's 1843:** Ludwig Feuerbach, *Principles of the Philosophy of the Future* (New York: Bobbs-Merrill, 1966).

118 **between I and Thou:** Ibid., p. 109.

118 **a true word?:** Ludwig Feuerbach, *The Essence of Christianity* (New York: Harper, 1960), p. 78.

119 **"into human misery":** Ibid., p. 87.

119 **is usually associated:** The Jesuit theologian Henri de Lubac describes how Feuerbach influenced the Russian revolutionary Mikhail Bakunin (1814–1876), who believed that "Communism is only Feuerbach's humanism carried into the social field." Henri de Lubac, *The Drama of Atheist Humanism* (New York: World Publishing Co., Meridian Book, 1963), pp. 12, 14.

119 **Isaiah Berlin's:** Isaiah Berlin, *The Magus of the North: J.G. Hamann and the Origins of Modern Irrationalism* (New York: Farrar, Straus, & Giroux, 1993).

119 **Friedrich von Schlegel:** Ibid. As Berlin puts it on p. 1: "[Hamann's] influence, direct and indirect, upon the romantic revolt against universalism and scientific method in any guise was considerable and perhaps crucial." On p. 92: "[Hamann] is a true forerunner of Schelling, of Nietzsche and of the existentialists, and a dangerous ally of any supporter of organized religion."

119   **hear Schelling's lectures:** Kireevsky visited Berlin in 1830, where he met Hegel and attended Schelling's lectures. Abbot Gleason, *European and Muscovite: Ivan Kireevsky and the Origins of Slavophilism* (Cambridge, MA: Harvard University Press, 1972), pp. 83-87.

120   **"the 20ᵗʰ century":** Harold Stahmer, *"Speak That I May See Thee!": The Religious Significance of Language* (New York: Macmillan, 1968), p. 106.

120   **leaps, and hints:** Berlin, *The Magus of the North: J.G. Hamann and the Origins of Modern Irrationalism*, pp. 18-19.

120   **of his time:** Ibid., p. 1.

120   **his greatest creations:** Ibid., p. 2.

120   **come into being:** Ibid., p. 105.

120   **writings on language:** For references to Schelling, Goethe, and Schlegel, see Stahmer, *"Speak That I May See Thee!": The Religious Significance of Language*, pp. 106-144.

120   **"mankind itself":** Rosenstock-Huessy, *Out of Revolution*, pp. 5 and 611.

120   **"in one process":** Rosenstock-Huessy, *Speech and Reality*, p. 68.

121   **and living action:** Friedrich Schlegel, *The Philosophy of Life and Philosophy of Language*, trans. A. J. W. Morrison (London: Henry Bohn, 1847), pp. 385-387.

121   **"New Principles in Philosophy":** Ivan Kireevsky, "The Possibility and Necessity of New Principles in Philosophy," in *The Complete Works of Kireevsky*, p. 238.

121   **(the unity of consciousness):** Abbott Gleason, *European and Muscovite: Ivan Kireevsky and the Origins of Slavophilism*, p. 285.

122   **"intuitive reason". . . . meaningless to him:** *The New York Review of Books*, Oct. 21, 1993, Nov. 18, 1993.

122   **"by Karl Marx":** Rosenstock-Huessy, *Speech and Reality*, p. 1.

Transition to Part II

125   **would be "argonautic":** Rosenstock-Huessy, *Soziologie, Bd. II, Die Vollzahl der Zeiten*, pp. 698-700.

126   **"to professorial dogmas":** Page Smith, *Killing the Spirit: Higher Education in America* (New York: Viking, 1990), p. 5.

126   **"antagonistic distemporaries":** Rosenstock-Huessy, *Speech and Reality*, p. 44.

126 **"values (gods)":** Rosenstock-Huessy, *Speech and Reality*, p. 44.

127 **New Middle Ages?:** Rosenstock-Huessy, *The Christian Future*, p. 142.

CHAPTER 9: BRIDGES FOR PEACE

128 **and all countries:** Eugen Rosenstock-Huessy, *Planetary Service* (Norwich, VT: Argo Books, 1978), p. 13.

131 **ideological divide:** Clinton C. Gardner, *Letters to the Third Millennium: An Experiment in East-West Communication* (Norwich, VT: Argo Books, 1981).

131 **the Russian Spirit:** Clinton C. Gardner, *Between East and West: Rediscovering the Gifts of the Russian Spirit* (Norwich, VT: Norwich Center Books, 1982).

133 **best-known book:** Mikhail Bakhtin, *Problems of Dostoevsky's Poetics*, Caryl Emerson, ed. and trans. (Minneapolis, MN: University of Minnesota Press, 1984).

133 **"polyphonic novels":** On page 34 of his *Problems of Dostoevsky's Poetics*, Bakhtin writes: "In our opinion Dostoevsky alone can be considered the creator of genuine polyphony." Earlier, on p. 6, he wrote: *"A plurality of independent and unmerged voices and consciousnesses, a genuine polyphony of fully valid voices is in fact the chief characteristic of Dostoevsky's novels."* [Italics in original.]

133 **Bethge's biography:** Eberhard Bethge, *Dietrich Bonhoeffer* (New York: Harper & Row, 1970), p. 47.

133 **Matthew Fox:** Matthew Fox, *Original Blessing* (Santa Fe, NM: Bear & Company, 1983), pp. 76, 90.

134 **"that ever has":** Whereas this quotation is widely attributed to Margaret Mead, it apparently is not found in one of her works.

136 **a nuclear war:** Under the leadership of Paul Nitze, the Committee on the Present Danger ran big newspaper advertisements, in 1977–1978, with the message that the USSR was preparing to launch a nuclear war, one that they expected to win.

136 **"the Soviet government":** George Kennan in the *New York Times Magazine*, May 7, 1978, p. 43.

138 **almost every state:** A history of the movement for citizen diplomacy, and the role of US-USSR Bridges for Peace in that movement is provided in *Building Bridges: US-USSR—A Handbook for Citizen Diplomats*, Clinton C. Gardner, ed. (Norwich, VT: Norwich Center Books, 1989).

139 **a "Bridges" activist:** Tony Ugolnik has written a fascinating introduction to the life of Russian Orthodoxy in Russia today: Anthony Ugolnik, *The Illuminating Icon* (Grand Rapids, MI: William B. Eerdmans, 1989).

140 **our Russian president:** A brief report on The Transnational Institute is available at: www.valley.net/~transnat/transnat.html.

140 **Solovyov Society:** See page 99 note on the Society, which refers to the Burchardi book about its history. That book notes that the society was refounded in 1991. See also: www.valley.net/~transnat/burchardi.html.

CHAPTER 10: THE SOLOVYOV SOCIETY

143 **and as we:** Sergei Bulgakov, *The Orthodox Church* (Clayton, WI: American Orthodox Book Service, 1935), p. 124.

144 **ratio or reason:** Alexei Losev in his 1923 article, "Russian Philosophy," reprinted in the Soviet journal, *XX Century and Peace*, February 1988.

144 **cosmos of speech:** Humboldt is generally recognized as the first to perceive that all languages share inherent grammatical rules, ones which tell us a great deal about human nature.

145 **"of its disciples":** Alexei Khomyakov, *Complete Works, Vol. III* (Moscow, 1891), p. 348.

145 **the name Sophia:** Solovyov, *Lectures on Divine Humanity*, p. 45.

145 **"will be recognized":** Re the "divine principle": Nikolai Berdyaev, *The Destiny of Man* (London: Bles, 1955), p. 54. Re the "third age": Nikolai Berdyaev, *The Divine and the Human* (London: Bles, 1947), p. 221.

145 **of the Trinity:** Pavel Florensky, *The Pillar and Ground of the Truth*, Boris Jakim, trans. (Princeton, NJ: Princeton University Press), p. 37.

146 **"and as we":** Bulgakov, *The Orthodox Church*, p. 124.

146 **including the religious:** Katerina Clark and Michael Holquist, *Mikhail Bakhtin* (Cambridge, MA: Harvard University Press, 1984), p. 121.

146 **"nature is dialogic":** Bakhtin, *Problems of Dostoevsky's Poetics*, p. 293.

146 **His "chronotope":** M. M. Bakhtin, *The Dialogic Imagination*, Michael Holquist, ed. (Austin, TX: University of Texas Press, 1981), p. 84.

147 **"of spiritual vision":** Kireevsky, "The Possibility and Necessity of New Principles in Philosophy," in *Complete Works*, p. 238.

152 **Stahmer's 1968 book:** In addition to Stahmer's book, there is a summary of Rosenstock-Huessy's thought in George Morgan, *Speech and Society: The Christian Social Philosophy of Eugen Rosenstock-Huessy* (Gainesville, FL: University of Florida Press, 1987).

152   **Holland is the country:** There is a Rosenstock-Huessy Society that is active in both Holland and Germany. The Dutch pastor, Lise van der Molen, has produced *A Guide to the Works of Eugen Rosenstock-Huessy* (Essex, VT: Argo Books, 1997).

152   **"said that himself":** Rosenzweig, "The New Thinking" in Nahum Glatzer, ed., *Franz Rosenzweig: His Life and Thought*, p. 201.

153   **"appeared only once":** Rosenstock-Huessy, *Die Sprache des Menschengeschlechts, Bd. I*, p. 696.

153   **was going to write:** Vitaly Makhlin, "Farewell to Descartes or the Cross of Reality Between East and West," *Problems of Philosophy*, No. 3, 1993, pp. 145-148.

154   **Between East and West:** Clinton Gardner, *Mezhdu Vostokom i Zapadom: Vozrozhdenie darov russkoi dushi* (Moscow: Nauka, 1993). (Translation into Russian of *Between East and West: Rediscovering the Gifts of the Russian Spirit.*)

155   **ate that apple:** St. Irenaeus (ca. 130-202), Bishop of Lyons, is considered a Father of the church in both East and West.

157   **"Russian philosophy":** *Problems of Philosophy*, No. 10, 1993.

158   **Moscow University Press:** Harold Berman, *Law and Revolution: The Formation of the Western Legal Tradition* (Cambridge, MA: Harvard University Press, 1983).

158   **acquired an imprimatur:** *The Way of Orthodoxy*, Monthly Journal of the Department for Religious Education and Catechism, Moscow Patriarchate, Feb. 1994, pp. 8-22.

CHAPTER 11: A HIGHER SOCIOLOGY

160   **space and time:** Rosenstock-Huessy, *I Am an Impure Thinker*, p. 94.

160   **the world symposium:** Bakhtin, *Problems of Dostoevsky's Poetics*, p. 293.

161   **the natural sciences:** John Kemeny's lecture, "A Look at the Future Prospects from Three Decades of Rapid Change," was delivered at Dartmouth College on August 2, 1977.

161   **"truly human society":** Rosenstock-Huessy, *Out of Revolution*, p. 793.

162   **world around us:** Caryl Emerson, *The First Hundred Years of Mikhail Bakhtin* (Princeton, NJ: Princeton University Press, 1997), p. 213.

162   **"any unitary truth":** Pauline Marie Rosenau in *The New York Times Book Review*, Feb. 20, 1994, p. 6.

163 **calls "polyphonic":** Rosenstock-Huessy, *Out of Revolution*, p. 801.

166 **to the United States:** Some organizations active in that 1980s movement are *still* bringing Russians to the US or sending Americans
to Russia. For an example, see the website of Project Harmony:
www.projectharmony.org.

Transition to Part III

171 **"come of age":** Bonhoeffer, *Letters and Papers from Prison*, p. 326.

Chapter 12: Transforming Christianity

173 **in the present:** Borg, *The Heart of Christianity*, p. 14.

174 **"everything that is, is":** Ibid., p. 66.

175 **"again some day":** Ibid., p. 11

175 **"Pentecostal Christians":** Ibid., p. 6.

175 **four primary meanings:** Ibid., pp. 28-37.

175 **"level, to God":** Ibid., p. 36.

176 **Kingdom of God:** Ibid., p. 131

176 **war in Iraq:** Ibid., pp. 143-145.

176 **"is the time":** Rosenstock-Huessy, *The Christian Future*, p. 189.

176 **"it is realized":** *Collected Works of Vladimir Solovyov*, Vol. VI, p. 335.

176 **anthology of them:** Rowan Williams became Archbishop of
Canterbury in 2003, and thus head of the worldwide Anglican
Communion. His book on Bulgakov's thought is: Rowan Williams,
Sergii Bulgakov: Towards a Russian Political Theology (London: T & T
Clark, 2000).

177 **pleasant land:** These are the last four lines in William Blake's short
poem, "And did those feet in ancient time" (1804).

177 **literalist-fundamentalist camp:** Borg, *The Heart of Christianity*, p. 104.

177 **a committed Christian:** Borg reported on his conversion experience during his lecture at St. Simons Island, January 23, 2007.

177 **"let yourself die":** Borg, *The Heart of Christianity*, p. 119.

177 **attacks on God:** Harris, *The End of Faith*.

178 **created the universe:** Ibid., p. 17

179 **"degree of evidence":** Ibid., p. 65.

179   **"physical universe":** Ibid., p. 294.

179   **right on the mark:** Ibid., p. 2.

180   **by that name:** Armand Nicholi, *The Question of God* (New York: Free Press, 2002).

181   **flaming atheist:** Hitchens, *God Is Not Great.*

181   **"blasting rehetoric":** *Wired* magazine, Issue 14.11, November 2006.

181   **to my definition:** Dennet, *Breaking the Spell*, pp. 9-10.

182   **the 2001 book:** Rodney Stark, *One True God: Historical Consequences of Monotheism* (Princeton, NJ: Princeton University Press).

182   **"we greatly desire":** Dennett, *Breaking the Spell*, p. 191.

182   **"or a thing":** Rosenstock-Huessy, *The Christian Future*, p. 94.

182   **including us:** Dawkins, *The God Delusion*, p. 31.

183   **ground of our being:** Paul Tillich, *Systematic Theology, Vol II*, (Chicago: University of Chicago Press, 1957), pp. 11-12.

183   **call themselves Christians:** Dawkins, *The God Delusion*, p. 237.

184   **"dreary and absurd":** Hitchens, *God Is Not Great*, p. 7.

184   **"a straw man". . . . "in our time":** Ibid., p. 119.

184   **in such books:** Diana Butler Bass, *Christianity for the Rest of Us: How the Neighborhood Church Is Transforming the Faith* (New York: Harper-Collins, 2006).

184   **"was a Christian". . . . "joined any church":** Hitchens, *God Is Not Great*, p. 179.

184   **"nebulous humanism":** Ibid., p. 7.

185   **his recent book:** Kevin Phillips, *American Theocracy*, (New York: Penguin Group, 2006).

185   **literally accurate. . . . Noah's Ark. . . . six days. . . . and the Antichrist:** Ibid., p. 102.

185   **in relative decline:** Ibid., pp. 113-120.

185   **"no longer marginal":** Ibid., p. 218.

185   **growing most rapidly:** Karen Armstrong, *The Battle for God: A History of Fundamentalism* (New York: Ballantine Books, 2001).

185   **"a wrong society":** Rosenstock-Huessy, *Out of Revolution*, p. 744.

186   **Athanasian Creed:** An Internet source for this creed's text is www.elca.org/communication/creeds/athanasian.html.

186 **"from the beginning"**: Rosenstock-Huessy, *The Christian Future*, p. 98. While the quotation on the Father appears on that page in *The Christian Future*, the other references, to Son and Spirit, are based on my class notes and general reading of Rosenstock-Huessy's work.

186 **published a book**: Kenneth Cracknell, *In Good and Generous Faith: Christian Responses to Religious Pluralism* (Cleveland: Pilgrim Press, 2006).

186 **Franz Rosenzweig. . . Martin Buber**: Ibid., pp. 72-73, 103.

187 **Christians are "saved"**: Ibid., pp. 41-95.

187 **Socrates and Heraclitus**: Ibid., p. 50.

187 **with the *Logos***: Ibid., pp. 86-93.

187 **who trust Christ**: Rosenstock-Huessy, *The Christian Future*, p. ii.

188 **one action**: Raymond Bernard Blakney, *Meister Eckhart: A Modern Translation* (New York: Harper & Brothers, 1941), p. 181.

188 **with creatures**: Ibid., p. 228.

188 **this or that**: Ibid., p. 230.

188 **Luther called *Schwärmerei***: See John M. Todd, *Luther: A Life* (New York: Crossroad Publishing Co., 1982), Chapter 12.

189 **"experience. . . . or piety"**: See *The Place of Bonhoeffer—Problems and Possibilities in his Thought*, Martin E. Marty, ed. (New York: Association Press, 1962).

191 **"without escort"**: Rosenstock-Huessy, *The Christian Future*, p. 110.

CHAPTER 13: THE NEW TRANSCENDENCE

192 **truth be divided**: Barbara Brown Taylor, *The Luminous Web: Essays on Science and Religion* (Cambridge, MA: Cowley Publications, 2000), p. 9.

192 **"only supernatural"**: Rosenstock-Huessy, *Der Atem des Geistes*, p. 37.

193 **"one but two". . . . "entirely on God"**: Taylor, *The Luminous Web*, p. 8.

193 **"reality be two"**: Ibid., p. 8.

193 **engaged by**: Stephen Hawking, *A Brief History of Time* (New York: Bantam Books, 1996).

193 **"of all diversity"**: Taylor, *The Luminous Web*, p. 9.

193 **the mind of God**: Hawking, *A Brief History of Time*, p. 191.

194 **"a Universal Mathematics"**: S. V. Keeling, *Descartes*, (Oxford: 1968).

194 **"laws of physics"**: Wilson, *Consilience*, p. 291.

194   **"and the future":** Hawking, *A Brief History of Time*, p. 148.

195   **"backward in time":** *Columbia Encyclopedia*, Paul Legasse, ed. (New York: Columbia University Press, 2000).

195   **we might call *kairos*:** Tillich, *Systematic Theology*, Vol. 3, pp. 369-372.

195   **"ground of being":** Ibid., Vol. I, pp. 155-157.

195   **is not "natural":** Rosenstock-Huessy, *Soziologie II*, p. 737.

195   **"has no yardstick":** Rosenstock-Huessy, *Out of Revolution*, p. 137.

196   **"of the past":** Rosenstock-Huessy, Dartmouth Lectures, Comparative Religion - 1954, Vol. 8, Lecture 4, Oct. 5, 1954.

196   **his 1929 classic:** Alfred North Whitehead, *Process and Reality: An Essay in Cosmology*, (New York: Macmillan, 1929).

197   **exclusively for Caesar:** Ibid., pp. 519-520.

197   **"for evermore":** Ibid., pp. 532-533.

197   **freedom of all:** Charles Hartshorne, *The Divine Relativity: A Social Conception of God* (New Haven: Yale University Press, 1948), xvii.

198   **his own perspective:** John B. Cobb, Jr., *God and the World*, (Philadelphia: The Westminster Press, 1969).

198   **outstanding resources:** "Living the Questions" at: www.livingthequestions.com.

CHAPTER 14: ON CEMETERY HILL: IN CONCLUSION

203   **birth of Christ:** Rosenstock-Huessy, *Soziologie*, Bd. II, p. 759.

204   **"law and theology":** Rosenstock-Huessy, *Out of Revolution*, p. 193.

204   **"all earlier philosophies":** Rosenzweig, "Das neue Denken," in Nahum Glatzer, ed., *Franz Rosenzweig: His Life and Thought*, p. 198.

INDEX

A

Abélard, Pierre, 125

academia, academe, academic(s), 33, 35, 44, 57, 67, 77, 80, 88, 104, 125-26, 133, 139, 151, 162, 177, 205-06

Adam, 116

Adam & Eve, 155

Agafangel, Bishop, 129-30, 134

Age of Exploration, 87

Albom, Mitch, 20, 226

Allah, 108

American Academy of Religion, 44

American Committee on US-Soviet Relations, 136

American Revolution, 48, 86, 90-91, 93

American Theocracy (Phillips), 185, 244

analysis, analytics, 67-68, 153

anarchy, 79, 209

Anashvili, Valeri, 156

Andropov, Yuri, 132, 159

Angewandte Seelenkunde (Practical Knowledge of the Soul) (Rosenstock-Huessy), 55, 230

Anglican Communion, Anglican(s), 14, 19, 112, 117, 180, 243

Anselm of Canterbury, 52, 125

Anthony, Bishop, 130

Anthony, Metropolitan, 128

anthropology, 60, 118, 145, 235

Arbatov, Georgy, 136

architecture, 62

Argo Books, 41, 74, 83-84, 125, 152, 220-23

Argonauts, argonautic, 125-26, 205, 239

aristocrats, 89, 95

Aristotle, 48, 69-70, 196

art, 64, 87, 88, 116, 210

Ascension Church, 165, 167

Athanasius, Bishop, 186

atoms, 164

"Aubade" (Auden), 72, 232

Auden, W. H., 21, 41, 51, 72, 151, 171, 206, 226, 232

Augustine, St., 19, 155, 226

Auschwitz, 23-24

autism, autistic, 78

Averintsev, Sergei, 132, 154-156, 165, 167

Axial Age(s), 48, 180

B

Bach, Johann Sebastian, 88

Bakhtin, Mikhail, 132-33, 144, 148-55, 159-62, 165, 171, 192, 207, 216, 220-22, 240-42

Bakunin, Mikhail, 238

"Ballad of the White Horse" (Chesterton), 33, 227

Barth, Karl, 43, 50, 153

Baum, Gregory, 14, 21, 111, 113-14, 117, 183, 237

Beethoven, Ludwig van, 61, 88

belief, 13, 18, 20, 39, 52, 56, 79, 91, 194, 107-08, 114, 171, 175-76, 178, 180-81, 185, 205

believers, 13, 66, 137, 185-86

Benjamin, Father, 148, 156, 165, 167, 215

Berdyaev, Nikolai, 9, 14, 18, 21, 23, 28-19, 37, 96-105, 109-10, 112, 117, 119-20, 127, 131, 133, 139, 141, 145, 151, 154, 157, 167, 171, 173-76, 183, 188, 192, 198, 200, 216-17, 219-21, 225, 227, 229, 234-36, 241

Berger, Peter, 233

Berlin, Isaiah, 119-20, 122, 221, 238-39

Berman, Harold, 12, 94, 158, 206, 242

Berthold, Fred, 12, 155, 191

Between East and West (Gardner), 110, 131-32, 134, 136-37, 139, 141, 148, 150-51, 153-55, 157-60, 166, 171, 207, 210, 215, 222, 240, 242

Bhagavad-Gita, 108

Bible, 17-18, 23, 87, 108, 153, 174, 178-80, 183-85, 215

biblical literalism, 17, 22, 174-75, 177, 180-81, 183-85, 188, 243-44

Blake, William, 44, 176, 243

Bodrov, Alexei, 167

body, 9, 44-45, 47, 51, 59, 80, 82, 97, 106, 108, 155, 160, 164, 190, 199, 202

Bonhoeffer, Dietrich, 1, 7, 13, 17, 19-20, 22-23, 41-42, 73, 82, 93, 133, 141, 171, 175, 184, 189, 204-206, 221, 225-26, 228, 234, 240, 243, 245

Bonhoeffer, Sabine, 18, 41, 206, 228

Bohr, Niels, 164

Borg, Marcus, 12, 14, 17-18, 20, 82, 171, 173-77, 180, 183-84, 186, 193, 198, 204, 221, 225-26, 243

born again, 175, 177

Boston, Bruce, 44, 229

Brahman, 108

Brand, Stewart, 84, 233

Brief History of Time, A (Hawking), 193, 245-46

Briggs, David, 12, 220

Brinton, Crane, 93, 234

Brothers Karamazov, The (Dostoevsky), 32, 64, 127, 131, 219, 231

Bryant, Darrol, 12, 152, 233

Buber, Martin, 13-14, 21, 73-75, 117, 171, 174, 186, 217, 221, 232, 238, 245

Buchenwald, 1, 7, 14, 22-24, 97, 101, 203, 227

Buddha, 48, 71, 108

Building Bridges: Middle East-US, 126, 214

Bulgakov, Sergei, 99-101, 110, 117, 119, 141, 143, 145, 157, 167, 176, 198, 200, 219, 223, 235, 241, 243

Bush, George Herbert Walker, 144

C

Calvin, John, 155

Camp William James, 31-33, 84, 98, 127, 134, 177, 203, 205, 220

Camp William James (Preiss), 222

capitalism, 89, 91, 163

Cartesian method, vision, insight, 29-30, 36, 51-52, 59, 68-70, 75, 79, 125, 162, 193-94, 201, 242, 245

Catholic Church, 11, 37, 85, 87-89, 114, 117

Chaadayev, Peter, 101

Charles I, 88

Chesterton, G.K., 33, 227

China, 47, 93, 95, 163, 185

Chomsky, Noam, 80, 233

Christ, 19, 22, 47-48, 70-71, 96, 105, 113, 116, 128, 180, 185, 187, 199, 204, 237, 245-46

Christendom, 23, 85-87, 92, 97, 111, 112

Christian Century, The, 43, 228

Christian Creeds
Athanasian, 186, 244
Nicene, 185-86, 217

Christian fundamentalists, 34, 175, 177, 188

Christian Future, The (Rosenstock-Huessy), 43-44, 50, 71, 92, 103, 116, 127, 186-87, 190, 220, 222, 225, 227-30, 232, 243-45

Christianity
emerging paradigm, 17-18, 174, 184
new paradigm, 15, 18-22, 73, 175, 186, 188-89, 192, 198-200, 204

religionless, 17, 94, 133-34, 141, 171, 189, 225

transformational, 20, 226

Christianity, Eastern, 106, 111, 126-27, 200, 234

Christianity, Western, 126

Christianity and Crisis, 20

Christianity for the Rest of Us (Bass), 184, 244

Christians, 13, 17, 39, 44, 48, 82, 104, 108, 127, 173, 175, 177-80, 183-87, 189, 199, 243-45
Pentecostal, 175, 243

chronos, 146, 194-95, 201

chronotope, 146-47, 153, 160-61, 241

church, the, 13, 17, 20, 23, 32, 44, 85-89, 95, 97, 115-16, 141, 146, 187, 191, 197, 207, 225, 227, 242

Churchill, Winston, 36

citizen dialogue, 129

civil service, 88

Civilian Conservation Corps (CCC), 31, 33-34, 91

Cobb, John, 196-98, 246

Coffin, William Sloane, 136

Cogito ergo sum, 52, 68

coincidence, 63, 159

Cold War, 110, 129, 136, 141, 144, 163, 166, 236

Colima, 33

Committee on the Present Danger, 136, 240

Committee on US-Soviet Relations, 136

common sense, 12, 34, 61

communism, communists, 28, 34, 91, 135, 144, 221, 227, 234, 238

community, 33, 41, 55, 68, 94, 118 135, 160, 179, 217

Comte, Auguste, 29-30, 49, 106, 236

Conkling, James, 184

conscience, 48, 87, 93, 189

conservatives, 185

consilience, 40, 194, 228, 245

Consilience: The Unity of Knowledge (Wilson), 40, 194, 228, 245

Copernicus, Nicolaus, 125

Cox, Harvey, 14, 42, 77, 83, 113-14, 156, 206, 221, 228, 233

Cracknell, Kenneth, 15, 185-86, 245

creation (Creator), 18, 35, 40, 51, 55, 59, 65, 77, 79, 82, 105, 107, 109, 111, 115-16, 120-21, 157, 164, 183, 186, 189, 200-201, 207, 209, 218, 230, 239

Credo ut intelligam, 52

Creed, Christian (*see also* Christian creeds), 186

Cristaudo, Wayne, 214, 228

Cromwell, Oliver, 88

Cross of Reality, 7, 25, 27-33, 35, 37-40, 42, 45-47, 49, 51-53, 57, 63, 69, 71, 74, 76-82, 84-85, 87, 90, 97, 103, 106-07, 109-10, 115, 120-21, 132, 144, 147, 152-53, 160-65, 174, 177, 194-95, 198, 201, 203-04, 206, 209, 215, 227, 234, 242

Crusaders, 86

Cupitt, Don, 180

D

Dalai Lama, 179

Dartmouth Christian Union, 28, 32

Dartmouth College, 11, 18, 177, 215, 218, 232, 242

Davidson, Frank P., 31, 127, 220

Dawkins, Richard, 22, 171, 181-84, 206, 227, 244

D-Day, 14, 23, 37-38, 204

D-Day and Beyond (Gardner), 221

death, 21, 28, 38, 56, 62, 67, 158, 189-90, 203, 207, 216, 128, 226, 230

decadence, 63-64, 69, 79, 209

Declaration of Independence, 63

deists, 57

Dennett, Daniel, 22, 171, 181-82, 184, 206, 227, 244

Descartes, René, 29-30, 43, 51-52, 57, 59, 68-70, 125, 193-94, 201, 242, 245

Destiny of Man, The (Berdyaev), 156, 221, 241

Deutsch, Karl, 84, 233

devil, the, 71

Dewart, Leslie, 14, 21, 113-15, 117, 183, 237

dialogical method, 58, 73, 75-77, 79, 81-82, 84, 147, 162, 164-65

dialogue, 11-12, 21, 55-56, 61, 73, 106, 129, 132, 135-36, 146, 160-61, 165-67, 171, 186, 212, 232

dictatorship of the proletariat, 91

Dictatus Papae, 86

distemporaries, 126, 166, 239

Divine Humanity, 29, 96, 99, 101, 103, 105, 132, 145, 204, 223, 227, 234-35, 241

Divine Relativity, The (Hartshorne), 197, 246

Dominicans, 87

"Doonesbury," 61, 231

Dostoevsky, Fyodor, 28, 32, 61, 99, 127, 132-33, 137, 148, 151, 155, 181, 217, 219, 221, 240-42

dramatic, 68, 209

dual, 35, 46, 65

E

Eastern Christianity (Ehrenberg), 101-02, 133

Eastern Orthodox Church, 106, 111, 137, 155, 200, 204

Eckhart, Meister, 187, 200, 245

economics, 162-63, 209

education, 31, 33-34, 39, 64, 88, 126, 139, 155, 167, 212

Egyptians, 200

Ehrenberg, Hans, 101-02, 110, 118, 235

Einstein, Albert, 18, 44, 192-94

Emerson, Caryl, 140, 150, 158, 167, 221, 240

empires, 47, 85, 200

empiricism, 40, 205, 228

Engels, Friedrich, 234

England, 27, 31, 34, 37, 89, 112

English, 46, 68, 128, 150, 171

English Revolution, 90

Enlightenment, 35, 40, 44, 57, 90, 93, 102, 119-21, 192, 201, 217, 223

entrepreneur, 89

epic, 68

Episcopal, Episcopalian, 11-12, 14, 18, 20

Ermarth, Michael, 214

Esprit magazine, 102-03, 110, 173

Essence of Christianity, The (Feuerbach), 118, 122, 217, 238

eternal life, 190

Eugen Rosenstock-Huessy Fund, 152, 228

Europe, European, 14, 31, 85-87, 91, 101, 137, 151-52, 218, 233

Exeter, 32, 140, 205

experiment, 40, 53, 88

Experiment in International Living, 32

F

faith, 1, 9, 18, 22, 28, 32, 36, 45, 50, 63, 79, 94, 108-09, 131, 173, 175-76, 178-80, 184, 189, 194, 199, 206, 217

Falwell, Jerry, 19

Faraday, Michael, 164

"Farewell to Descartes," (Rosenstock-Huessy), 43, 242

fascists, 34

feral child, 73

Feuerbach, Ludwig, 104, 117-19, 122, 217, 238

Fiering, Norman, 12, 228

Filatov, Sergei, 135

Florensky, Pavel, 99-100, 119, 145-46, 150, 155, 157, 200, 219, 235, 241

Ford, Henry, 34

Fox, Matthew, 133, 183, 221, 240

France, French, 14, 27, 31, 48, 83, 86, 89-91, 93, 119, 122, 133

Francis, St., 190

Franciscans, 86

French Revolution, 48, 86, 89-90

Freud, Sigmund, 30, 49, 180

Friedman, Maurice, 73, 221, 232

Frost, Robert, 32, 61

fundamentalism, fundamentalists, 11, 19, 22, 34, 40, 94, 126, 175, 177, 179, 185, 188, 190, 244

Future of Belief, The (Dewart), 113-15, 237

future time, 30, 35, 37, 45, 63, 107, 198, 209

G

Galileo, 125

Gardner, Elizabeth, 12, 39, 97, 104, 141, 159, 173, 203

Gardner, Margaret, 33, 104, 187

Gardner, Raymond, 33, 104

gentlemen, 89

Genisaretsky, Oleg, 149

genius, 42-43, 84, 221, 228

German Reformation, *see* Reformation

Germany, Germans, 27-28, 70, 88, 99, 118-19, 152, 204, 214

gnostic, 102, 109, 235

God, 1, 9, 13-15, 17-24, 32, 35, 37, 39, 45, 49-52, 55-60, 64, 70, 74, 80-83, 86, 93-94, 96-97, 101-08, 111-16, 118, 131, 133, 143-45, 153, 161, 171-89, 192-207, 217-18

as *Elohim*, 116

as Father, 51, 59, 82, 105-09, 113, 115, 183, 186-90, 199-200, 209

as Holy Spirit, 9, 21, 45, 51, 55, 59, 71, 81-82, 86, 93-94, 100, 102, 105, 107, 115, 146, 151, 186, 188, 190, 198-99, 204, 229

as living God, 32, 182, 186, 230

as Son, 51, 82, 105-09, 114-15, 180, 183, 186, 188-90, 199-200, 209, 236-37, 245

as supreme being, 1, 17-18, 23, 49, 57, 105, 111, 113, 115, 178, 182, 184, 197, 226

as whole humanity, *see* humanity, whole

as *Yahweh*, 116

see also Kingdom of God

God and the World (Cobb), 198, 246

Goddard College, 32

Goethe, Johann Wolfgang von, 44, 119-120, 239

Golden Age (Russian), 99-100

Gorky Institute, 132, 151, 171

Gormann-Thelen, Michael, 214

Gorbachev, Mikhail, 138, 141, 144, 154

grace, 43-44, 60, 82, 155, 174, 199

grammar, 45, 58, 71-76, 80-82, 118, 206, 218

grammatical method, 58, 75-76, 126, 233

Great Society, the, 92

Greeks, 47, 164, 187, 195, 219

Gregory VII, Pope, 85-86

H

Hamann, Johann Georg, 117, 119-22, 217, 221, 238-39

Harris, Sam, 11, 13, 22, 53, 171, 177-81, 184, 189, 206, 226, 229, 243

Hartshorne, Charles, 196-98, 200, 204, 246

Hawking, Stephen, 192-95, 245-46

Heart of Christianity, The (Borg), 174, 221, 225-26, 243

Hegel, Georg Wilhelm Friedrich, 75, 93, 217-19, 239

Heidegger, Martin, 104, 236

Heraclitus, 48, 69-70, 164, 187, 232, 245

Herder, Johann Gottfried, 119-20

Heschel, Abraham Joshua, 39, 213, 228

Heschel, Susannah, 213

Hinduism, 108

history, 27, 30-37, 45-51, 58-59, 62, 65-68, 71, 76-78, 82-86, 91-95, 105, 107, 109, 113-16, 194-95, 201-04, 209

Hitchens, Christopher, 13, 22, 171, 181, 184-85, 206, 227, 244

Hitler, Adolf, 28, 35, 41, 70, 115, 228

Hobbing, Enno, 98

Holquist, Michael, 222, 241-42

Honest to God (Robinson), 14, 19, 112, 188, 222, 226

Horujy, Sergei, 149, 158, 167

Hough, Joseph, 179-80, 189

Hough-Ross, Richard, 138

Huessy, Hans, 39, 77, 127, 159, 233

Huessy, Margrit, 55, 104, 203, 214

Huessy, Mariot, 39

Huessy, Mark, 152, 230

Huessy, Raymond, 12

humanities, 18, 40, 152, 162

humanity, whole, 9, 51, 102, 105-06, 112, 174, 198, 229, 235

humankind, 28-29, 47, 70, 86, 93-94, 102, 105, 144, 164, 186, 189, 201, 207, 234

humor, 61

hydrogen bomb(s), 50, 101, 138

I

I Am an Impure Thinker (Rosenstock-Huessy), 43, 212, 220, 222, 228, 232-33, 242

I and Thou (Buber), 21, 73, 117, 221, 232, 238

I-thou, 74

idealism, 93, 122, 219

ideologues, 34, 135-36, 163

idols, 19

immanence, 55-56, 115, 192

imperative(s), 46, 51-52, 58, 63-66, 68, 72, 74, 76-79, 81-82, 85-93, 107, 161, 166, 174, 207, 209, 231

In Good and Generous Faith
(Cracknell), 186, 245

indicative, 68, 209, 231

industry, industrial, 35, 91

infinity, 35, 46

inner space (-self), 29-30, 33,
35-36, 45-46, 64, 81, 107, 162,
201, 209

Institute for Lifelong Education at
Dartmouth (ILEAD), 11, 178, 181

Institute for the Study of the USA
and Canada, 135-37

Institute of Philosophy, 136, 140,
158-59, 167, 171

institutes of technology, 89

integral knowledge, 103, 121,
131-32, 147

intersocietal pioneers, 105, 205

investiture, 87

Ionian Enchantment, 40

Iran, 27

Iraq, 27, 176, 243

Irenaeus, Saint, 155, 200, 242

Isaiah, 48, 63

Islam, 108, 200

–isms, 102, 235

Israel, 47, 152

Ivanov, Konstantin, 139-41, 143

J

James II, 88

James, William, 31, 69, 156, 205, 227

Jaspers, Karl, 48

Jesus, 17, 30, 108, 113, 175-76, 180,
185, 187-88, 191, 199, 237

Jews, 23, 90, 196, 218

John Paul II, Pope, 111

Johnson, Carl, 12, 173

Jonathan, Father, 129-34, 154, 165

Judaism, 55-56, 71, 108, 200

Justinian, code of, 196

Jung, Carl, 49, 229

K

kairos, 194-95, 201-02, 246

Kant, Immanuel, 73, 217

Karamazov, Alyosha, 32, 64, 219,
231

Karamazov, Ivan, 64, 133

Karyakin, Yuri, 133, 148, 215

Kauchishvili, Nina, 158

Keep, Russell, 220

Keller, Helen, 62

Kemeny, John, 161, 164, 242

Kendal at Hanover, 11, 191

Kennan, George, 42, 110, 136,
228, 236, 240

Khomyakov, Alexei, 28, 98, 100,
131, 135, 144, 150, 156, 217-18,
235, 241

Kierkegaard, Søren, 104, 153

Killing the Spirit (Smith), 126, 239

Kingdom of God, 9, 39, 83, 86, 176

Kireevsky, Ivan, 28, 98, 100, 103,
110, 119, 121, 131-32, 145, 147,
192, 217, 218, 235, 239, 241

Klee, Paul, 61

Klimovskaya, Oksana, 154

Kline, George, 140, 143, 149,
158, 222

Kokoshin, Andrei, 135-36

Kolomenskoye Park, 165

Koppel, Ted, 21, 130

Koran, 108

Kozhinov, Vadim, 151

Kreisau Circle, 41

Krishna, 108

Kuhn, Thomas, 18, 226

L

lamina quadrigemina, 79-80

language, 20, 27, 42-43, 45-48, 53, 55-62, 68-76, 80-82, 91, 94, 100, 104-05, 114, 117-21, 132, 151-53, 160-61, 166, 192

(*see also* speech)

Ten Theses on, 81

Language Instinct, The (Pinker), 80, 222-23

Lao Tzu, 48, 71, 177

law(s), 88-89, 92, 162-63, 204, 209, 219

law of motion of the spirit, 57-58, 206, 231

Law and Revolution (Berman), 94, 158, 242

lawyers, 89, 196

Lectures on Divine Humanity (Solovyov), 29, 99, 145, 204, 223, 227, 234-35, 241

Lenin, 36, 99, 110, 122, 144, 165

Leningrad, 91, 128-30, 133, 137, 139-44, 148, 154

Letters and Papers from Prison (Bonhoeffer), 17, 133, 225-26, 234, 243

Letters to the Third Millennium (Gardner), 131, 221, 240

Lewis, C. S., 180, 184

life after death, 28, 38, 190

Life Lines (Rosenstock-Huessy), 222

Lilla, Mark, 57, 213, 231

Lincoln, Abraham, 184, 190

linguistic analysis, 153

Lippmann, Walter, 110, 236

literature, 53, 61, 64, 67-68, 87, 89, 99, 120, 164, 209, 216

Loewith, Karl, 44

Logos, 21, 69-70, 100, 110, 144-47, 164, 172, 187, 199, 202, 236, 245

Logos magazine, 156

Loseff, Lev, 140, 159

Losev, Alexei, 144, 241

Lukyanov, Oleg, 212

Luminous Web, The (Taylor), 193, 196, 223, 245

Luther, Martin, 63, 87, 188, 245

M

MacArthur Foundation, 148

machine age, 100,

Macquarrie, John, 75, 233, 237

Magus of the North, The (Berlin), 119, 221, 238-39

Makhlin, Vitaly, 149-54, 158-61, 165-67, 206, 210-11, 242

Maliavin, Vladimir, 154, 158

Martel, Leon, 220

Marty, Martin, 43-44, 51, 189, 206, 228-29, 245

Martyr, Justin, St., 187

Marx, Karl, 118, 122, 234, 238-39

mathematics, 67, 162, 194, 209, 244

Matlock, Jack, 156, 215

matter, 32, 37, 40, 49, 57, 80, 131, 155, 193-95, 207, 229

McCarthy, Joseph, 163

McGrath, Alistair, 183

McNamara, Robert, 163

Mead, Margaret, 134, 240

Men, Alexander, 167

Messiah, 108, 196

metalinguistics, 146, 161

metanomics, 30, 50, 75, 110, 125-26, 157, 160-67, 204-05, 212, 218, 227

metaphor, 116, 175

metaphysics, 70, 162, 210, 236

Mexico, 33

Meyer, Marshall, 75, 206, 232

Middle Ages, 48, 85, 127, 207, 240

millennium
first, 48, 86, 105, 115, 147
second, 82, 85, 95, 105-06, 125
third, 42, 93-94, 104-05, 125-26, 161, 205-06, 228
before Christ, 47

mind, 39, 49-50, 58, 60, 69, 73, 80-81, 205

miracle, 9, 18, 28, 45, 50, 62, 68, 175, 192, 206, 225

Mohammed, 108

Molen, Lise van der, 242

Moltke, Freya von, 12, 41-42, 125, 127, 152, 230

Moltke, Helmuth Caspar von, 152

Moltke, Helmuth James von, 41

Moltke, Konrad von, 152

Moore, Douglas, 178

"Moral Equivalent of War, The" (James), 31, 227

Morgan, George, 241

Morris, Sylvester, 204

Moscow, 96, 99-100, 110, 130, 134, 137-39, 140-41, 143-44, 148-50, 154, 156-60, 165, 167, 205, 210, 236

Motroshilova, Nelly, 158-59, 165

Mounier, Emmanuel, 102-03, 173-74

Multiformity of Man, The (Rosenstock-Huessy), 35, 43, 46, 223, 227

Mumford, Lewis, 84

music, 64, 68, 87

mystery, -ies, 109, 111, 113, 118, 199, 236

mystics, mysticism, 17, 39

N

natural science(s), 18, 29, 36, 39-40, 51, 57, 67, 73, 75, 77, 125-26, 131, 161, 195, 199, 204, 206-207, 209, 226, 228, 232, 242
see also science

nature, 9, 28, 30, 35-36, 42, 45-47, 50, 67, 101, 105, 112, 126, 155, 161, 175, 194, 201

Neidecker, Anthony, 140

neo-conservatives, 185

Neue Zeitung, Die, 98, 190

New Deal, 34, 91

New Jerusalem, the, 44, 177

"New Thinking, The" (Rosenzweig), 56-57, 230, 242

newspapers, 89

Niebuhr, Reinhold, 20, 83-84, 151, 171, 206, 233

Nietzsche, Friedrich, 104, 238

Nightline, 21, 130

Nitze, Paul, 135-36, 240

Non Sibi, 32, 205

Nordhausen, 227

Norwich Center, The, 127, 129

Norwich Congregational Church, 11, 19, 39, 113, 127, 203, 214

O

objective, objectivity, 29, 34, 46, 51, 58, 67, 77-79, 85, 89-90, 103-04, 109, 161-62, 206, 209
see also speech, objective

O'Flaherty, James, 122

Ohrdruf, 227

Omaha Beach, 38, 203

Omega Point, 49

One True God (Stark), 182, 244

110th Antiaircraft Artillery Battalion, 37

Ong, Walter, 152

Open Christianity, 137, 139-43, 151, 154, 171

Origin of Russian Communism, The (Berdyaev), 28, 221, 227, 234

Origin of Speech, The (Rosenstock-Huessy), 60, 231

Original Blessing (Fox), 133, 221, 240

Orozco, José Clemente, 6, 19-20

Orthodox reformation, 100

other world, 28, 35, 69, 95, 114, 131, 175

Out of Revolution (Rosenstock-Huessy), 30-32, 35, 61, 82-95, 102-03, 116, 120, 153, 157-58, 161

outer world, outward space, 29-30, 34, 36, 49, 59, 71, 76, 82, 147, 198-99, 209

P

Paine, Thomas, 35, 90

panentheism, 1, 7, 15, 17-18, 20-21, 100-02, 111-17, 133, 157, 174, 178, 180, 182, 187-88, 192, 197-200, 204, 237

Papal Revolution, 40, 85-87, 90

Paracelsus, 153

paradigm(s), 18
earlier, 18, 171
new (emerging), 1, 11, 15, 17-22, 73, 82, 127, 174-75, 184, 186, 188-89, 192, 195, 198-200, 204

parliamentarians, 89

Parliamentary Revolution, 86, 88-89

Pascal, Blaise, 45, 47, 51, 80, 117, 122, 238

past time, 30, 34-35, 40, 58, 65, 79, 107, 198, 209

patterns, 13, 50, 79-81, 84, 153, 161, 206

Paul, St., 17, 87, 180, 187-88, 190, 200

peace, 22, 40, 69-70, 78-79, 82, 105, 109, 126-27, 166, 177, 200, 205-07

Peace Corps, 134, 177, 205

peace of mind, 205

Pearl Harbor, 36

Pease, Donald, 214

Pelikan, Jaroslav, 111, 237

Perle, Richard, 136, 185

personalism, 102

Phenomenon of Man, The (Teilhard de Chardin), 49-50, 229

philosophy, 1, 27-28, 35, 47, 56, 59, 100, 104, 114-15, 118-19, 122, 152, 164, 185, 194, 207, 209
    Russian, 98-103, 110, 121, 143, 144-49, 151, 157, 167
    see also social philosophy

physics, 18, 40, 125, 129, 132, 162, 193-95, 228, 245

pietists, piety, 19, 34, 189, 217, 245

Pigalev, Alexander, 156-58, 165-67, 210-11, 212

Pinker, Steven, 80, 222, 233

Pister, Hermann, 23

Planetary Revolution, 90, 92-93

Plato, 48, 70, 125-26, 204

plural, 35, 46, 94

poetry, poetic, 30, 33, 47, 58, 61, 64, 68, 72, 121, 219

politics, 62, 135, 162-63, 179, 185, 209

Polyakov, Leonid, 157

polyphonic economies, 163

polyphonic novels, 133, 240

"Possibility and Necessity of New Principles in Philosophy, The" (Kireevsky), 145, 147, 235, 239, 241

Post, Avery, 12, 155

postmodernism, 162, 236

Practical Knowledge of the Soul (Rosenstock-Huessy), 55, 58, 225, 230-31

pragmatism, 69, 156

prayer, 38, 50, 58-59, 62, 64, 68, 86, 149, 181-82, 189-90, 203

Preiss, Jack, 222

prejective, 63, 77

Principles of the Philosophy of the Future (Feuerbach), 118, 122, 238

Problems of Dostoevsky's Poetics (Bakhtin), 132, 151, 221, 240-42

Problems of Philosophy, 153, 157, 166, 242

Process and Reality (Whitehead), 196-97, 246

"Promise of Russian Philosophy, The" (Gardner), 144, 150, 158

prophecy, 47, 68, 126

prosaic, 68, 209

Protestantism, Protestants, 18, 37, 89, 112, 114, 117, 133, 135, 185, 226

providence, 173

psychiatry, 77-78

psychology, 27, 49, 51, 60, 75, 77-78, 121, 162, 209

public schools, 88

Puritans, 88

Pushkin, Alexander, 99, 101, 137

Q

Quakers, 180

Question of God, The (Nicholi), 180, 244

R

Ratio (reason), 100, 144, 241

rational thought, 30, 67, 69, 103, 121-22, 147, 201

Reagan, Ronald, 141

reason, 48, 51, 59, 68-70, 89, 100, 117, 119, 122, 144, 192-93, 217

Goddess of, 102

redemption, 51, 55, 59, 82, 107, 209, 218

Reformation, the, 48, 86-88, 94

religion(s), 1, 9, 11, 13, 19, 31-32, 39-40, 44-49, 53, 56-57, 59, 64, 71, 94, 99, 103-04, 110, 114, 117, 119, 130-31, 135, 146, 152, 162, 171, 179, 181, 184-85, 189-90, 192-93, 196, 198-202

religious empiricism, 40, 205

Reshetnikova, Elena, 143-44

Respondeo etsi mutabor, 41, 43, 51-52, 157, 166

resurrection, 64, 190, 198

revelation, 51, 55, 59, 82, 102, 107, 114, 156, 209

revolution(s), 37, 48, 79, 83-95, 234

Riesman, David, 39

Robertson, Pat, 19

Robespierre, Maximilien de, 89

Robinson, John A.T., 14, 19-20, 112-13, 117, 182-83, 188, 204, 222, 226, 237

romantic, 30, 36, 121, 238

Roosevelt, Eleanor, 33

Roosevelt, Franklin D., 33

Rosen, Art, 178, 180

Rosenstock-Huessy, Eugen, 1, 9, 13-14, 18-21, 27-110, 113-28, 131-32, 147-53, 156-57, 160-66, 171-77, 182-87, 190-92, 195-207, 210-16, 218, 220, 222-46

Rosenstock-Huessy, Margrit, 55, 104, 203, 214

Rosenstock-Huessy Society, 152, 214, 242

Rosenthal, Bernice, 140

Rosenzweig, Franz, 13, 21, 55-60, 70, 73, 75, 101-102, 117-18, 120, 131, 150-53, 171, 186, 192, 204, 206, 213-14, 218, 220, 222-23, 230-31, 238, 242, 245-46

Rosenzweig, Rafael, 152

Rousseau, Jean-Jacques, 35, 89

Russia, 21, 23, 99, 101, 110, 126, 131-32, 136-37, 141, 144, 148, 150-51, 154, 156, 159, 162-63, 165-67, 173, 210, 212

Russian Idea, 98, 102-103, 132, 234

Russian Orthodox Church, 21, 96-97, 128, 130, 136-37, 158, 167, 217

reformation of, 100

Russian philosophy, 28, 98, 100-01, 103, 110, 119, 121, 143, 144-47, 149, 151, 157, 211, 219, 241-42

Russian Revolution, 48, 86, 91-93, 95

S

Saint Andrew's Biblical Theological Institute, 167

Saint Sergius Seminary, 96-97, 105, 110

Sancto Victore, Hugo de, 187

Sakharov, Andrei, 138-39

salvation, 87, 94, 190

Scanlan, James, 140, 223

Schelling, Friedrich Wilhelm Joseph von, 105, 119-20, 218-19, 238-39

Schlegel, Friedrich von, 117, 119-21, 219, 238-39

Schmemann, Alexander, 96, 98, 102, 110

Schoeps, Hans, 55, 230

Schwärmerei, 188-89

Schwartz, Morrie, 21

science, 29, 36-37, 39-40, 51, 57, 59, 67-68, 73, 75, 77, 85, 88, 103, 105, 125-26, 131, 153, 162, 192, 204, 206-07, 209, 228
    and religion, 11, 32, 39-40, 44, 51, 131, 192-95, 223
    Five Theses on Reconciling Science and Religion, 198-201
    see also natural science, social science

scientific method, 29-30, 42, 77, 238

"Secret of Progress, The" (Solovyov), 65, 231

Secular City, The (Cox), 14, 83, 114, 221, 233

secular, the, 17, 19-21, 38-39, 42, 47, 54, 71, 83, 85-88, 94, 99-100, 106, 131, 191, 206

sentimentalists, 34

Sergius, St., 96, 110, 137

Shaull, Richard, 152

Shmelev, Nikolai, 140-42, 148, 165

Shopping International, 41, 138, 151

Silver Age (Russian), 99-100, 136, 139, 159, 200, 204

sin, 70-71, 108, 155, 189

singular person, 35, 46, 65, 181

small group(s), 105, 122, 134

Smith, Adam, 163

Smith, Page, 31, 84, 126, 206, 233, 239

Sobchak, Anatoly, 141

sobornost, 103, 132, 135, 156, 217-18

Social Democrats, 191

social philosophy, 21, 31, 207

social science(s), scientists, 18, 29-30, 35, 38, 40, 67, 75-76, 125, 152, 161, 164, 199, 207, 218, 233

Social Security, 91

socialism, 91

society, 9, 20, 29-30, 35, 37, 39, 50, 53, 63-64, 76, 78-79, 83, 88-89, 91-92, 95, 105, 112, 126, 134, 143, 145-46, 156, 161, 164, 185, 207, 225, 228-29, 236-37, 242, 244

sociology, 29-30, 75, 135, 151,
    a higher, 30, 50, 79, 157, 160-64, 205

Socrates, 48, 187, 245

Solovyov, Vladimir, 1, 9, 14, 18, 21, 23, 28-29, 31, 37, 51, 61, 65, 98-99, 101-03, 105, 110, 117, 119, 127, 131, 133, 137, 139, 141, 145-46, 149, 151, 157-58, 167, 171, 175-76, 183, 188, 192, 198, 200, 204, 207, 217, 219-20, 223, 225, 227, 231, 234-35, 241, 243

Solzhenitsyn, Alexander, 134

Solzhenitsyn, Natalya, 134, 137-38

Sophia, 101-02, 145, 235, 241

soul(s), 35, 47, 57-58, 69, 80-81, 119, 121, 147, 160, 184, 189-190, 192, 198, 205-06, 225, 230-31, 233

Soviet Peace Committee, 130, 132, 138-40, 149

Soviet Union, 29, 130, 132, 136, 236

Soviet Women's Committee, 130, 134, 136, 138

space axis, 29

Spassky, Igor, 97, 100-02, 105, 109-10, 112, 165

"Speak That I May See Thee!" (Stahmer), 152, 223, 239

speech, 9, 11, 21-22, 44-52, 55-82, 85-93, 102, 104, 106-07, 109, 115, 118, 120, 144, 146-47, 150-53, 160-64, 172, 192, 195, 198-202, 204, 206-07, 209, 210

high, 59-63, 67-68, 72, 81-82, 86, 109, 195, 199

imperative (vocative), 30, 37, 46, 48, 51-52, 58, 63-72, 74, 76-79, 81-82, 85-91, 93, 107, 109, 147, 161, 163, 166, 174, 181, 207, 209, 231

low, 60-61

narrative, 46-47, 49, 51, 58, 63, 65-66, 68, 76-77, 81-82, 85, 107, 109-10, 161, 165, 209, 231-32

objective, 33, 46, 58, 63, 66-68, 76-77, 81, 85, 91, 104, 119, 125, 161, 206-07, 209, 231

subjective, 46, 51, 58, 63-66, 68, 76-79, 81-82, 85, 87, 107, 109, 10, 114, 161-62, 209, 231

Speech and Reality (Rosenstock-Huessy), 75, 80, 118, 223, 225, 229-33, 238-40

Speech and Society (Morgan), 222, 241

speech method, 58

Spengler, Oswald, 230

Spinoza, Baruch, 57

spirit, 9, 11, 21, 30, 32, 44-45, 47, 51, 53, 55, 57-59, 67, 71, 80-82, 86, 92-94, 100, 104-10, 112, 119-20, 131, 144-47, 155, 160, 164-66, 172, 174, 192, 196, 199, 202

Spiritual Foundations of Life, The (Solovyov), 31, 227

Spong, John Shelby, 14, 20, 82, 111-12, 117, 180, 183, 188, 198, 204, 223, 226, 237

SS *(Schutz Staffel)*, 23

Stahmer, Harold, 12, 159, 223, 239

Stalin, Joseph, 23, 35, 110, 165, 228

Star of Redemption, The (Rosenzweig), 55, 150, 218, 223, 230

statistics, 48, 67, 91, 184

Strada, Vittorio, 160-61

Strong, Robert, 32

subjective, *see* speech, subjective

subjectivity, 30

subjunctive, 58, 64, 68, 209, 231

Sullivan, Anne, 62

Sun Yat-Sen, 95, 234

supernatural, 13, 17, 19, 28, 39,
    50-51, 64, 111, 114, 119, 131,
    171, 174-75, 178, 181-83, 192,
    200-01, 205-06, 226, 229,
    237, 245

supra-rational, 69, 103, 119, 122,
    147, 235

T

Taylor, Barbara Brown, 173,
    192-93, 196, 223, 245

technology, 29, 36-37, 89

Teilhard de Chardin, Pierre, 49-50,
    183, 229

temples, 47

Ten Commandments, 63

theism, 13, 15, 17, 20-21, 51,
    100-01, 111-12, 115, 117,
    174-75, 178, 180, 192, 196,
    199-200, 226, 237

supernatural theism, 17, 174, 226

theology, theologians, 13-15, 19-21,
    37, 41-44, 50-52, 56-57, 59,
    69, 73, 75, 77, 82-83, 86, 96,
    111-15, 125-26, 133, 140, 145,
    153, 155, 167, 171, 179, 183,
    187, 192, 196, 198, 204-05, 207,
    217-18, 228, 233, 238, 246

thou (you), 21, 46-47, 58-59, 63,
    65, 67, 73-74, 76, 78, 81-82, 85,
    106-07, 117-18, 143, 145-46,
    161, 199, 209

Tillich, Paul, 13, 19-20, 42-43,
    49-50, 73, 82, 171, 179-80, 183,
    195, 200, 204, 226, 244, 246

time axis, 29-30, 34

Tolstoy, Leo, 99

Torah, 108

"Toward a Philosophy for the
    Third Millennium" (Gardner),
    160-61

trajective, 65

transcendence, 17, 43, 55-56,
    114-15, 192, 200-01, 205, 207,
    228

transcendentalism, 40, 205

Transnational Institute, The, 140,
    165, 241

tribes, 85, 200

Trinitarian thinking, 51, 103, 132,
    180, 235

Trinity, the, 97, 100, 103, 106-10,
    113, 115, 145, 180-81, 184, 186,
    189, 199, 200, 235-36

Trinity-St. Sergius Monastery, 96,
    110, 137

Trudeau, Garry, 61

Tuesdays with Morrie (Albom), 20, 226

U

Ugolnik, Anthony, 139, 148, 241

United Auto Workers, 91

United Church of Christ (UCC),
    18, 83, 138, 155, 176, 178

United States, 11, 14, 75, 90-91,
    94, 130, 132-33, 135-38, 140-41,
    148, 151-52, 166-67, 176, 185,
    188, 200, 204, 243

unity, axiom of, 40

universe, 39, 47, 50, 105, 111, 178-79, 182-83, 193, 197, 201, 207

"Uni-versity of Logic, Language, Literature," (Rosenstock-Huessy), 53, 120, 229, 231

Upanishads, 108

US-USSR Bridges for Peace, 11-12, 21, 122, 126-27, 128-42

USSR, 91, 122, 128, 130, 133, 136-38, 156, 159, 166, 240

V

Verdun, 27, 55

Vico, Giambattista, 153

Vietnam, 163

Virgil, 31

Vladimir Solovyov Society, 99, 140, 143, 148-50, 155-58, 165, 167, 215, 234, 241

Voltaire, 89

voluntary service, 27, 41, 127, 205

W

Walicki, Andrzej, 121, 140, 143, 223

war(s), 19, 31, 33, 36, 70, 79, 106, 128, 136, 209

Way of Orthodoxy, The, 158, 242

Weimar, 22

Whitehead, Alfred North, 112, 196-98, 200, 204, 246

wholeness (*tselnost*), 103

Why Christianity Must Change or Die (Spong), 20, 112, 223, 226

Williams, Rowan, 176, 223, 243

Wilson, Edward O., 40, 228

Wittgenstein, Ludwig, 104

Wolf, Ken, 12, 173-74

World Wars
World War I, 50, 55, 56, 60, 99
World War II, 13, 19, 22-23, 31, 36-37, 42, 92

Wright, Frank Lloyd, 61

Y

Yanayev, Gennady, 144

Yeltsin, Boris, 143-44, 154, 163

you, *see* thou

Z

Zacek, Lothar, 190-91

Zagorsk, 137

Zamoshkin, Yuri, 134-37, 157, 159, 165, 215

Zukav, Gary, 80, 233

Printed in the United States
203032BV00001B/172-312/P